JOHN BERRYMAN
A CRITICAL COMMENTARY

THE GOTHAM LIBRARY
OF THE NEW YORK UNIVERSITY PRESS

The Gotham Library is a series of original works and critical studies, published in paperback primarily for student use. The Gotham hardcover edition is primarily for use by libraries and the general reader. Devoted to significant works and major authors and to literary topics of enduring importance, Gotham Library texts offer the best in literature and criticism.

Comparative and Foreign Language Literature:
Robert J. Clements, Editor

Comparative and English Language Literature:
James W. Tuttleton, Editor

John Berryman
A Critical Commentary

John Haffenden

New York University Press. New York *and* London

Library of Congress Cataloging in Publication Data

Haffenden, John.
  John Berryman, a critical commentary.

  (The Gotham library of the New York University Press)
  Bibliography: p.
  Includes index.
    1.   Berryman, John, 1914–1972 — Criticism and interpre-
tation.   I.   Title.
PS3503.E744Z7   811'.54   79–3893
ISBN 0–8147–3404–9

Manufactured in Great Britain.

Table of Contents

Acknowledgements

I am greatly indebted to Kathleen Donahue (Mrs John Berryman) for giving me all possible help with my work, and for permitting me access to John Berryman's papers and library. This book has developed out of my postgraduate thesis at the University of Oxford, and accordingly I would like to thank my supervisor, Professor Richard Ellmann, for his guidance and firm counsel; also John Fuller, who substituted as my supervisor for a short period in 1973 and prompted further efforts; and my external examiners, Professor Geoffrey Moore and Mr Christopher Butler, who encouraged me to publish.

For putting information at my disposal, for interviews, or for help in many other capacities, I owe thanks to: the late Mrs Jill Berryman, Nancy Jewell Aldrich, A. Alvarez, Van Meter Ames, Sarah Appleton, Saul Bellow, Elisabeth Bettman, Brian Boydell, John Malcolm Brinnin, Bryan Burns, J. Alister Cameron, C. D. Corcoran, Brenda Engel, Robert Fitzgerald, Robert Giroux, E. M. Halliday, Edward Hoagland, Mackie Jarrell, Richard J. Kelly, Jean Lanier, Alan Lathrop, William Meredith, Charles Monteith, Florence Miller, Howard Munford, Howard Nemerov, Timothy O'Sullivan, Sergio Perosa, Victoria Pope, Ernest C. Stefanik, Allen Tate, Boyd and Maris Thomes, Valerie Trueblood, the late Mark Van Doren, Andrews Wanning, and Richard Wilbur; Sue Haffenden for her help and interest; my father, and Andrew and Geraldine Hillier, for their kind chivvying; Rosalind Duckmanton for promptly and unflaggingly typing and retyping the manuscript; and my colleagues in the Department of English Literature at Sheffield University for their good fellowship.

I read Chapter 4, in slightly different form, at a John Berryman Special Session during the Annual Convention of the Modern Languages Association of America in New York, December 1978, where I was happily able to meet other scholars in the field—specifically Gary Q. Arpin, Jack V. Barbera, Peter Stitt, and Larry Vonalt—whom I had otherwise known only by name and reputation; my warm thanks also to Kathe Davis Finney, for her able and enthusiastic presiding at the Session.

I am grateful to the Staff Research Fund of the University of Exeter for a grant-in-aid which first helped me to the USA, and to the University of Sheffield for grants awarded from the Research Fund and the Foreign Travel Fund.

I should also like to thank the following institutions for providing me with essential documentation: Manuscripts Division, University of Minnesota Libraries; Princeton University Library; Berg Collection, New York Public Library; Chicago University Library; Office of the Registrar, Columbia University, New York; Columbia University Library; and Washington University Library.

While completing this study, I have had the pleasure of reading Sergio Perosa's edition of selected Dream Songs and other poems (*Canti onirici e altre poesie*, Torino: Einaudi, 1978), which includes an elegant and helpful Introduction, and good notes to the poems. Readers should savour the Italian renderings, for which Professor Perosa deserves congratulations and thanks.

The author and publishers are grateful to Faber & Faber Ltd and Farrar, Straus & Giroux Inc for permission to quote from *Delusions, Etc.*, copyright © 1969, 1971 by John Berryman and © 1972 by the Estate of John Berryman; *The Dream Songs*, copyright © 1959 to 1969 by John Berryman; *Homage to Mistress Bradstreet*, copyright © 1956 by John Berryman; *Love and Fame*, copyright © 1970 by John Berryman; *Sonnets*, copyright © 1952, 1967 by John Berryman; *Short Poems*, copyright © 1948 by John Berryman, renewed © 1976 by Kate Berryman; *Henry's Fate and Other Poems*, copyright © 1969 by John Berryman, renewed © 1975, 1976, 1977 by Kate Berryman; *Recovery*, copyright © 1973 by the Estate of John Berryman; *The Imaginary Jew*, copyright © 1945 by John Berryman renewed © 1973 by Kate Berryman.

February 1979   JOHN HAFFENDEN

1 . Introduction

All the way through my work . . . is a tendency to regard the individual soul under stress. The soul is not oneself, for the personal 'I', one with a social security number and a bank account, never gets into the poems; they are all about a third person. I'm a follower of Pascal in the sense that I don't know what the issue is, or how it is to be resolved—the issue of our common human life, yours, mine, your lady's, everybody's; but I do think that one way in which we can approach it, by the means of art, coming out of Homer and Virgil and down through Yeats and Eliot, is by investigating the individual human soul, or human mind, whichever you prefer—I couldn't care less. I have tried, therefore, to study two souls in my long poems.[1]

The two souls whom Berryman had in mind were Anne Bradstreet and Henry, the personae of his most significant works. It is my view that the soul under stress, and under observation, is Berryman's, and that the poet is everywhere at the centre of his work. His poetry may be regarded as the mythopoeic recomposition of his own experience. Berryman directs his attention always to versions of his own self. Robert Fothergill's term 'serial autobiographer' is applicable to Berryman, in the sense that such a writer 'constantly mediates between a provisional interpretation of his life's meaning and direction, and the fresh experience which may modify that direction'.[2] In *The Dream Songs*, the work by which Berryman's reputation will ultimately stand, the persona 'Henry' acts as the focus for what may be called (borrowing a phrase from Roy Pascal) 'ideas and actions as effluents of a personality and a situation . . .'.[3] Henry enacts Berryman's subjective response in states of identity-consciousness which are continually altering, always insecure, demanding and defining. When all other schemes are exhausted, Henry is the unifying principle of the work. In an article on Ezra Pound, Berryman took a view which was to be realised in his own work:

'Does any reader who is familiar with Pound's poetry really not see that its subject is the life of the modern poet? . . . it is the experience and fate of this writer . . . that concern him.'[4]

This book aims to give a reading of what I believe to be the works of Berryman's maturity: *Homage to Mistress Bradstreet*, *The Dream Songs* (*77 Dream Songs* and *His Toy, His Dream, His Rest*), and *Love & Fame*.[5] My discursive chapters are centrally concerned with a study of Berryman's working drafts and note pages—the genesis of the poems—in order to understand the ways in which he gave artistic shape (exploring gradually emerging structural themes) to the events and other stimuli of his inspiration. In *Love & Fame*, for example, the circumstances of composition make for acute problems of interpretation, since a double time scheme is in operation of which even Berryman himself was only partially aware. In much of *Love & Fame* he seems to be selecting and formulating experiences and episodes from an earlier stage in his life, but the final structure of the volume was strictly contingent upon changes in Berryman's life at the time of writing: that is, in his contemporary outlook. The second half of the volume stands to the first as Spenser's *Hymne of Heavenly Love* stands to his *Hymne in Honour of Love*, or as Blake's *Songs of Experience* stands to *Songs of Innocence*. What is in question is not a pattern of preconception (in which the last poems in the book repudiate the values of the first), but the fact that Berryman changed his heart during the process of composition. It must be inferred that Berryman came sincerely to regret the secular indulgence of poems written not above a few weeks earlier. Similarly, in the writing of *The Dream Songs*, Berryman was often fashioning immediate events, concerns, and responses into aesthetic form, but he needed constantly to revise his plans for the structure of the poem as a whole, under the pressure of changing conditions during a thirteen-year period. Any analysis must take stock of that process of evolution and revision.

I have chosen not to write a separate discursive chapter on *Delusions, Etc.*,[6] mostly because the volume is not as unified as Berryman's earlier works; it presents much less sense of cohesion or necessity of structure, and more of a compilation of poems (one or two reserved from earlier years, some being highly accomplished, and others of poor technical quality). It is possible to see that, even in composing the volume, Berryman tended to be desultory and uncoordinated, and that he had it in mind to repeat what was the relative success of *Love & Fame*, as we may infer from this letter to a friend:

. . . writing Offices . . . I began to 'do' them last month but found you really can't—or I can't—in the world; so started composing— a 'Lauds' and then 'Matins'—interrupted then by a political anti- prayer I called 'Interstitial Office'—broken off then by sudden absorption in a scale-poem on Guevara—and I only got back to *Opus Dei* (the 9-poem sequence) day before yesterday, w. the opening stanza of 'Prime' and the last 3 for 'Nones' . . . my sacred poems . . . There are as many more of those now, occupying the same position—Part IV—in my next collection, *Delusions*.[7]

I have worked on annotations to the volume in order to alleviate some aspects of its abstruseness. In addition, I have reserved an appendix for an analysis of the poem 'Scholars at the Orchid Pavilion' from that volume. This needs little justification, except to say that Berryman began the work in 1948 and worked on it purposefully if intermittently for more than twenty years, and that the poem was immensely important to his emotional and spiritual needs, for it recapitulated many of the crucial concerns of earlier work (notably, *The Dream Songs*)—the relation of father to child, filial respect, death, and the nature of immortality in the aspects both of life and of art. It is evident that the finished length of the poem (as Berryman chose to publish it) is not in proportion to his grand sense of the work, to which he referred for many years as being of the scale and significance of *Homage to Mistress Bradstreet*.[8]

My discussion of *Berryman's Sonnets* will be found in the authorised biography (which should complement this book), since Berryman's life and the writing of that sequence unfolded *pari passu*. The real events of the summer of 1947 need to be distilled from the fictional construction which Berryman put upon them. He seems to have exercised at once a dissociation from the immediate pulse of experience and a form of double-consciousness which led him to arrogate life to art. The sequence of the sonnets can be seen as corresponding to a paradigm, but Berryman's procedure may be described more properly as being to annex the incidents and responses of his own life to a creative pattern. The moral scheme of the sonnets (which begins in reciprocal passion and ecstasy, and leads on to reproach and remorse) was in fact fortuitous, and not a premeditated plot. The end was not implicit in the beginning (as might have been the case with a fictional design illustrating perhaps the workings of nemesis), but corresponds to the outcome of a real relationship. The actual state of affairs was more complex than a summary can suggest, for certain sonnets do appear to apprehend the fate of the affair which is their subject, and so to imply a prevenient moral and aesthetic purpose. Several of the sonnets seem, that is to say, to have taken the measure of all the others, as though the whole story were mapped at any interim stage. Each poem seems naturally to find its point on a narrative progression whose culmination is known and needs only to be reached. Yet such a sense of prehension, of a foreknown and presumably forejudged pattern of events, is no more than an illusion. It is a curious but radical aspect of Berryman's mentality that even when involved in love and remorse he could divorce himself from his responsibility to life in order to capitalise on a situation which was opportune to his creative efforts. In what I consider a perceptive analysis, Milton Gilman takes the view that Berryman's 'Lise'

. . . is, of course, a provisional deity, created by the speaker to shape his predicament as he suffers his way into, through, and out of the affair.

. . . the structure is based on a number of narrative 'opportunities' that allow detailed exploration of various themes and help to objectify the sensibility of the speaker.[9]

It is understood of perhaps most fictions that a character in the work is at the mercy of situation or an experience from which the author (to a greater or lesser extent) is exempt. In respect of *Berryman's Sonnets*, Berryman is both character and author: in the former case, he is subject to a situational irony from which Berryman-as-author places himself at a remove; in the latter, he is involved in a double irony, being able to compose each sonnet—in turn—in the order of art, but capable of anticipating the natural order of events less by pre-arrangement than by intuition. He has to scrutinise himself with what amounts to a morally dubious intensity. After suffering and assessing his emotions and thoughts, he does more than record them (as a diarist), he formulates them—fabricating a myth of self—in an arrangement of fixed (if striking) attitudes. The true nature of what he does express in *Berryman's Sonnets* is that of an inventory of his being, mind and moods, at stages on a blind road.

While I take the sequence to be a *tour de force*, a critical analysis of the sonnets *qua* sonnets is beyond my immediate interest. As to the example and influence of such a sequence, it seems likely that

Berryman's Sonnets will prove a lost leader, both for their strained technique and for chance of circumstances.

Much critical commentary on *Homage to Mistress Bradstreet* has assumed that Berryman tried to recover the personality and community of the historical Anne Bradstreet, and freighted the poem with historical information to that end. Some critics have taken it for a weakness or a foolishness that Berryman deliberately distorted the historical record, even to the point of calumniating his heroine.[10] My view is that Berryman embraces Anne Bradstreet to quite a different purpose, and that he himself figures in the poem not only in the disembodied voice of the 'poet' but also (in many respects) as Anne Bradstreet herself. The poem, which was begun in 1948, may be seen as, in a sense, the purgative recapitulation of his experience of adultery the year before. He sets the historical scene so thoroughly that it appears as if the social environment incites Anne Bradstreet's adulterous feelings. In terms of her contemporary culture, physical illness was often construed as divine retribution for such sinfulness. For Berryman's purposes, that physicality (which he captures so passionately) serves as the image, the objective correlative of the spiritual pain that he himself suffered during the late 1940s and early 1950s. In a letter dating from mid-February 1953, he described the middle section of the poem, in which the 'poet' discourses with Anne Bradstreet, as 'an emotional unit', and went on advisedly to use the term 'the passional and spiritual range' when speaking of the poem's 'ambition'.[11] Berryman tried in *Homage to Mistress Bradstreet* deliberately to reinterpret a personal liaison, with its concomitant psychological tensions and distress, as a form of metaphysics. In another letter, written when the poem was finished, he told how 'over the years by accretion and development the subject seemed to attach and embody the whole world'.[12] Robert Fitzgerald (in whose house in Connecticut Berryman spent two weeks completing the poem) is able to confirm that the work had a 'very direct relationship with [Berryman's] personal existence'.[13] Although some reviewers have suggested hints and guesses, there seems to have been little attempt as yet to reach behind the subject and the metaphysics of the poem to the essential personalism of its theme.

In his National Book Award Acceptance Speech, Berryman announced,

I set up the *Bradstreet* poem as an attack on *The Waste Land*:

personality, and plot . . . I set up *The Dream Songs* as hostile to
every visible tendency in both American and English
poetry. . . . The aim was the same in both poems: the repro-
duction or invention of the motions of a human personality, free
and determined, in one case feminine, in the other masculine.[14]

Almost from the beginning of his work on *The Dream Songs*,
Berryman felt urged to confer a structure upon the poem. He
succeeded best in commending certain models to the interest of its
unfolding. Provoked by what he took to be the conventional
exigencies of the long poem, he tried to inject a plot into material
which had little intrinsic narrative direction apart from that of the
natural order of events.

> Art sex truth money and children
> in what order may well yet work out
> somebody, sometime, somewhere[15]

He wanted to submit the Songs (the sections of the poem) to the
discipline of sequence and succession. He felt it important for them to
imply a story. Continuity alone, whether of form and style, or of the
creative life which the Songs composed, was just not enough. His aim
was to impose an absolute form on a poem constituted by multiple
occasions. For example, it included lyrics on transitory topics which
could not readily be made transcendent and general. It depended for
its composition on the fact that Berryman's writing closed leech-like
with his life. Even as early as September 1958, Berryman sketched
this (unpublished) 'Note': 'Nothing in the poem is imaginary. It all
happened. The character of Henry—who generally writes in the first
person but often, of himself, in the third—is based upon deeply
sympathetic, almost incredulous study of several of my closest friends
and most venomous enemies.'[16] To have imposed an absolute form
would have been to foretell ten years of his life. In an interview with
Joseph Haas, Berryman disclosed that his reason for becoming
interested in the character of Henry 'was completely self-obsession.
It's all about me . . . and God . . . and friends . . . and God
. . . and . . . well, that's still going on.'[17] He could not help looking ahead, however, trying to anticipate the nature of the work.
He needed to control the direction of its progress (which was a type
of wanting to control his own life), not to surrender it; to project its

plot (and then to enforce it), rather than to allow it self-definition. The effort to chart the poem to a determinative point was in most respects a losing one, for its true character was that of chance, of segmented insights, and of occasional lucubrations. While working on his second volume of Dream Songs in 1966, Berryman told Jonathan Sisson that *His Toy, His Dream, His Rest* 'has to be composed out of whatever I save'.[18] The statement may be seen as tantamount to an admission that his structural principle was one of elimination, of chance and discovery. During the following year he gave all his time to writing more and more Songs, with the result that Book VII came to be seriously (and perhaps pointlessly) distended with sections ordered and written more on the principle of a diary.[19] Because of that difference of approach, the work as a whole is unbalanced and desultory in structure. The evidence which I am able to assemble tends to confirm Denis Donoghue's fair argument that (in the later Songs)

> Mr. Berryman found the rules too hard, and sought an easier course, at some cost to the poems. . . . There is no classic order among the materials; order is to be imposed rather than discovered. In Song 305 the aesthetic procedure is given as attention to the means rather than the end; presumably because a projected end implies a classic order waiting to be unfolded . . . in the middle and later Songs it has become increasingly difficult to take Henry seriously as a character distinct from his maker . . . the gap between Henry and his maker is closed: Mr. Berryman's effort to maintain a distance is perfunctory. The hotspur materials are the same materials, and there is no sense of a receiving self different from his own.

> It is my impression that in the later Songs attention to other voices has receded. Increasingly, there is one voice, doctrinaire, edgy, magisterial . . . it may mean that, as the poems progressed, Mr. Berryman found the sole indelible interest was his own emotion.[20]

In September 1966 Berryman implied to William Meredith that narrative had failed him in *77 Dream Songs*: 'Some of my new Irish Songs are extremely beautiful: I'm relaxing in that direction from the first volume, where narrative and beauty were largely excluded.'[21]

Three months later he gave the impression that he was giving much more attention to shape and story:

> Bk VII is practically done; it is very long, 80 or 90, mostly from recent months—I have killed some but most I need, for the narrative, such as it is. The end of it, 12 or 15 Songs built backward, is good; about the rest I can't tell yet, though I have in effect judged, by admitting them.[22]

The Songs accumulated relentlessly over that period. The structural principle turned unavoidably into one of selection rather than of necessary order or narrative, as we may reasonably infer from a letter that Kate Berryman wrote after yet another three months:

> We have been burdened with Dream Songs all winter and now every day is a day of reckoning. Me typing and John organizing and not writing any more which is a good thing since there are over 300 contenders for *His Toy, His Dream, His Rest.*[23]

Nonetheless, while *The Dream Songs* may be described as a poem subject more to fortune than to predetermination, it is of crucial importance to appreciate the formative validity of Berryman's wish for it to be more than the sum of its parts. By so doing, he created the preconditions of the poem—local device, viewpoint, moral dynamic—of which the form was then ultimately and inevitably a function. While looking in his work for patterns of consequence, of cause and effect, Berryman produced, in fact, a poem based quite successfully not on sequence and development, but on complex patterns of coordination. It does seem likely, however, that the finished poem compromised Berryman's first feelings for predesignation. Like most of his other works, the essential character of *The Dream Songs* derives from Berryman's habit of studying and treating selectively his life, attitudes, reading, and contacts, not *a posteriori* as an accomplished whole but as a developing and changing pattern of immense complexity.

2. 'Bitter Sister, Victim!'— *Homage to Mistress Bradstreet*

John Berryman was very fond of declaring that it took him exactly five years to write *Homage to Mistress Bradstreet*,[1] from 22 March 1948 until 22 March 1953. One of the earliest of his journal references to the poem occurs on 4 April 1948, the next not until 1 August 1949, when he 'drafted half a dozen stanzas for "Bradstreet poem".' He determined at that time to 'fool' the poem into 'being and beauty', but he was not to do so until 1952. Elisabeth Bettman remembers his torment from the time when he first got down to the work in earnest early in 1952:

> He talked of *Homage to Mistress Bradstreet* in terms of his doubts as to being able to complete the work; he worried about a poem of that length, could he sustain its tone of intensity? Would it be of the quality he hoped it would be? He felt the strain of overwork very keenly . . . He discussed his creative difficulties at length and in detail . . . feeling that he couldn't sustain the burden of trying to be scholar, teacher, poet.[2]

> Anne Bradstreet was a real presence in his life. It was almost as if he was 'in love' with this dead woman. Whatever, she haunted his nights and days, and sometimes he could talk of nothing else. He worked in spurts. Sometimes he could go for hours on end, into the night without any sleep. At other times he would have a dry run that lasted for days. He was in torment at those times.[3]

Stirred by feelings of guilt for his own adultery in 1947, Berryman had become deeply preoccupied with the subject. In 1948 he was already working on what was to have been a series of poems—a pastoral sequence in an urban setting—in which the hero was to be sexually unfaithful and to recover. The work was too absorbing for him to make progress on a new poem. In that year also, when the idea for the Bradstreet poem first struck him, he was perhaps too close in time to his own extra-marital affair to be capable of dramatising a poem about just such a liaison—apparently from the woman's point of view. The notion of a tryst at an impossible distance in time suited his need for a form of objectivity: the poem was to be a dramatic subterfuge rather than a personal lyric.

To a degree less complex but more conscious than Tennyson's *Maud*,[4] *Homage to Mistress Bradstreet* is properly Berryman's mono-drama which, in the interests of poetic economy, subsumes perhaps more than one relationship sustained during the process of com-position. As he depicts her, Anne Bradstreet is compounded of the woman he calls 'Lise' in *Berryman's Sonnets* and at least one other lover who followed her, in 1948. The poem represents Berryman's effort to make trans-subjective a predicament which he had scarcely resolved in his own person. In his work *John Berryman*, J. M. Linebarger has correctly pointed out that 'Anne seems to realize what no critics have noticed about *Homage*—that the modern poet and his age are as important to the poem as Anne Bradstreet and the Massachusetts colony.'[5]

Critical attention to the poem has been remarkably slight, but a number of critics have followed the false trail taken by Alan Holder: ' . . . Berryman is trying to reconstruct the person behind the text . . . is trying to burrow into the past, to give us a sense of the way it was for America's first woman poet.'[6] A similar misapprehension about the work informs Gabriel Pearson's view that 'Society as destiny and self as completed life coincide beautifully in the figure of Ann [sic] Bradstreet. She partakes at the foundation of white America while the idea of its destiny is still simple and uncompromised. The integrity of Anne's life approximates to the grounds on which a more complex, contemporary integrity might be founded.'[7] While Holder draws towards a conclusion which gives the lie to his earlier remarks (and which strikes me as right), that 'the poet has fallen in love with a woman that he has not so much recovered as created',[8] I would say that the theme of the poem is less the travails of either the historical or the fictive Anne Bradstreet than the emotional turmoil of the poet himself. Although Linebarger discerns that 'Anne Bradstreet is in some ways a mask for Berryman', he hesitates to enlarge upon the insight, 'she reveals very little about him'.[9] Berryman is in fact treating his own guilt feelings by shedding them in the person of Anne Bradstreet. Her phases of rebellion and submission,[10] and her consequent sufferings, are correlative to his own sense of remorse; his guilt, that is to say, is materialised in her diseases of the flesh. The true perspective on this state of affairs is illusorily reversed within the poem, since the figure of Anne Bradstreet is highly realised, while the poet himself is attenuated—no more than a voice. She is substantiated in order that Berryman may introduce himself almost as a projection of her fantasy.

The terms of reference of the Puritan community provide Berryman with a metaphor for externalising the moral complexities of his own consciousness. The dense local detail of much of the poem—although, as Gary Q. Arpin has pointed out, 'distorted for thematic reasons'[11] – serves less for the sake of historicity than for setting a scene which is sufficiently realistic as not to beg important biographical questions. The setting is, in a sense, a local distraction, to provide an environment cognate with but radically distanced from Berryman's own.

Saul Bellow's novel, *The Adventures of Augie March*, gave Berryman a sense of liberation to spur his own writing: he called it 'a breakthrough—namely, the wiping out of the negative personality that had created and inhabited [Bellow's] earlier work'.[12] He had also just re-read *Anna Karenina*, which he considered 'the best portrait of a woman in world literature'.[13]

A further incentive was that he had just been through the experience of group therapy in New York, which he found 'shattering'. It had left him, he said, 'blazing with hostility and feelings of gigantism, defeated gigantism'.[14] During the course of that group therapy late in 1952, Berryman had decided to write a novel, to be called *The Group*, in tandem with the process of his own treatment. The notion was to be more fully realised in his later novel, *Recovery* (published in 1973), since only seven typewritten pages survive of the first effort. In a preliminary note made at the time, Berryman declared candidly,

You *begin* a group – at the actual beg'g, that is, you are paralyzed with reluctance . . . & fear, wh. destroy curiosity, but *before* that: you begin w. a sense of women being fascinatingly accessible, etc etc BUT: there they are, utterly unattractive – as one quietly perceives that one is oneself – and thenceforth any idea of emotional sex-involvement, inside the group is *inconceivable*, not even to speak of the dislike one develops, & how boring they are.

me: (I was madly nervous, resistant, insufficiently considerate, oppressive; I exag'd)

Similarly, he says of himself in a doggerel verse, 'John hates women' and is 'abrasive & boring'. In order to understand Berryman's sense of frustration during the period of writing *Homage to Mistress Bradstreet*, and the urgency of his desire to expose raw feelings, it is enlightening to extrapolate at some length from the draft chapter of the novel:

Dr Wade was not sitting in his chair; probably he was in the w.c. B. was talking audibly about something to J., Florence listening. The level, failing, late-September light lay across the long room high over the invisible Park with its useless fireplace and he was too angry to listen even to E. talking. E. seldom talked. She was the only member of the group he could bear, except X. whom he positively liked. About B. there was nothing to like because nothing showed, but when she wept he felt miserable and friendly. It was clear life seemed a nightmare to her. The group otherwise, and including these two, he detested, feared, and felt superior to in degrees exceptional even in his experience of these powerful emotions. The group made him want to laugh with contempt and horror – nearly every week lately more so. Why he was still a member he did not know. As he chiefly with passion put it to himself, the group *bored* him and he'd as soon be dead.

But in fact the group (although it was extremely boring) did not bore him. It interested him unbearably, a fact he resented with his whole being.

Dr Wade moved easily in, greeting the women and him with nods and unintelligible words, and busied himself, still standing, at the low table beside his large chair. Dr Wade was a tall roundfaced tweedy wellfed *calm* looking man. He did not hate Wade, and he had not even, exactly, lost faith in Wade, but he was convinced, hopelessly, that he could not look to him any longer for anything.

The women were absolutely chatting.

His nerves stretched and twanged. He lit a cigarette. There was more room in this office for smoke, it was a rather larger office, Wade must be thriving and small wonder. . . . But this was the third office and in a fortnight it would be five years since he had sat down opposite Wade in the small green office and torn his ears off for one breathless hour with the excrucation of those months. He was an old hand, getting nowhere. Any of these others know the green office? But the stupid prints had followed – cartoons and bright, fake, pseudo-child pseudo-Leger works. Unsolved that ancient puzzle, whether Wade was a philistine. As for these others—

. . .

'It's very *boring*, it seems to me,' John said suddenly. 'The world *is full* of *unreasonable* people. What of it? *Too bad.* What can *we* do about it? I've had to work with such people myself, what's the point of complaining about it?' He was looking directly and savagely down at Florence, whose face was charred with resentment.

Everyone had turned astonished eyes on John except Wade who was watching Florence. Nothing like this had happened in the group before.

'I'm sorry I bore you,' she said angrily. 'You've been boring me for weeks about your friends and relatives. I should have told you before now.'

'Listen,' he went on with undiminished fury, 'with the possible exception of X, nobody in this group has talked less than I have *about his own problems*, and if I once mentioned my brother and have several times drawn illustrations from the lives of friends of mine *relevant* to some problem you or somebody else here brought up, *in an effort to be helpful*, that is a little different from a long and boring complaint about something that nobody can help. What the hell can *we* do about Rosen?'

'Don't shout at me! If you just sit tight and feel superior that's your own fault,' Florence said bitterly, 'but you have no right to attack me!'

'John's just angry about something himself——' Bill began calmly.

'Yes you're damned right I am,' John said to him. 'I admit it, with pleasure. I'm tired of wasting my time in a group where there is not the slightest point in my saying something *about myself* because nothing I say or could say is understood, as when last week, in regard to one of my dreams, you had to ask Dr Wade whether it was *possible* to have a dream involving a knowledge of Roman history (of the most elementary sort) and learn from him that it *was.*'

. . .

John, not through at all, broke in again. 'You *see*,' he said, 'what I said was pure anger, as I said, *but* it had truth in it also. This is what none of you will admit. And you needn't' – facing Florence again – 'feel so superior; if you've wanted to attack me for a long time and haven't dared to, you're no better than I am.'

'It's true,' she said, as Dr Wade resumed:

'This is the first time anything of this sort has happened in the group, and I'm interested in how the rest of you would have felt if you had been attacked in this way instead of Florence. . . .'

This charge of frustration, hostility, and excoriation, helped to concentrate Berryman's mind on the theme of putting a woman to a severe test.

The unravelling of the process of composition of the poem forms the substance of this chapter. The poet's approach to his purpose provides a valuable avenue towards a tentative explication of the poem. In his introduction to *The Monk*, by Matthew G. Lewis, Berryman applauds the way in which the novelist handled his hero's compulsion towards dissipation and inexorable doom. Lewis, he says, 'is interested in the *progress* of Ambrosio utterly to damnation'.[15] This insight is a key to a proper reading of Berryman's purposes in his long poem. The edition of *The Monk* for which Berryman wrote his introduction was issued in 1952, the year when *Homage to Mistress Bradstreet* began to take shape. Noting that Coleridge disliked the lust displayed by the friar in his pursuit of the heroine Antonia, Berryman himself takes the opposite view that, 'It seems to me that it is just in the presentment of the Monk's flickering affections and lusts that Lewis is most steadily natural.'[16] What is postulated of *Homage to Mistress Bradstreet* is that an innately rebellious woman is enabled to move towards the consummation of her rebelliousness; the logic with which Berryman pursues and exposes her is similarly natural. 'Lewis', Berryman said, 'makes available a chain of deepening terrors and enchantments intended to exhibit, to test, his characters.'[17] Berryman's aims in *Homage to Mistress Bradstreet* seem quite like that; we can discover the involvement of his theme by following the steps by which the poem came to be.

From the start, certain themes became clear to him, most notably the dilemma of a poet (i.e. both Anne Bradstreet and Berryman himself) in an anti-poetic society. The poem would show real sympathy for a woman who was 'prevented by the age *as we are* from using her Talent'. In 'One Answer to a Question: Changes', Berryman wrote, 'one point of connection, at any rate, being the almost insuperable difficulty of writing high verse at all in a land that cared and cares so little for it'.[18] He saw his heroine as a type of Demon Lover and La Belle Dame sans Merci, an emblem of the 'Great Goddess', and an 'ancestress', as well as being the 'first poetess' of America. Quintessentially, she was to be seen as a mother figure; her name itself, Anne, reminded Berryman of the mother of the Virgin Mary. As a mother, she should be regarded in a prospect of children. It would become necessary to account for the background, the circumstances and conditions of Anne Bradstreet's life in the first settlement of the New World. Once established as a real person, with personality, duties and devotions, she could encounter the 'poet' in an innominate area of being. The terms of existence would be hers, the time of transgression his.

Another premise to the engagement was that *she* should be innocent, 'we' guilty, by which Berryman meant that he would be playing fast and loose with the historical facts. He knew well that Anne Bradstreet had been a remarkable woman married to a remarkable man, and that 'she loved him, with a passion that can hardly be described, through their whole life together, from the age of sixteen on. I decided to tempt her. I could only do this in a fantasy; the problem was to make the fantasy believable . . .'[19]

At quite an early stage in drafting the poem, Berryman envisaged its conclusion as an 'elaborate, extreme, clinical, dreadful, account of her death; and (in it) (with despair) faith'. That is to say, her dying was to have religious—namely, theological—repercussions. For the purposes of the poem, Anne Bradstreet should feel rebellious towards God. An early draft of stanza 14 provides this example:

> I was not
> We ~~became~~ one.
> God ~~then~~ to me ill lingeringly, learning to shun
> A bliss, a lightning blood
> vouchsafed, what did seem life. I bled with mystery.   [sic]

That Anne rejects both her husband and her father (and the sense of religion they embody) is evident from the finished version of the stanza:

> That year for my sorry face
> so-much-older Simon burned,
> so father smiled, with love. Their will be done.

He to me ill lingeringly, learning to shun
a bliss, a lightning blood
vouchsafed, what did seem life. I kissed his Mystery.

$$(14:3-8)^{20}$$

Her disparagement of both men, and the God with which they sort, is
intensified by her profane allusion to the Lord's Prayer in the third line
quoted. A later description of Simon as 'Drydust in God's eye' (15:1)
confirms that impression. Her marriage, sanctioned in heaven and by
her father, was to seem a mixed penalty, an ambiguous grievance.
Similarly, an early draft of part of lines 2–3 of stanza 19 runs, 'Below
my waist /God is a hell's vice. To no end.' The image associates sexual
intercourse with a theological blight. Stanza 19, along with stanzas 20
and 21, was eventually to express—although not unmixedly—the
physical and emotional experience of childbirth, but was originally
imbued more with a sense of marital restlessness: 'I *press* and love and
will, /I must be free.' The speech is addressed to her husband, Simon,
who is seen as covenanted with God. God and Simon together
represent a mutual force to which she finds herself opposed.

Berryman decided that this God was to be like Empedocles', whose
'speculative theology was like that of Xenophanes and also of
Anaxagoras, for he speaks of God as a "sacred and unutterable mind,
flashing through the whole world with rapid thought"'.[21] In
borrowing the latter phrase for stanza 47 of the poem, Berryman
altered 'rapid thought' to 'one thought', and so implied that God is
single-minded in meting out death:

Sacred & unutterable Mind
flashing through the universe one thought,
I do wait without peace.
In the article of death I budge.   (47:1–4)

Apart from seducing Anne Bradstreet, the 'poet' would aggravate
her sense of lapsing from religious faith. His blandishments were
nihilistic, predicated on human ignorance of eschatalogy: 'Time,
which poisons love, keeps ours rude and gay, /Being hopeless.' These
lines suggest that their love is hopeless (impossible) for reasons of time
and space—more than 300 years—and function as a *memento mori*
persuasive finally of despair: 'We are lost anyway; be lost, together.'
The 'poet' argues that, 'I cannot feel myself God waits' (35:1). Anne
throws 'hostile glances towards God' (36:3), and then betrays the

dubious and ambivalent knowledge that she is 'sifting, nervous, and bold' (38:4). Berryman took his sense of 'sifting' in this passage from the Gospel of St Luke (22:31): 'And the Lord said, "Simon, Simon, behold, Satan hath desired *to have* you, that he may sift you as wheat".' When she considers sin and death, that is, Anne Bradstreet is to confuse her own fate with a sublimated allusion which addresses a 'Simon' (her husband's name) to Hell and damnation. The phrase subtly involves personal rebelliousness and maliciousness.[22]

However, another early draft of the poem suggested that the final movement of the poem might allow for forgiveness:

> *end*   (in Heaven)
> And your voice is transfigured
> And interesting to God

On the other hand, in other drafts, Berryman was to subject Anne Bradstreet to a passage of· what he called 'delirium,' as in these sections:

> He smells the rifle and lifts it. It is long.
> It points at my heart.   (48:6−7)

> I image a fire burning without outlet,
> consuming acrid its own smoke. It's me.
> I do writhe and choke.[23]

He relieved the pressure towards mortification by his understanding of the first part of the final stanza:

> O all your ages at the mercy of my loves
> together lie at once, forever or
> so long as I happen.   (57:1−3)

He explained that these lines begin 'perhaps the transition from her end (sick, dead) to my poem's (loving) end'.

To convey these psychological and physical devices, Berryman rightly felt that he needed 'a more living, looser, flexible syntax', which was to appear less artful, but in fact to be more so. It needed to be tenuous and sensuous, and able to accommodate 'bulks of facts'.

The poem began to take shape as a three-part structure: scene-setting;

crisis; resolution. Anne Bradstreet would establish a physical presence 'in some very carefully described homely operation' such as supervising a servant. The exchange with the servant was to be one of 'fierce, calm detail' which Berryman compared to that of Degas' painting 'Jockeys'. The 'poet's' opportunity for seducing her was to be provided by the fact that the historical Anne Bradstreet had actually to suffer a 'long separation' from her beloved husband. During that period she would long for a child. At one point Berryman drafted seven stanzas on child-longing, which he then considered too many. A draft of this sort made the direction of her thought too explicit and blunt:

> O childless, childless, from the roaring waves,
> year after year, as if that crossing'd shockt
> A timorous womb.

These two factors, the combination of spousal separation and of longing for a child, were then to be consummated in the rigours of childbirth followed by a liaison with the 'poet'. Another of her attitudes or motives, her feeling of rebelliousness against God, husband and father, summed up in a fragment 'O Father galled', was to lead the poem towards its final phase. What Berryman called 'a *jagged* passage *downward* (psychological; at first medical and ambiguous) into her father's extremity, "jealous and just"', would be followed by a general dying away in the poem, 'out of which the end of her life gradually arises'.

When he had charted the poem to this point, he felt that after undergoing the crisis of acquiescence with the 'poet's' inducements, Anne Bradstreet should naturally feel extreme guilt. Berryman had recorded on 5 September 1948 that he himself felt a sense of 'despair over my innocence irrecoverable': Anne Bradstreet should share the feeling. But the 'poet' was also to experience a concomitant feeling— a resentment towards the woman as the object of his sinfulness. On 6 June 1952, Berryman dreamt that he had murdered a number of women and was burning their bodies on bars over a fire, an action which merited capital punishment. So vivid was the dream that Berryman included it as part of the 'poet's' speech:

> I trundle the bodies, on the iron bars,
> over that fire backward & forth; they burn;

> bits fall. I wonder if
> *I* killed them. Women serve my turn.   (34:1−4)

Despite the fact that Anne Bradstreet next says, 'Dreams! You are good', the point of the exchange is that the 'poet' is in effect saying to her that, while other women were prey to him, she could count herself safe. After this episode, she recoils and recedes from the 'poet' into emblematic scenes of ghastly punishment, of her father's terrible death and of her own ambivalent fate.

It is crucial to a deeper understanding of the poem to appreciate Berryman's close and personal sense of the subject, not only in stanza 34 but throughout the drama. On another occasion, for example, he dreamt of 'cached murdered bodies', and recorded afterwards his feeling that 'it is my *daysense* of *not* having having [sic] murdered that is false,—not my nightsense of having murdered'. In other words, the 'poet' expresses in stanza 34 Berryman's own feelings of having exploited women: 'Women serve my turn', after a section detailing the association of murder and sexual opportunism. The sense of guilt and withdrawal which the 'poet' and Anne Bradstreet share, was to be sustained to the end of the poem and to infect the whole modern world through an elaborate simile of atomic processes—a nuclear reactor generating chaos—an image that remained discernible in the abstruse phrase, 'reactor piles wage slow upon the wet brain rime' (55:8).

By 25 July 1952, the poem had advanced to the point of adumbrating the notion of withdrawal, of diminishment towards death:

> when we *are* all together, and exhausted bones
> And brains must stir and brood no more.

Berryman had finished studying Helen Campbell's biography of Anne Bradstreet[24] by 7 April. The twenty-eight pages of notes that he had taken from the biography, together with additions from Winthrop's *Journals*, Perry Miller's *New England Mind*, and other works, were to provide the factual and historical background of the poem. One of the problems for Berryman was how the poem might ingest so much real detail and still remain, not a historical compendium but a fictitious drama. By 28 July 1952, he had seventy-five or eighty pages of notes, and more than 125 draft lines of poetry. It was also on 28 July that he began to make progress on the poem from the point at line 9 where he had stalled after his first efforts four years earlier. At that time, he had one complete stanza and the first line of the second stanza. Having progressed that far, Berryman needed to regroup his ideas, study the sources, and undertake the long period of gestation that would eventually yield a conceptual basis and dramatic structure. Now, he determined, to 'POUR IN what-is-*already-done* FAST, or the poem will flap away.' One of the important corrections at this time involved the last line of the second stanza, which originally read: 'Times' flood I fly carried thro' one short arc.' From being a romantic and atemporal notion, Berryman revised the line as a direct statement of alienation and of affiliation with Anne Bradstreet: 'Both of our worlds broke each of us. Lie stark' (January 1953). (The verb 'broke' was alternately 'rooked' and 'racked' before he settled on the final, superior choice of 'unhanded'.)[25]

When he had drafted the first five stanzas, Berryman decided to focus attention on the settlers for a while, 'up thro' the *fact* of her not becoming preg[nant]—("Something keeps on not happening, I shrink")'.[26] He felt that perhaps the crucial fact of her apparent failure to conceive a child should not even be made clear. Accordingly, the poem would display her repining in girlhood, followed by a movement towards the line, 'then the pox blasted, when the Lord returned' (14:2)—clearly to associate physical suffering with religious punishment[27]—and only then to her admission of grief at childlessness. After such a measure of waiting, Anne Bradstreet would have a child at the right psychological moment (the natural fulfilment of a period of apprehension and anticipation shared by the reader), followed by what Berryman called 'my love (describe her then)'.

Throughout the process of drafting fragments, he had gradually outlined the structure of the poem, as we have seen. Next he schematised it as a three-part process:

1) her life – towards close of (1) allow high spirits, wit.
2) my black love
3) her resistance and (hatred? and) anti-religion, e.g. and modern life (war) and my penitent love and her death.

By six o'clock on 24 January 1953, Berryman had successfully drafted the first seventy-five lines of the poem, to the third line of stanza 10. Anne Bradstreet's community had weathered the initial hardships and seemed to be stabilising itself. But the 'sea' (which apparently the settlers had crossed in safety) was now to generate more of the qualities of a symbol, to be emphasised in the context of her barrenness, of religious sectarianism, and of her own verse:

> mistress neither of fiery nor velvet verse, on your knees
>
> hopeful & shamefast, chaste, laborious, odd,
> whom the sea tore. . . .   (12:8−13:2)

The meaning here, as other notes verify, is that the sea should be 'wounding' (a word which, Berryman knew, has Freudian connotations of sexual intercourse) to Anne Bradstreet and the 'poet', her lover, and that eventually, as Berryman's notes record, 'the sea wins'.[28]

When he had completed what is now stanza 12, Berryman moved straight on to draft stanza 15: 'Drydust in God's eye . . .' It had taken him a long weekend, ending on 27 January, to write what he called the 'honeymoon' of the poem – the worthy hardships of the New England settlement. Then occurred 'the Hump of the first part of the poem': he had to backtrack and integrate the nexus of stanzas 13 and 14, the grievous association of father, husband, and God the Father. I quote from the fifth line of stanza 12:

> – To please your wintry father? all this bald
> abstract didactic rime I read appalled
> harassed for your fame
> mistress neither of fiery nor velvet verse, on your knees
>
> 13
>
> hopeful & shamefast, chaste, laborious, odd,
> whom the sea tore. – The damned roar with loss,
> so they hug & are mean
> with themselves, and I cannot be thus.
> Why then do I repine, sick, bad, to long
> after what must not be? I lie wrong
> once more. For at fourteen
> I found my heart more carnal and sitting loose from God,
>
> 14
>
> vanity and the follies of youth took hold of me

Berryman questions the egregious quality of her verse, and asks whether it was written to please her 'wintry father?'. His observation about her verse is taken from Helen Campbell's remarks about Bradstreet's *Four Seasons*, which (since they have not been located elsewhere) need to be recovered in their context:

> With the final lines a rush of dissatisfaction came over the writer, and she added certain couplets, addressed to her father, for whom the whole set seems to have been originally composed, and who may be responsible for the bald and didactic quality of most of her work.[29]

It is important that Berryman lays such stress upon the negative influence her father wielded over her. Earlier, Anne Bradstreet had herself lamented that 'Versing, I *shroud* among the dynasties' (12:1) (my italics), a remark which clearly conveys the deathly power of her father. Berryman discloses the direction his poem is to take by extrapolating phrases from Bradstreet's letter 'To My Dear Children',[30] used in the last three lines of the passage quoted (13:7– 14:1). For Berryman the dominance of Anne Bradstreet's father and her own sexual rebelliousness are grimly united, the one being almost the begetter of the other. It is then by way of retaliation that Berryman causes her father to die the awful death of stanza 43:

> Father is not himself. He keeps his bed,
> and threw a saffron scum Thursday. God-forsaken words
> escaped him raving.

In his comments on the passage, Alan Holder misapprehends its personal vehemence: 'The poet is exhibiting a characteristic American response to the Puritan fathers, desiring to judge Dudley's harshness harshly . . .'[31] Berryman himself gave a gleefully malicious account of the matter: 'The third pleasant moment I remember is when one night, hugging myself, I decided that her fierce dogmatic old father was going to die blaspheming, in delirium.'[32] To appreciate the implications of that outrageous death, the last lines of stanza 7 give evidence:

> The Lady Arbella dying—
> dyings – at which my heart   rose, but I did submit.
>
> (7:7–8)

These lines, which significantly violate the possibilities of conventional grammar,[33] juxtapose the death of Lady Arbella Fiennes to Anne Bradstreet's initial religious protestations:

> After a short time I changed my condition and was married, and came into this country, where I found a new world and new manners, at which my heart rose. But after I was convinced it was the way of God, I submitted to it and joined the church at Boston.[34]

The Church at this time had become divided into the 'Prelatical or Hierarchical' headed by Laud, and the Nonconformist or Puritan. On arrival in New England, Anne Bradstreet adhered to the former, but presently she was converted to the new way of Puritanism. What strikes me as remarkable in *Homage to Mistress Bradstreet*, however, is that Berryman refuses to signify the context of Bradstreet's apostasy, but transposes the matter of her rebellion and submission to that of 'dyings', the syntactically disconnected first word of line 8. The most likely interpretation is that stanza 7 presents an acute impression of religiosity as death. As we have seen, that religiosity is intimately connected with Anne Bradstreet's father, with her marriage, and with her potential for sexual rebellion.[35]

The next step was the poetic representation of Anne Bradstreet's parturition, an undertaking almost unprecedented in literature. For the sake of authenticity, Berryman determined to consult any or all of the real-life mothers that he knew, including his own mother and a friend, Betty Mackie. In the event, Brenda Engel laboured again for Berryman, as she recalls:

> J. B. called me one afternoon and said he needed some advice; could he come over and ask me some questions; his 'mistress was having a baby.' I was in some confusion until it became clear that he was referring to his poem.
>
> He came over and I remember answering, to the best of my ability, his very specific and intense questions: how long did the strong labor pains last; what kinds of pains were they; what kinds of thoughts went through my head during labor; how the pains changed as labor progressed; and so on.
>
> He seemed to be trying to understand, as clearly as possible, *exactly* what a woman went through, both physically and psychologically in the course of giving birth—every step of the

way. He tried to understand so clearly that he himself almost
seemed to be trying to empathize. His questions were very
detailed. Some he repeated and seemed dissatisfied with my
answers. It was difficult to put into words just what birth pains felt
like and, under J. B.'s questioning, I must have spent an hour or so
trying.[36]

The critic Carol Johnson has said that 'The first complicating
mistakes are in the preternaturally speedy and literal parturition
recounted in the space of three stanzas (19–21).'[37] But the point
about the passage is that not only was Berryman true to his source,[38]
as in the lines,

> everything down
> hardens, I press with horrible joy down
> my back cracks like a wrist   (19:5–7)

but also that the literalness of the movement—heavily-stressed, an
anguished stream-of-consciousness verging upon hallucinatory
intensity—is precisely Berryman's object. The final line of this stanza,
'shame I am voiding oh behind it is too late', seems to present one of
Berryman's oddities of consciousness. Sergio Perosa writes that 'It
must be taken, apparently, both in a figurative and a literal sense. As
John Ciardi has written, in this stanza "there are clues enough, and
more, for putting all the elements not only in order, but in *various
possible simultaneous orders*—which is precisely the effect the poet has
sought."'[39] Childbirth is related to incontinence, for example,
through the non-predicational collocation of 'shame I am voiding oh
behind'.

Drafting proceeded through stanzas 19 and 20. But Berryman
struck a wrong note in stanza 21, which was designed to register
'ECSTASY', without rhetoric, as characteristic and exalted. This is the
draft version:

> Drenched and powerful, I did it with my body!
> One blinding stroke greens Heaven, marvellous,
> Unforbidding majesty.
> What horror, down stormy air,
> Warped towards me—whence I fought free.[40]

The transition from the third to the fourth lines quoted is a shock, an unannounced swing from bliss to horror, unsubtle and ambivalent. The transition of mood, if it had been left in that form, would have been gratuitously blunt, since it would have disturbed the psychological pattern of the poem, in which motherhood was to be the *real* fulfilment of the first period of yearning. The last two lines of the draft were eventually held over until stanza 38, at a point when Anne Bradstreet is becoming disabused of her sinful relationship with the poet. In that context, the last four words—'whence I fought free'—were eliminated, to be replaced by a rendering of Berryman's own feeling, as he expressed it in a note, that the 'poet' should be given 'the last part of this line, as his last black word?':

What horror, down stormy air,
warps towards me? My threatening promise faints

(38: 7– 8)

An awareness of this revision helps us to make sense of the phrase, 'My threatening promise faints', which seems otherwise to be syntactically disconnected and unaccountable. There is no indication, from punctuation or characterisation, that this phrase is spoken by the poet, but it does seem probable that 'threatening promise' denotes the desperate mendacity of the seducer–'poet'.

When Berryman read back over the stanzas written so far, he felt that a portentous lull was needed in the intense onrush of the plot, and provided it in a wholly new stanza 16, which is quiet in tone but surges with aspects of religious fear and local superstition.

On 27 January 1953, Berryman sent Allen Tate the first ten stanzas in typescript. Three days later Tate responded: 'Your poem is *very* fine, and I await the finish. I've read these stanzas about ten times with an increasing sense of luminosity . . . There's nothing like this being done; you've never done anything like it; and you've got to slug it out.' On 3 February, Berryman sent him a further instalment, to Tate's mounting excitement: 'Page 4 of the poem [the published stanzas 17 to 21, which include Anne's parturition; what is now stanza 16 had not yet been written] creates real suspense: I've got to have the rest . . . You've never written any poetry before within 6 light years of this. There's great technical mastery and (if you will allow the phrase) a mature command of life.'[41] After another three days he told Tate how much heart-ache the composition gave him:

I feel like weeping all the time. What keeps me from weeping is partly my ecstasy and partly a daily necessity of the hardest, most calculated work I have ever done—and (though it never came to anything) I have done hard work.

By the way: I regard every word in the poem as either a murderer or a lover and I am not much less avid abt every mark of printing as destructive of or loving to the subject and I know there are stupidities and crimes in the stanzas you have, but I won't bother you now with those I've expiated.

You understand that the reason I am moving at this merciless speed is that I have been on this ground since 1948. One of my worst worries is that there still remain of *pages* of sketching, aesthetics, and notes, some 50 unexamined and so all of their parts unapportioned even to sections, much less to section-parts. Lord have mercy on us and bless you.[42]

In July 1952, Berryman seems not to have thought through the role that the 'poet' was to take in the drama. He had not yet devised an adequate means of interaction between his protagonists. In fact, he talked of 'my relief at her distance (therefore inaccessible)'—three centuries' distance. Although he determined that the 'poet' should love Anne Bradstreet through all stages of her life, even as a grandmother, he yet lacked a tense involution of plot. Instead, he set about to group themes. On the one hand was a great deal of description: the voyage to America; the fight with the wilderness; Anne Bradstreet's patience in Sarah-like childlessness; the suffocation of provincial culture. On the other hand, Berryman dwelt much on the theme of dispossession—of England, of King, of homes, of friends, children and parents, and (since the poem was to draw towards Anne Bradstreet's end) of life. The poem would close with 'trumpets of obliteration, non-Christian—and a consolation after all'.

Anne Bradstreet was to be very much a woman of her time. Specific points of relation were needed, so that she should be seen 'not in a mist, nor now', but as real and temporal, confined to her own age by the mortal span of flesh and blood. One such point is provided when she compares her skin to 'the crabs and shells of my Palissy ewer' (28:2). In one way, this image is an example of what Berryman called 'the *relieving* grotesqueness'—signifying, that is, her reality as a not necessarily fetching woman, rather than as a symbol of romantic ideality, of the disembodied fair. The comparison with the decorative style of the potter Palissy was singularly appropriate to the concept. Bernard Palissy (*c.* 1510–90) made earthenware which, by his own description, aimed less at beauty than at the 'estrangeté et monstruosité' of a vision or dream, his decorations being often moulded from the *nature morte* itself. His technique, a kind of horrifying naturalism, was intended specifically *ad aemulatione della natura*. What became known as the 'style rustique' continued after him for about a century.

Anne Bradstreet should also be real, however, as a person subject to painful doubts of her identity and of the direction of her life.

> Distrusting who I am, mother, daughter, wife,
> Myself, victim of cold, nostalgia,
> Inattention, and heroine of mad joy
> Forbid, I hate to let my poems be seen
> Pride to make—I think, I admit; but

The next movement of the plot was to present 'A love forbidden by Time and Space, and the laws of God and man, and death', but how was the language to accomplish it? Berryman knew that the chief problem was to portray the 'poet' himself, who, up to this point, really has not said anything—is just a presence so much less material than even Anne Bradstreet—and 'hence has no *tone*, and naturally it's hard to construct it'. Berryman compared the difficulty with Tolstoy's mistake in making Vronsky so passive towards Anna in *Anna Karenina*. 'I can't hear him,' he complained of the 'poet'. 'Yet he can't just fit between her speeches!' At this point, Berryman realised that the location for their liaison was finally unimportant, since the emphasis of the tryst was psychological, not geographical-historical: 'the consent of the will is the sin.' Both characters could, then, temporise with the exigencies of what was really a conceptual device: Anne Bradstreet could move forward in time, the 'poet' backward:

> a twanging, an unusual fatigue,
> slips our eras backward and forward.

Finally, at noon on Friday, 30 January, Berryman fully perceived that the second movement of the poem would have to be a dialogue 'between them (her and me)'. Looking back on the poem after several years, he remembered that realisation as being one of his moments of

'special heat': 'I realized that the middle of the poem was going to
have to be in *dialogue*, a dialogue between the seventeenth-century
woman and the twentieth-century poet—a sort of extended witch-
seductress and demon-lover bit.'[43] My own judgement of the passage is to second Ian Hamilton's qualified approval: ' . . . her
voice . . . meets with his in an almost hysterical dialogue of
temptation and guilt that has moments of extraordinary power.'[44]

On 3 February, Berryman typed an extensive programmatic note
for the poem:

> Perhaps a way of getting into Part Two is this: the poet describes
> her, with increasing detail and assurance and tenderness, and
> suddenly she says something showing (to the reader's amazement)
> that she *hears* the poet. Then the poet can at once speak to her
> absolutely directly. For a time the love is—innocent? The poet asks
> nothing, recognizes it as hopeless; so, she is surprised but not
> frightened. Guilt grows unaware until it hurls itself on her, and on
> him.
>
> Yes. But by that time she is locked in desire.
>
> 'I *want* to take you for my lover.' *Do*. And he does not help her.
> Instead he argues that *since* they are lost anyway, *be* lost together,
> wholly. (He misses the whole point of the Will involved and
> crucial.) This point of Will is what she finally returns to—besides
> revulsion, and hatred of *desiring* Evil, and suddenly cries out that
> she is not God's any longer! then
>
> 'Torture me, Father, lest not I be thine.'
>
> Upon her turn away from evil, with her help, *he* finally turns. And
> she continues alone into Part Three.

Stanza 27 began with the four lines published in the finished
version, but then the fifth line introduced this exchange: 'I *want* to
take you for my lover.—Do.' Again, the emotional advance was too
precipitate, for this dialogue had its source in a real exchange between
Berryman himself and the girl referred to as 'Lise' in *Berryman's
Sonnets*. Sonnet 42 dates from 30 June 1947:

> 'I want to take you for my lover' just
> You vowed when on the way I met you: must
> Then that be all (*Do*) the shorn time we share?

The exchange can best be glossed by a note Berryman wrote at the time, referring to the girl's declaration as 'that unreproducible intonation'. In Berryman's own words, the rhythm of the statement implies: 'I can see myself as your *lover*: I *am*: but not your husband.' At this point the drama of *Homage to Mistress Bradstreet* required a more neutral aspect: accordingly, he gave Anne Bradstreet a symbolic but housewifely line: 'A fading world I dust, with fingers new' (27:5). The line apparently represented to Berryman what he later described as being the 'tactical solution of a problem arising out of this [the dialogue in which he had engaged his protagonists]: how to make them in some measure physically present to each other.'[45] In the same place he adds that 'Later on it appears that they kiss . . .', but it should be understood that Berryman's comment is best construed with particular stress on the verb 'appears'. What is in question are four words spoken by Anne Bradstreet—'Kiss me. / That once.' (30:1–2)—which are clearly marked for ambiguity. It is surely important to the success of the conceptual poise of the poem that whether or not the characters are physically present to each other remains in doubt.

By Sunday, 8 February 1953, Berryman had drafted the three stanzas which begin the second movement of the poem, being particularly pleased with what he called (in his diary) her first 'real speech'—about her hair (26:4–8). He then wondered why Section II should not be 'all her? (He is suggested, the love and assault, and that's enough).' In the event, the poem was to be entirely voiced; that is, every word of the way is spoken by someone. For one important matter, such a device avoided a confrontation other than by verbal intercourse. Anne Bradstreet and the 'poet' are physically present to each other, talk to each other, but do not actually make physical love to each other. An account of their love-making would have necessitated descriptive narrative, which the ruse of direct speech decorously avoids.

A problem that remained through the excitation of the dialogue between 'poet' and Anne Bradstreet was for Berryman 'to get feelingly down' and through, as he put it, to the idyl of her unconscious mind, 'then back up and agony'.[46] In consequence of such an oppressive form of scrutiny, she would become madly nervous, even ill, 'under my pressure', as Berryman put it. These notations give the psychosomatic dimension to Anne's lines about her smallpox—' . . . a manic stench /of pustules snapping . . .'—in stanza 29. At about this time too, Berryman decided to introduce what he called an 'aria stanza', originally to have been spoken by Anne Bradstreet. It then became evident that she should in fact invite the 'poet' to address her, to which he might respond with a vivid, nervous, emotional stanza describing spring, subtly interwoven, as Berryman himself described it, with '*images* of erection, longing'. The result was stanza 31, which contains a melody appropriate to the 'poet's' blandishments, since, as Berryman put it in this connection, the 'poet' is 'the damned seducer'.

He next decided to incorporate their 'idyl', followed by what he called 'back-n-forth laceration'. The idyl was rightly to be brief and precarious, since, as one draft stated, 'my /Desire to be dissolved, and be with Thee' was 'a weakness and a darkness'. Despite the fact that this phrase carried in Berryman's mind a double burden—as sexual and Christological—the motif of being 'dissolved' directed the inclusion of what a note calls 'Images of drowning, undersea, in *senses*, in the past'. Using that notation, it is possible to deduce that the idyl in point is stanza 33, where Berryman represents the rapture of love /lust through the use of what are called 'délires des grandes profondeurs', an expression explained in the published notes to the poem: ' . . . a euphoria, sometimes fatal, in which the hallucinated diver offers passing fish his line, helmet, anything.' The hallucinatory aspect of this experience backfires on the 'poet', who is impelled towards his own visionary or eidetic account (in stanza 34 discussed above) of exploiting women. He betrays his sinfulness through his own words, and instantly reawakens Anne Bradstreet towards reparative steps: 'Dreams! You are good.' The outburst is melodramatic, but its necessary dramatic function is to shock her into an awareness of the 'poet's' evil influence. From that point onwards, what little the poet says to sustain his case, as in stanza 35, is unavailing.

Stanza 36 introduces the rigours of self-chastisement, displaying what Berryman called 'the *emptiness* of sin; its *dis*harmony':

> —Hard and divided heaven! creases me. Shame
> is failing. My breath is scented, and I throw
> hostile glances towards God.
> Crumpling plunge of a pestle, bray:
> sin cross & opposite, wherein I survive
> nightmares of Eden. Reaches foul & live
> he for me, this soul
> to crunch, a minute tangle of eternal flame.

The word 'survive' in line 5 originally read 'enjoy', a change which dramatises the acuteness of this shift of emphasis. The irony of this

reversal must be appreciated, since the 'poet's' self-betrayal in stanza
34 is caused by what Berryman called 'her anxiety about "losing"
him, which she expresses ambivalently as a wish for reassurance:
"Straiten me on."' The manuscripts at this point also indicate that the
poet too should feel a sense of pointlessness from the whole
arrangement: 'Here am I tied to/A service athwart Time, and to no
end.'

The rest of this movement mingles fact and fantasy in a morbid
decline. The poet fades from the scene, and illness and old age afflict
Anne Bradstreet, as instanced in Berryman's use of the English
proverb, 'Gray Hairs are death's blossoms':[47]

> Death's blossoms grain my hair; I cannot live.   (37:2)

Through stanza 43, where her father dies in a terrible psychological
nadir already referred to, and on to stanza 53, almost a quarter of the
whole poem is given over to the facts of the historical Anne
Bradstreet's declining years, supplemented by the grotesqueries of
religiose excess. The poem ends in a historical quietus and fatalism.
Originally, Berryman was to propose a balance: 'His vision to her of
her "country's" future is both good and bad—*Immoderate cities loft.*'
The last stage of the poet's homage to Anne Bradstreet is in fact
ambiguous, suggesting the perseverance of their relationship either in
the enjoyment of an afterlife or as long as the poet is alive to
memorialise his heroine:

> O all your ages at the mercy of my lives
> together lie at once, forever or
> so long as I happen.   (57:1−3)[48]

The poem was actually completed by Sunday, 15 March 1953, and
Berryman gave the first public reading in Princeton on 23 March.

Various aspects of the poem show how close it was to Berryman's
own experience. It was at one time to have been dedicated 'To
Adamine', a name that concealed the identity of a girl for whom
Berryman hopelessly longed in 1954− more than a year after he had
completed the work, when he was preparing it for book publication.
Anne Bradstreet's intimacy with her children is illustrated in these
lines:

Sam, your uncle has had to
go from us to live with God. 'Then Aunt went too?'
Dear, she does wait still.
Stricken: 'Oh. Then he takes   us one by one.' My dear.

(23:5—8)

Berryman's source for this exchange was a letter written to him long before—on 27 February 1943—by his sister-in-law, Marie. She had just told her son Jimmy about her uncle Charles's death, and was relieved to find how readily the boy accepted the naturalness of death—that God takes us 'one by one'. She concluded her letter with a devout sense of thankfulness that her son should be spared any fear of death. It was a moving statement of faith in God's providence to which Berryman responded profoundly.

The conditions informing Berryman's own affairs of 1947 and 1948 (if not of others), and their essential likeness of character, obtain in the poem; only the surroundings are changed. Anne Bradstreet is the type of Berryman's desubstantiated self. His breath is mixed with her agony and consolation.

Alienated from her husband, her father, and her religion, unable to quench her longing in the bliss of childbirth, Anne Bradstreet seeks to realise her needs in adultery with the 'poet'. A fundamentally curious feature of the poem is that Berryman takes such pains to capture her as a mother, and *only then* to express the febrile tensions of her purposed affair with the 'poet'. The explanation of that strategy is found in Berryman's own life. Probably all of his mistresses during the late 1940s—certainly of the two crucial affairs during 1947 and 1948— were married with one or more children. Berryman's own wife had been childless all the years of their marriage (since 1942). The order of events in the poem is of utmost importance in this respect, since Berryman sees the figure in the poem as no woman's lover unless she is gifted with children. By depicting a relationship beyond space and time, he is attempting to transcend the subjectivity of the autobiographical nisus. The consummation of the affair is uttered but unattained. Anne Bradstreet admits the wish, which is the sin itself, and recoils almost in the same moment, and then survives many more years of penitence and penance. After displacing his own sense of blame upon Anne Bradstreet, that is to say, Berryman goes on to absolve her of his own ill spirit. 'The point of the Bradstreet poem', he told Richard Kostelanetz, 'was to take an unbelievably conventional woman and give her every possible trial and possibility of error and so

on, and wind her up in a crazy love affair, and then get her out of it—
better, get her out of it in ways that will allow her forgetting of it after
a long period of time.'[49] Berryman's synopsis may be glossed as at
once whimsical and painfully ironic.

On 19 December 1954, Berryman wrote this entry in his *Journal of
Self-Analysis*: ' "Listen, *Sister Anne*" I was just saying to myself in an
imaginary conversation with Eileen—.' He was referring to stanza 25
of the poem:

> Bitter sister, victim! I miss you.
> —I miss you, Anne,
> day or night weak as a child   (25:2—4)

Berryman realised just how ambivalent his feelings had been in
connection with adultery and his marriage, both sublimated in the
poem. The Anne Bradstreet of his poem had absorbed the identities of
mistress/mother and childless wife. A fictional mistress had borne the
child that the real wife had not. The concept, as Berryman himself
then fully acknowledged, had been made prominent and ambiguous
in the poem—even, as he pointed out, down to the use of the terms
'victim' and 'child'. The poem was both a lament for a doomed
marriage—John and Eileen Berryman split up later that year—and a
homage to a figure uniting mistress and wife.

3. 'The Care & Feeding of Long Poems'

Early in his work on *The Dream Songs*, Berryman wondered whether to provide them with an 'argument' in the classical sense, or else to borrow the attitude of Juan Maria Cecchi (1518–89), 'who in *La Dote* refused to tell the Argument "since men today are so intelligent that they understand without having so many arguments before-hand"'.[1] If Berryman had employed Cecchi's policy, it would have been in a spirit of self-defensive irony combined with sarcasm. Problems of form and structure in *The Dream Songs* have vexed all Berryman's critics, not least because of his self-declarations in a number of interviews, such as: 'I was aware that I was embarked on an epic.'[2] No extended study of Berryman's work has been able to avoid the question, mainly because of the poet's insistence that *The Dream Songs* must be taken as *one* poem, not as an accumulation of lyrics with certain features of diction or theme in common. The fact that Berryman has taken pains to divide the Songs into seven books of unequal length, in the midst of which—the fourth book—the hero of the work is dead, arouses expectations of clearly discernible narrative or, at least, that each book might be, as Berryman put it pro-vocatively, 'rather well unified, as a matter of fact'.[3] In the same place, he declared:

> The narrative such as it is developed as I went along, partly out of my gropings into and around Henry, and his environment, partly out of my readings in theology and that sort of thing, taking place during thirteen years—awful long time—and third, out of certain partly preconceived and partly developing as I went along, sometimes rigid and sometimes plastic, structural notions.[4]

Berryman remained open to all the theories his critics propounded—'one of them, a woman, sees it as a series of three odysseys, psychological and moral, on the part of Henry'—but all

34

critics must feel disarmed by his disclaimer of anything like a categorical imperative of epic structure: 'I don't know whether she is right or not, but if so, I did not begin with that full-fledged conception when I wrote the first dream song.'[5] He never did manage to solve or waive the question of whether or not the Songs function as a single poem. In March 1959, for example, he wrote a draft fragment for a Song:

> where thought, word kiss,
> what makes Henry hard is due
> rei magnitudine, doctoris
> imperitia, audientis durita.[6]

The obscurity of the poems was not deliberate, that is to say, but comparable to St Jerome's task in biblical commentary: obscurity was due to the enormity of the task, the teacher's lack of skill, and the indifference of his listeners.

What may reasonably be inferred from such efforts at justification is that Berryman himself was not aware of the framework that the Songs were designed to fit, especially when even his more searching and appreciative critics began to share the opinion that little sense of story or development is perceptible. One of the finest among the more recent attempts to discern that shape has been made by Jack Vincent Barbera, who bases his findings on a study of Berryman's manuscript drafts. His conclusions support the case for an absence of form, but without prejudice:

> Although patterning is everywhere in the poem, it is everywhere local. There is the structured movement within Songs and the groupings of Songs; but there is no actual or implied overall pattern by which all the groups are ordered, the whole finished and sealed.[7]

Barbera proceeds lucidly to show that 'Berryman arranged many of them into clusters of varying cohesion',[8] and to explode what he calls the 'fiction of prevailing chronological order'[9] which seems to be a structural device of the last three books. As for the first books, he has this to say:

> Berryman's method in these first three Books seems to have been not so much writing Songs to fit a preconceived theme as writing

Songs and then selecting among them and figuring out some plan
by which to organize them.
. . .

   When asked if the Opus Posthumous Songs were in the center
(as Book 4) to conform to epic convention, Berryman denied it:
the placement of the Songs, he said, 'is purely personal' (*Advocate*,
5). Aside from inter-Book transitions, Book 4 could just as well be
earlier or later in the poem than it is (and it would be an easy matter
to change around the transitions).
   This does not mean the whole poem is without plot, but the plot
is of casual rather than necessary order—variations on the
personality of Henry as he lives, remembers, and dreams at various
times over a decade. Any *ulterior* overall structure, Berryman
emphatically denied. . . .[10]

Although Barbera's discriminations are excellent, it does seem to me
that his findings are in some sense neglectful of Berryman's best
endeavours. The conclusion that has been almost universally
reached—that the Songs were discontinuous in the writing and
unpremeditated in overall structure— is invariably shuffled off with
the explanation that it finally does not matter, and that the binding
qualities of the poem inhere in qualities quite other than the formal
structural or philosophic ones. It is not surprising that, among all the
reviews of *77 Dream Songs*, Berryman found Adrienne Rich's
uniquely satisfying, for her perceptions seemed to validate his
procedures:

   . . . it is the identity of Henry . . . which holds the book together,
   makes it clearly a real book and not a collection of chance pieces
   loosely flung under one cover. None of the poems (except possibly
   the elegies) carries in isolation the weight and perspective that it
   does in relation to the rest; partly because the cumulative awareness
   of Henry is built from poem to poem.[11]

She concludes that the work is truly original because of its superiority
in 'inner necessity and by the force of a unique human character'.[12]
But her phrase about 'inner necessity' tends to beg rather than to
answer questions operative on the level of story: the direction in
which a long poem may be seen to move (according to customary
expectations) and its reasons for that movement.
Berryman certainly did try to model the Dream Songs on

traditional epic structures, but he failed on his own terms to achieve that end. His lack of prevenient purpose gave him hundreds of hours of unrest—indeed, distress—for what seemed to be in question was the notion less of 'preconceived theme' than of a preconceived plot. While he was not terribly worried about the problems of cohesion within the individual Songs (since it did not seem to him too difficult to bind each eighteen-line unit), the relationship between all units grew ineluctable even to Berryman himself. The problem was how to order the sequence on the principle of necessity and not just of catenation? Like many of his critics, Berryman thought it needful to have some idea of narrative or inevitability to the sequence. The models he turned to most resolutely included Dante's *Divine Comedy*, the liturgical structure of the Bible as explicated by Archbishop Philip Carrington, the categories set out by Joseph Campbell in *The Hero with a Thousand Faces*, and the *Iliad*. None of those paradigms provide a strict equivalence for the unfolding activities of Henry, but all of them gave Berryman insights into structure which were to inform his own epic. He was not above forcing a mould upon his Songs, but it is important to recognise that Berryman's failure to impose a narrative structure gave him a deductive sense of the form proper to the peculiarities of his hero. In June 1963 he wrote an enthusiastic letter to Randall Jarrell (who had recognised that the poem was unified) insisting that 'there's one thematic norm, one personality, one diction, one set of dramatic arrangements',[13] but he felt unable to applaud himself for the singleness of its structure and story.

While Berryman was writing the first of the Dream Songs, he had not long completed *Homage to Mistress Bradstreet*, his first major poem. He later told Martin Berg that it took him 'two years' to recover from the momentous task of writing *Homage*: 'But, I didn't blow my brains out either.'[14] He was also at that time fashioning a prior long sequence called 'The Black Book'—a cycle of poems about the Nazi persecution of the Jews. The Songs, as he then looked on them, were to be a new venture, almost (in his own word) 'an interlude' between *Homage* and 'The Black Book'. Four sections from 'The Black Book' had seen print in *Poetry* magazine in 1950.[15] Although the subject nagged him for some years, Berryman was never able to complete the project, for which his original plans (as he told Jonathan Sisson in 1966) were awesome in scope and intensity:

The subject was—it was more than I could bear. I wrote about eighty parts, I guess. It was in the form of a Mass for the Dead. It was designed to have 42 sections. . . . But I just found I couldn't take it. The sections published—there were eight of them in Poetry—are unrelievedly horrible. I wasn't able at this time—that was about twenty years ago—to find any way of making palatable the monstrosity of the thing which obsessed me.[16]

Between 1955 and 1957, therefore, Berryman moved to develop new resources in terms of style and content.

He began at an early stage to establish within individual Songs patterns and meanings that appear to be often inaccessible. The burden of 'A Stimulant for an Old Beast' (Song 3), for example, must be guessed at; it seems to comprehend Berryman's abhorrence of decadence and of being divorced from the experiences of real life, but even such tentative construings instantly fall foul of the difficulties of paraphrasing the incoherent. When such poems accumulated, each patterned according to its own internal demands of thought and emotion, Berryman had to admit that the larger problems of organisation became all the more acute. As time went on, he grew less concerned with the specific intensity of the individual Songs. His change of approach works to benefit the whole poem, for it is clear that the density of *77 Dream Songs* militates against its success. In 1971, Berryman told Joseph Haas that 'it takes about three Songs in Books 5 and 6 and 7 to get done what I was doing in one in the first volume'.[17]

It should be said, however, that some of the difficulties and obscurities of *77 Dream Songs* are more apparent than real, and may depend only on the identification of specific names or references for the pattern and meaning to emerge. Song 11, for example, seems to be a poem as abstruse as 'A Stimulant for an Old Beast', but it actually expresses a more finely controlled meaning.

His mother goes. The mother comes & goes.
Chen Lung's too came, came and crampt & then
that dragoner's mother was gone.
It seems we don't have no good bed to lie on,
forever. While he drawing his first breath,
while skinning his knees,

while he was so beastly with love for Charlotte Coquet
he skated up & down in front of her house
wishing he could, sir, die,

while being bullied & he dreamt he could fly—
during irregular verbs—them world-sought bodies
safe in the Arctic lay:

Strindberg rocked in his niche, the great Andrée
by muscled Fraenkel under what's of the tent,
torn like then limbs, by bears
over fierce decades, harmless. Up in pairs
go we not, but we have a good bed.
I have said what I had to say.

In the second line, the name 'Chen Lung' should, I think, read
'Ch'en Jung', who was the artist of one of Berryman's favourite
works, the great scroll of 'Nine Dragons' executed in 1244.[18]
Charlotte Coquet, who figures in line 7, was a classmate of
Berryman's at Public School 69, Jackson Heights, New York. It was
after 1926, when his father committed suicide, that Berryman's
family first moved to New York City. Fraenkel, Strindberg, and
Andrée, who are the subjects of the last stanza, were members of a
balloon expedition to the North Pole in 1897.[19] The expedition was
lost, and their bodies not retrieved until August 1930, when they
were discovered frozen to death and partly mutilated by bears. The
poem may be seen as an exercise in the contemplation of the relativity
of time. The context is that of Berryman's childhood, a time when he
skated up and down in front of Charlotte Coquet's house in a
rapturously pubescent trance, 'wishing he could, sir, die'—for love.
During that period, when he was growing up, the three explorers
were literally dead, and accordingly, in Berryman's terms, enjoyed a
paradoxical security (like childhood in that respect alone) because of
being 'safe' from the depredations of time, immortalised in ice and so
immutable. The bears that marauded their bodies were, strictly
speaking, 'harmless' to them. While Berryman grew through
childhood, safe in a different way, cared for by his mother, those men
transcended time altogether, unknown to him. When Berryman says
that 'Strindberg rocked in his niche', he is imaging the explorer's
makeshift grave—a narrow crevice between rocks covered with a
thin layer of loose stones—as a type of cradle; the word 'rocked' is,
therefore, a pun. Andrée, the leader of the expedition, and 'muscled
Fraenkel' (an athlete and gymnast, not a scientist like the others), died
side by side in their tent. Similarly, Ch'en Jung has passed not only
beyond the time of his childhood, made secure by his own mother,

but he too has transcended all time in the passage of several centuries, and shares the notional time of death with the explorers.

My exegesis need not exhaust the possible meanings of the poem, but I put it forward to counterbalance the evidence for poor internal structure which some critics have lamented.

What must be recognised, however, is that Berryman himself (only too well aware of the density and abstruseness of certain individual Songs) knew from the very first that he needed to arrest the career of the poem, and to channel its course. My argument in fact balances William Meredith's evidence, which Barbera adduces in support of his argument:

> He reports that at summer's end 1962 Berryman took a suitcase of manuscripts to a Vermont cabin to begin assembling *77 Dream Songs*. It was Berryman's first serious attempt, Meredith says, 'to find the structure of what I think had been, up to then, an improvisational work'.[20]

Berryman's awareness of the need to devise a new technique on the level of the individual Songs is evident as early as April 1958, in a letter to his mother: 'I have a style now pared straight to the bone and can make the reader's nerves jump by moving my little finger.'[21] As for the organisation of the work as a whole, it was in September that year that he was admitted to the Regent Hospital, New York, where, as he told his doctor in Minneapolis, he was at work on 'some general thinking abt my poem (not writing: structure)'.[22]

Berryman compared the new poems with another of his own earlier sequences, 'The Nervous Songs',[23] poems which had themselves been modelled on Rilke's. *The Dream Songs* were to be, as he described them, 'much "rougher" and more "brilliant"'. There was to be less obvious lyricism. Eschewing sentimentality, the emotion of each Song was to rise out of the facts. Like Patmore's poems, they were to combine gravity of matter with gaiety of manner. There was to be 'one stroke of damned serious *humour* in each'. Berryman had in mind twenty-five or thirty poems—a whole book, or the major part of one, each poem having its own title, subject, and theme. 'Do anything crazy,' the poet advised himself, 'and see how it feels and sounds, and builds.' Even at this stage, he decided, they would be 'like a *series* of dreams, some funny etc., bitter but some, and especially late on in the series, designed to lift the reader *out of the* world'. Partly, at least, the poems would chart the history of a marriage, their themes including religion, sex, power, politics, psychology, childhood, youth and age, and memory.

Yet another model that Berryman proposed to imitate for *The Dream Songs* was his own earlier attempt to write a sequence of *Eclogues* (again begun in 1948). That sequence, which was to tell the tales of a group of characters in and around New York, would have treated the themes of loyalty and freedom. By April 1948, 'the Action had resolved itself into a Treachery, a treachery and a recovery.'[24] Like all Berryman's major poems, the sequence would have had a substantial basis in fact: in this case, the subject stemmed, like *Berryman's Sonnets*, from his adultery in the previous year, with other treacheries taking place in political and artistic spheres. The characters in this urban-pastoral sequence were to approach real-life counterparts, Berryman himself being 'Robin'. 'Colin', a 'dedicated, powerful' figure, was to be based on Robert Lowell. Other *dramatis personae* were to include an 'insistent, quarrelsome, renegade Marxist' (Dwight Macdonald), a 'light, rapid, brilliant, witty' person (Delmore Schwartz), and one characterised by the words 'sex, slang, fire, dense' (Dylan Thomas).[25] Concerning pastoral as a convention, what was important to Berryman in 1948—and again in 1955, when he saw these *Eclogues* as a model for *The Dream Songs*—was that it could

. . . still be made a way of dealing with human beings dramatically in poetry, assisting distance and transformation, admitting equally solemnity and vivacity, opening the way (with luck) for a richness and *consistency* otherwise unattainable in a long poem at present. . . . The worst dangers perhaps are affectation, excessive irony, the appearance of ingenuity. . . . Continuous pressure towards the dramatic (as a mode) will work against them. I ought to say clearly that my poem, if I am successful, will be something very different from, (though I hope continuous with) Pastoral as we know it. A new form.[26]

While these prescriptions did not work out in 1948, the poem that they prefigured put the example to good use.

Since the proposed subjects of the Pastoral poem were treachery, guilt, disengagement, and return-escape, it would have worked to demonstrate that man 'is redeemable *in time* if not in history or eternity'. The context was a 'collapsing society, worst in the best individual. Only the will-to-health can recover him to work.—*One man's story*: crime and return.' These terms of reference for that poem, written in 1948, may be applied, with considerable exactitude, to *The Dream Songs*. In both poems, the poet was to recover through his wife, who would be explicitly analogous to the Muse sustaining the poet, or a Goddess holding man in her arms while he undergoes 'terrifying metamorphoses'—'betrayals and languor and rage and despair'.[27]

Berryman decided in the mid-fifties to make his own experiences, since 1953, available to the Songs, including what he regarded as the chaos of his life in New York City, Iowa, and Cambridge, Massachusetts.[28] He had the raw materials to hand in two works to which he applied himself for at least a year after his arrival in Minneapolis, Minnesota, in 1954. He had quit Iowa after a drunken altercation with his landlord which left him unwanted as a university teacher there, and came to Minneapolis in October of that year. After three months of joblessness and frantic self-appraisal, he succeeded to Isaac Rosenfeld's teaching post in Humanities at the University of Minnesota. Those first months in Minneapolis were a watershed in his life. For one thing, he had to contain his feelings for a devout, inaccessible Catholic girl, and undertook a radical reassessment of the direction of his life and of his psychological malaise. The results were two long, often bizarre, and rigorous works of introspection. The first, *Journal of Self-Analysis*, is, after a fashion, a running commentary on the other work, a far more inchoate, exoteric study which was to be entitled *St. Pancras Braser*.[29] That second work, on the face of it a crazy outpouring of uncoordinated dream transcriptions, is a morass of private references, social, literary, and familial ideas, and multitudinous associations. The plot appears to be an incomprehensible autobiographical maelstrom which rivals the extravagances of *Finnegans Wake*. The point of mentioning the work in this context is to stress the importance of this self-examination, its devices and resources, as a compelling and informing background to the style, content, and even idioms of the Dream Songs. In or about 1955, he persuaded himself to 'use *real* dream-technique for some of these poems'.[30] In a footnote to a draft of an unpublished Song called 'Henry's Nightmare', he added: 'Some of my dreams in *St. Pancras Braser* will probably touch off songs, examined.'[31]

It is important to appreciate that between the form and style of 'The Nervous Songs' (after Rilke), the earlier venture in the Pastoral mode, the dramatic success of the style developed in *Homage,* and the bizarre procedures and substance of his self-analysis, Berryman gave *The Dream Songs* their conditions and frame of being.

By virtue of the themes of sexual treachery and recovery at the hands of a woman, muse or goddess, and by introducing fresh preoccupations—resentment at personal and professional setbacks, introspective analysis, and a certain malignity towards the father—the earliest of the Dream Songs derive and progress from the *Eclogues*. By a logical extension into the religious sphere, Berryman's malicious and inquisitorial feelings towards his father reached also to the Heavenly Father manifested in Christ, and to the Catholic Church, his father's Faith. Since Berryman had recently endured a crisis of conscience and self-respect which included being out of work for some months, *The Dream Songs* may be seen as an attempt to resolve his problems of personal identity through the facilitation of new styles, new forms, and new areas of creativity. In a loose diary note from that time, Berryman wrote out what he called *The Argument* of the poem: 'Henry, in the face of enemies and considering his great loss, sulks, who had been a favourite and happy; suffers new losses, voluntary and not.'

Early 1958, Berryman felt that probably *The Dream Songs* would have to end with 'dreams of' death. It was not, that is to say, to end with suicide, nor in suffering, but simply in what he called 'a resigning from all this stuff', which would include 'NOT seeing POO [his son Paul] succeed'.[32] The conclusion was to be enigmatic, but not specific, since he was still making vague strivings towards a felt design. His notes exhibit a groping toward the imperceptible in structure, and sometimes even in content; he applauded the notion of 'tinkering' for 'power' and 'delicacy'—'something like the first turn in the first part of Opus III may lie ahead.'

On 4 April that year, Berryman planned a programme for *The Dream Songs*. 'When I come to write,' he devised (even though he had been fashioning the Songs for nearly three years already), 'restrict composition (as with *Anne Bradstreet*) to one every 2 days, say and spend most of that time on construction, plan-ahead.' To that end, he decided for a while to read only philosophy. All his verse fragments and notes, not only of Dream Songs, but also left-over fragments from *Homage*, could be incorporated in the new work. 'For instance,' he said, 'I don't see why there can't be flashbacks into Henry.' But, in consideration of the fact that several reviewers of *Homage* had failed readily to discern its 'plot' and 'voices' (and how, as he consoled himself by reading in H. T. Wade-Gery,[33] it took 2,000 years for the form of the *Iliad* to be recovered), he decided to have a 'clear narrative-and-meditative line', together with structural notes like those provided for the book version of *Homage*. Most of the Dream Songs written so far he already regarded as 'interludes, or fragmented'. (The language was to present just as difficult a problem as in *Homage*. One analogous usage could be seen between the archaisms in *Homage* and the 'kid-talk' in the Songs: 'This stuff (private language),' he decided in another place, 'is in fact a development from my *syntax in Anne Bradstreet*.')[34] The major problem outstanding in early April, 1958, was the overall organisation of what he called '*journey, action, structure*'.

Another early view of the structure of the Songs took the form of an Inferno–Purgatorio–Paradiso pattern, but only, Berryman advised himself, as a 'general' plan.[35] 'Clearly', he determined, helpless love *vis-à-vis* Mabel was to be a feature of Part I of the poem: Henry, that is to say, like Berryman himself, already had a wife. He was to get a divorce and then to marry Mabel in Part II; afterwards to have 'a Pouker'. Perhaps, he considered further, this sequence—divorce, second marriage, and the birth of a child—would be the basic action of Part II, corresponding to what was to be the basic action of Part I, a world tour. Furthermore, he felt as a conclusion to this rudimentary Dantesque plan on 5 March 1959, he would absolutely need a 'terminal date as of John Berryman/Henry'. A particular year should be such a terminal date, 'as 1300 was for Dante'.

Apart from the knowledge that Henry is still married to his first wife in the poem 'Henry sats' (Song 5), traces of this early scheme cannot be said to have remained dominant in the completed *Dream Songs*. In fact, the only other annotation that I have been able to find in support of Berryman's plan to structure *77 Dream Songs* as a type of *Divine Comedy* is a marginal comment on the manuscript of Song 103 (*His Toy, His Dream, His Rest*, Book V), written at the turn of the New Year 1959, which suggests that the Song might serve to conclude the *Purgatorio*, Book II of the poem, or (less likely) Book I.[36]

As an analogue of the *Inferno*, at least, *The Dream Songs* might have measured up.[37] Henry would begin in the Circle of sullenness (Circle 5), his vice of drinking would find its mark in the gluttony of Circle 3, and, for the avarice and improvidence equivalent to Circle 4, Henry would be a 'rolling stone' (an image to be used as a 'key expression', as in 'No moss! No moss!'). Henry is carnal, decidedly a heretic from Catholicism, violent towards his neighbour, treacherous—

necessarily, Berryman felt—towards his kin, but not (except involuntarily) a hypocrite (Circle 8). 'Henry's Confession' might be equated with Canto 13. Despite the closeness of this parallel, it was not one that Berryman went on applying with any resolution, and he continued to look elsewhere for an exact format—perhaps, as at one time he considered doing, to creation epics (Babylonian, Amerindian, or Hindu), except for the timely awareness that the *Dream Songs* was evolving as a 'Survival-epic'.

One of the problems facing him in the poem was that of continuity, which included aspects of pace, subject, imagery, form and diction. In other words, how was he to unite the separate components into a poem that would function as a whole? It seemed clear to him that he needed Part I to be 'hard, vast, accumulating',[38] Part II 'dark, lustful, strange' (an extreme vocabulary for what was to be the remarriage and childbirth section), but Part III was not yet clear, except for the fact that it should be 'climactic' (unlike *Homage*) and 'summary'. (At this stage, there was no thought of a sequel to the three-part structure of the Songs.) One point of narrative movement had been solved during 1958 with Song 5 ('Henry sats') and Song 24 ('Oh servant Henry'): these two songs were to advance the 'plot' (such as it was) by having Henry travel towards a lecture tour.

By September/October 1958,[39] the Songs stood in this provisional state: Part I, 'finisht, more or less. In order.' ('With notes'?) Part II was far advanced, with many poems more or less complete, but, according to the poet, 'inferior'. Part III consisted only of 'Programmatic notes'. He felt that to put his Far Eastern tour (which actually occurred in 1957) late in Part I was the correct arrangement, as well as to split the three hospitalisations—corresponding to Berryman's own periods of hospitalisation—through the three books. (Hospital visits were periods at once of crisis and recovery for Berryman: structurally, as a device within the poem, they may be seen to approximate to Henry's interludes of affliction and heroic indirection.) He had also decided that Song 75, 'Turning it over' (its theme: the publication of a book), and Song 76, 'Henry's Confession', both belonged late in Part III of the book.

—You is from hunger, Mr. Bones,

I offers you this handkerchief, now set
your left foot by my right foot,

shoulder to shoulder, all that jazz,
arm in arm, by the beautiful sea,
hum a little, Mr. Bones.
—I saw nobody coming, so I went instead.   (76:12–18)

Despite a theme of ironic reconciliation and a movement towards an enigmatically new phase of experience in 'Henry's Confession', Berryman already had a notion that the culmination of the volume should be more positive. 'The end,' he said, 'will have to grow out of the poem, probably very high-keyed indeed, unimaginable beforehand.' Even though the poem which eventually came to stand last in the volume, 'Seedy Henry', was written in November 1958, Berryman had not yet selected it for the close.

Also in November that year, he began to exercise more control over what he called mock heroically 'The Tragical History of Henry'. He determined not to continue with episodic, hurried, 'occasional' work, but to make it more *withdrawn, meditative, methodical*— 'which, after all, I don't see why I *might* not be able to do'. It was characteristic of his exasperation—with himself, with the poem, and with the state of being an American—that, early in 1958, he had considered dedicating the work 'to the miserable men and women who have dared to practise the art of poetry in the United States of America'—variously, in May 1961, 'for the honour of the United States of America'.

Anticipating incomprehension and criticism, he found himself 'sick' of the Songs by 25 November 1958. They were 'going and not going', besides (as he said) 'keeping me on edge, getting me nowhere, killing me'.[40] Again, on 25 April 1959, he recorded, 'I'm in despair tonight over this whole poem, going on with it or publishing it. It's *too personal*, like my bloody sonnets of '47; too accidental.' He bewailed the fact that he had still 'never yet really faced the fundamental *inter*dependence and sequence *essential* to the notion of a long poem'.[41] One binding device could be that of a continuing dialogue between Henry—Mr Bones—and a friend. 'Find out about the Mr. Bones business,' Berryman told himself in January 1959, a date from which it may be inferred that Mr Bones and his friend, the interlocutor, had not before figured very consciously in his plan. (Possibilities began to open up: Henry and his friend could be, for example, types of Gilgamesh,[42] in the Babylonian *Epic of Gilgamesh*, and of his friend and companion in adventure, Enkidu, the primeval man. Despite having traces of the wild, primitive Enkidu, Henry himself would have to stand for Gilgamesh.)

Recalling the fact that Delmore Schwartz used to call him 'Don Quixote',[43] Berryman saw that Henry and his friend might parallel Cervantes's heroes, an analogue which has been recently explored by Paul John Kameen:

> Is not Henry a sort of twentieth century Don Quixote out on his own bizarre quest?
>
> A close comparison between these two characters does indicate so—while it also recommends a more comic view of *The Dream Songs* than the poem is generally granted. . . . Across vast physical and mental settings their hapless adventures proceed from one courageous folly to another. The Don is insane with his visions of a world of chivalry long since dead. Henry is insane with the loss of innocence, family and friends, all now dead. Both superimpose their own fantasies, their own dreams, over 'reality'. But in spite of their personal delusions and lack of sense, both heroes are ultimately engaging in their lunacies.[44]

Berryman himself felt that Henry's friend, or 'pal', a type of Sancho, could be characterised as 'inquisitive, reproachful, choric'.[45] This nameless interlocutor, Henry's friend, accordingly became a character in the poem, what Berryman himself called the second 'real' character—'Mabel' being the third,[46] later to be dropped. He was to be Henry's 'enemy' at the start, later his 'friend' and 'confidant', and therefore to have 'a history beginning *here*'.[47] (The 'operation' poem (Song 67) might prefigure an improved relation with the Friend, similar to that of the Don and Sancho Panza in Part II of *Don Quixote*.)[48] Like their prototypes, Mr Bones and his friend would debate their proposed adventure and its early details. By this means, the Songs could take on a serial character, and cohere better. Although Henry is assuredly a type of Don Quixote, it does seem, however, that the idealism that accompanies the Don's suffering is not so apparent in Berryman's hero. The manifestation of what Berryman called 'humorous agony' is nevertheless common to both. Apart from that specific likeness, however, Berryman found that the details of his arrangement were still recalcitrant: 'where', he asked himself in some perplexity, 'does "Bones" stuff begin?'

For the disposition of Mr Bones and his interlocutor Berryman borrowed features from the stage pattern of minstrel show tradition,

for which his source was Carl Wittke's *Tambo and Bones*, a work
published in 1930. As with the structure of his 'epic' as a whole,
however, the relationship between Henry and his friend is compounded of more than one paradigm. Berryman has described
Henry's friend as a 'Job's comforter', a likeness which needs to be
borne in mind. Henry himself, Berryman dubbed 'simple-minded.
He thinks that if something happens to him, it's forever; but I know
better.'[49] He added that he was more lenient with Mistress
Bradstreet, in whom he had created the same dilemma (in her case, by
means of her responsiveness to a sexual trial), but whom he chose to
exculpate 'in ways that will allow her forgetting of it after a long
period of time'.[50] Henry is absolutely unable to forget his 'irrever-
sible loss'—that composite of father and of womb.

In 1963 Berryman wrote an appreciative notice of W. H. Auden's
collection *The Dyer's Hand*,[51] but long before then he had discriminated for himself the artistic strategy that Auden analyses in one essay,
'Balaam and His Ass'. Auden treats of the master−servant relationship
in literature, Quixote−Sancho, Lear−Fool, Giovanni−Leporello, in
what Berryman calls 'the show-piece of the book'. The essay is
lapidary in style and inclusive in range, and proceeds to the crucial
consideration that 'To present artistically a human personality in its
full depth, its inner dialectic, its self-disclosure and self-concealment,
through the medium of a single character is almost impossible.'[52]
Auden concludes part of the essay by insisting that, to express the
inner dialogue of a human personality, two characters must be
employed and the relationship between them must be of a special
kind; they must be similar in certain respects and they must be
inseparable. The only relationship which satisfies all these conditions
is that between master and servant. It seems to me that, on those
terms, Henry's friend may be regarded as, in a loose sense, a servant to
Henry. (It is salient to remark that Henry's friend always expresses
himself in blackface idiom.)

Although his presence is felt everywhere in *The Dream Songs,*
Henry's friend figures in direct speech remarkably little: only
eighteen times in *77 Dream Songs*, and thirteen times in *His Toy, His
Dream, His Rest* (a volume which comprises no less than 308 Dream
Songs). His voice is that of democracy, of what commonly passes for
common sense, of sanity, of religious orthodoxy, of admonition, and
of exhortation. Occasionally, as in Song 26, he is no more than an
instrument to feed Henry with questions. More often he expostulates
against what he considers to be Henry's contrary philosophy, 'Now

there *you* exaggerate, Sah. We hafta *die*' (36:7), 'Mr. Bones, / you makes too much / démand' (64:8–10), desires him to 'Come away, Mr. Bones' (77:7), snaps at him to 'stop that damn dismal' when Henry becomes morbid, is briskly optimistic about Henry's chances with the opposite sex, 'That's enough of that, Mr. Bones. *Some* lady you make' (143:1), is exasperated—'I really gotta go. You don' make sense' (272:13)—when Henry keeps him from his bed, and has more than one remark to make about putting faith in God and the life hereafter. This is not to say that Henry's friend is right in his sentiments; merely that the consciousness of Berryman's compound hero oscillates between the possibilities of doubt and belief, of hope and despair, advanced by each of the characters in turn. To an extent, Henry's friend is blunt and inconsistent in order that Henry's 'gripes' may have more edge; that ambivalence is a necessary part of Berryman's dialectic.

In respect of Henry and his friend, one further point to be kept in mind is Berryman's ambiguous statement, on 6 April 1960, that 'Mr. Bones' is *Death*, Henry's friend—who at the end takes him off-stage.'[53] The issue is not quite clarified, however, since Berryman arrogated the identification to Bones *ex post facto* by borrowing this passage from a novel by R. V. Cassill, *Naked Morning* (New York: Avon, 1957):

> 'I thought you was trying to kill me,' she said. 'I *thought* I heard you sneaking up on me the other way. *Something* did.'
> 'That was Bones,' Martin said. She had heard—she was sensitive enough to hear and know what saner people would never hear— the actual step of death coming after her, death coming exactly like the black hooded figure of medieval paintings. (p. 89)

For the name of his protagonist, Henry, Berryman absorbed several exemplars. There was Frederic Henry, Hemingway's character in *A Farewell to Arms*, who, as Berryman had it, 'fought, lost all'.[54] Similarly, Stephen Crane depicted a Henry Fleming at war, in addition to the Henry Johnson of his story 'The Monster'. Prince Henry was Ralegh's patron (who, as Berryman recalled, had criticised his own father), 'dead, so young, paragon'. Finally, there was a Henry reformed, the 'victor king' Henry v. There was, however, no single prototype of the name Henry in *The Dream Songs*: Henry House, Mr Bones, may have assumed many aspects of others, but I find no evidence for a singular provenance.

When, on 8 April 1958, Berryman wrote 'Huffy Henry', the Song that was to become the first of the published canon (it appears to have been written and published almost without revision, except, most notably, for the last line which originally read 'and my friends grow still or mad'), he believed that it exhibited a 'very doubtful' style, but eased one crux of the Songs. It defined, as Berryman himself put it, 'better than ever before the relationship between the poet and Henry.—The poet *knows all about Henry*.' From the beginning, however, Berryman confused himself with his protagonist.

In a journal beginning in December 1957, he wrote: 'I am a strange man, not unitary like other people. I am really Henry Pussycat, and I am also a bastard, and I am hopeful and good-natured, and I am a man insulted and injured, and I love Ann and the Poo.' This identification was reinforced on 23 May 1958, when Berryman wrote of himself: 'I am Henry Pussy-cat. My whiskers fly.'[55] Even in a letter of 16 January 1960 to his wife Ann, Berryman referred to himself as 'Henry Pussycat'.[56] He remained ambivalent at all times about his relationship with Henry, as in a letter of 5 April 1958 to his doctor, enclosing a copy of Song 54 (then called 'Room 333'): 'You understand: this is (not me, but) Henry, the—hero?—of my next poem, begun in 1955 and *nowhere*.'[57] In his article 'One Answer to a Question: changes', Berryman was ready to acknowledge that in the first Dream Song, 'the "I", perhaps of the poet, disappears into Henry's first and third persons (he talks to himself in the second person, too, about himself).'[58] In view of Berryman's published declarations, it seems best to concur with Ernest Stefanik's fine judgement that, in Song 1, 'the speaker's voice is clearly identifiable as Henry's, with Henry's in the third stanza, and that he is both speaker and subject.'[59] It seems also necessary to reserve judgement about the features which may or may not make Henry discrete from Berryman himself, especially in the light of Berryman's self-contradictions, such as this early unpublished prefatory 'Note' to *His Toy, His Dream, His Rest*:

> Read me loud and clear, ladies and gentlemen: Henry is not me, either. The poet does not enter the poem at all, even in Songs like the initial one and "Life, friends".

In April 1959, Berryman wrote: 'Jon Silkin's "Death of a Son" is the best poem I've read since Elizabeth Bishop's about Ezra Pound about 2 years ago ("Visits to St. Elizabeths"). This piece-meal composition of *Dream Songs* makes utterly impossible that organic kind of writing.

STOP, till I can write uninterrupted.' It was clear from a comparatively early stage (77 *Dream Songs* was not published for a further five years)[60] that he should apply yet more resolute thought to structuring the poem.

By 1 September 1962 he had considered a fairly elementary disposition: the volume he was originally to publish as a group of 72 Songs might be divided into two parts. The first group of thirty-six Songs could be predominantly minstrel. In that section, according to the minstrel tradition that he had learned from Carl Wittke, he might include dances, jokes, superstition, fear, ballads, weird costumes, and burlesques of opera and personalities, all of which would end 'in a "walk around" of ALL'. It would seem, in fact, that the arrangement could accomodate just about every one of the Songs then written, which otherwise took on the appearance of a rag-bag.

One more searching and sophisticated plan employed a calendar framework, being measured by high days and holidays, including 4 July, Christmas, and Paul's birthday. (Thanksgiving had already been used in *Homage to Mistress Bradstreet*, and Berryman would return to it in Song 385, the last of *The Dream Songs*). At the back of his mind, he valued the notion that, while our present civilisation celebrates birthdays, the Greeks exulted over death-days, the idea being glossed by this observation by G. R. Levy: ' . . . every hero's tomb was the scene of rites, such as still belonged to the spirits of nature, and at an earlier time to the ancestors.'[61]

Berryman was fascinated by the unity of the year, in terms of the seasons, but also as dreamlike—in the sense, it seems, that time itself is illusory. In consequence he decided late in August 1962 to try a temporal arrangement, which would be other than what he called 'fiscal or academic or calendric'. 'Huffy Henry', the first Song, would be located in 'broad summer', the season in which he first started writing Dream Songs. The Songs could then trace a single year, in a fashion analogous to Archbishop Philip Carrington's discoveries about St Mark's Gospel. In 1963 Berryman reported to A. Alvarez (in connection with Song 48, which *The Observer* was then printing): 'Archbishop Carrington's amazing discovery (The Prim. Xtian Calendar, and his edition of Mark since) that the structure of Mk, on which Mt. and Lu wholly rely is liturgical.'[62] As Archbishop Carrington[63] interprets it, St Mark's Gospel reformulated the events of Christ's ministry—for liturgical purposes—to the term of precisely a year. For a while Berryman took the hint in attempting to create a blinding feature of *The Dream Songs*. To an even greater degree, however, Berryman's discovery from Archbishop Carrington that St Mark's Gospel was in some sort an artifice or fiction served to confirm the metaphysical underpinning of the Songs, as the philosophical thrust of his own work was both anti-Christian and anti-eschatological.

Since most critics have agreed with William J. Martz's bald pronouncement that *The Dream Songs* 'lacks plot, either traditional or associative', [64] it strikes me as important to appreciate the definition of 'plot' and 'structure' in the crucial aspect of 'coherence'. In addition to such themes as kinship and loss, a consuming interest of the *Songs* (so prevalent as to be a dominant theme) is the very nature of godhead and immortality. It is my contention that Berryman's disquisitions on the subjects of Christology and eschatology are so insistent and cohesive as to function as a principle of structure. He reiterates his observations about divinity and death so earnestly that he constructs a sufficiently close-knit schedule of meanings which does bring all the Songs—from the whole twelve-year span of their composition—into a relation with one another. My object is accordingly to make some answer to Jack Barbera when he observes (also in the context of estimating the poem's structure):

> I suggest that any critic who proceeds by analysis of the metaphysical stance of poems cannot significantly discuss a poem such as *The Dream Songs*. Different Songs provide different stances, and it is questionable whether the whole poem's openness can be said, itself, to imply a stance. [65]

When Berryman asserted to John Plotz, 'It has no plot. Its plot is the personality of Henry as he moves on in the world', [66] he was trying manifestly to forestall criticism of the book's lack of structure. The effort seems, in fact, to have been arrant and ingenuous, a type of compensation for the fact that he had failed on his own terms to describe a narrative continuity in the work. My point is to the contrary—that the force and basic consistency of Henry's views on godhead and eschatology amount to a scheme which is ultimately ratiocinative; his 'plot' and 'structure' may be seen as the conduct of an inquiry which is coherent enough to give the poem a type of structure. Even though thematic harmony is not quite structural unity, it is not less functional.

In his search for a sound, more overt structure Berryman discovered what seemed to him a promising model outlined in Joseph Campbell's *The Hero with a Thousand Faces*.[67] Campbell categorises the Adventure of the Hero of myth as a three-part sequence: Departure (subdivided into five parts); Initiation (subdivided into six parts); Return (subdivided into six parts). The cycle of activities corresponds to what Berryman himself called 'out', 'into', and 'back'. Within this broad structure, Berryman tried to plot a sequence of Songs equivalent to the series of activities. In a table form, these approximations were:

DEPARTURE

'Huffy Henry'	The Call to Adventure
	Refusal of the Call
'Muttered Henry' (17)	Supernatural Aid
'Turning it over' (75)	The Crossing of the First Threshold
'There sat down once' (29)	The Belly of the Whale

INITIATION

'Henry sats' (5)	The Road of Trials
'Filling her compact' (4)	The Meeting with the Goddess
'During his father's' (6)	The Woman as Temptress
'No visitors' (54)	Atonement with the Father
'Nothin' very bad' (76)	
'Of 1826'	Apotheosis
'I don't operate often'	The Ultimate Boon

RETURN

'Silent Song' (52)	Refusal of the Return
'The greens of the Ganges' (27)	The Magic Flight
(An unparticularised Song about the Friend)	Rescue from Without
'The glories of the world' (26)	The Crossing of the Return Threshold
	Master of the Two Worlds
'Seedy Henry' (77)	Freedom to Live

Broadly speaking, within the three-part structure, Berryman felt that 'Departure' was to be jaunty and hellish, 'Initiation' to be concerned with 'sex, money, learning, art', and 'Return' to be solemn and exalted. Henry's own return was to be a return from 'outer space'—from his obsession with grandiosity and paranoia. In this structure, according to Campbell's categories, he would also allow for diversions and interludes, as well as for what he called 'enforcement'.

One particular example remains to us: Berryman specified that the following passage from *The Hero with a Thousand Faces* should gloss Song 64:

> For those who have not refused the call, the first encounter of the hero-journey is with a protective figure (often a little old crone or old man) who provides the adventurer with amulets against the dragon forces he is about to pass.[68]

When Henry requests, 'Anybody's blessing?' it is his friend who responds as the 'little old crone or old man':

> Mr. Bones,
> you makes too much
> démand. I might be 'fording you a hat:
> it gonna rain.　　(64:8−11)

I do not know, however, whether Berryman designed the equivalence or discovered it after writing the Song.

Nevertheless, despite the approximations between Henry's adventures and Campbell's categorical Hero, Berryman did not adhere to this schema. It is evident from a glance at the list above that the final ordering of the Songs fell away from Campbell's structure.

The last and perhaps major influence on the structure of the poem was that of the *Iliad*. The three parts of the *Dream Songs* might correspond to the three grand parts of the *Iliad*.[69] In each book, there would be numerous coincidences of time and place for dealing with, in Berryman's words, 'humiliations, losses, sacrifices, loves, *fights*, triumphs, blasphemies, and magnanimities'. The hero, like a type of Achilles or King Lear, is cast out by real enemies, but he is also cast out by himself. His vulnerability is therefore self-inflicted. The quest, which is also in a sense the plot of the work, the object of the process, might not be reached or attained, because it is a self-quest. Like Job, the hero is suffering, and at war with God, but he does not know if he will survive until survival has been achieved. His friends, Job's comforters, are akin to Henry's friend: they provide occasions for the

study of his plights and gripes within a partially controlled environment. The hero may choose to determine his destiny and to undertake
actions towards that end, but his choice might be void. 'Remember
the three who pretend to be Job's friends,' Berryman apprised
Richard Kostelanetz in an interview. 'They sit down and lament with
him, and give him the traditional Jewish jazz—namely, you suffer,
therefore you are guilty. You remember that. Well, Henry's friend
sits down and gives him the same business. Henry is so troubled and
bothered by his many problems that he never actually comes up with
solutions, and from that point of view the poem is a failure.'[70]
Berryman regarded *Job* as a questioning, a trial of God's justice: as of
himself, the justice in question was that of his father's death. Henry
combines elements of Job and Achilles, and is perhaps most like
Achilles in the actualities of his experience: 'Insult, unused power,
loss, viciousness, generosity.'

Berryman made his own thoroughgoing comparison of Henry
and Achilles in 1958 and 1959. As an archetype of 'Huffy Henry' the
sulky Achilles is a hero, he understood, who is needed and yet
reluctant because he is insulted.[71] The chief enemy, in Achilles'
case, was Hector, whom Berryman explicitly equated with Henry's father.
His is also a 'crummy society'. The basic action of *The Dream Songs*
would accordingly be a war, possibly even undeclared, running hot
and cold by turns. Berryman indicated that the object of both *Homage
to Mistress Bradstreet* and *The Dream Songs* was to 'kill Hector', even
though Henry too would die. The hero will win, but die in doing so.
Berryman decided that Henry should die like Achilles, and yet Henry
need not die *in* the poem. His fate could be kept mysterious, like
Oedipus' in Sophocles, or (as Berryman himself said) like *'mine in
Anne Bradstreet'*.[72] Henry's death would also be seen as health-giving,
a relief and a blessing.

In a conspectus dating from October 1958,[73] Berryman pursued
the parallels between Henry and Achilles, describing Henry as 'a man
(hero) *deprived*, and *insulted*, sulks (poor will) with enemies *inside* as
well as *on* his side'. Specifically, he identified the enemy 'on' Henry's
side as his mother, a type of Thetis, as well as academic colleagues and
American philistinism in general. Song 14 sets the scene of Henry's
unrest:

> Life, friends, is boring. We must not say so.
> After all, the sky flashes, the great sea yearns,
> we ourselves flash and yearn,

> and moreover my mother told me as a boy
> (repeatingly) 'Ever to confess you're bored
> means you have no
>
> Inner Resources.' I conclude now I have no
> inner resources, because I am heavy bored.
> Peoples bore me,
> literature bores me, especially great literature,
> Henry bores me, with his plights & gripes
> as bad as achilles   (14:1– 12)

It is relevant here to know that, at a poetry reading in Spoleto, Italy, Berryman informed his audience that the name 'achilles' was deliberately 'spelt with rage with a small letter at the beginning'.[74] (In conversation, Berryman's mother told me that she had felt outraged at being mocked in that Song, and bitterly pained to have heard it once at a public reading.)[75]

Unable to sleep in the early hours of 26 February 1959,[76] Berryman wrote from his hospital bed: 'The poem 'ought' to be organized in (narrative or implicit) *actions*—if I can do it, and if it seems truly *suitable* to the stuff—like pieces of a novel (scenic, panoramic, descriptive, monologue) or Books of *The Iliad* or Canto's.' What was suitable 'to the stuff' could not be decided until, by definition, the poem had been written. For Henry, there was no literal, overt, and massive conflict between opposing forces, as in the *Iliad*. His major conflict was internal, in the ups and downs of his attempts to resolve neurotic conflicts. Despite geographical movements to Japan, India, or Ireland, Henry's quest was inward, taking the form of a fight to identify and control his own behaviour-as-destiny.

Berryman felt at the time that a major illness, or despair, should perhaps grow out of, and climax, each large part of the poem, one example being 'No visitors' (Song 54), written almost exactly a year before, also in hospital. Perhaps one part should even end 'gladly, or in the kind of *doubt* Homer goes in for'? He was convinced too that some form of non-despair approaching ecstasy was required, as well as what he called 'a large smooth-muscled ceremonial section at the end of 1st section'. At the back of his mind was the scene in Olympus at the end of the *Iliad*, Book 1. (The notion of Olympians suited his vein of anti-theology, his distrust of one Absolute God.)

On 15 July 1963,[77] Berryman attempted to chart the equivalences between the episodes of the *Iliad* and Henry's chronicle. Of the twenty-four books of the epic, he found eleven approximations to his own Songs, sometimes in a more than one-to-one relationship:

I.	Quarrel	'Huffy Henry' (1)
V.	Diomedes vs gods	'God bless Henry' (13)
VIII.	Trojans to wall	'Silent Song' (52)
IX.	Overtures to Achilles	'A Capital at Wells' (6) and 'Life, friends' (14)
X.	Doloneia	'I met a junior' (98) and 'Her properties' (115)
XII.	Hektor storms wall	'Henry is old' (7)
XIV.	Zeus conned	'Filling her compact' (4) and 'Love her he doesn't' (69)
XVIII.	Achilles' armour	'Supreme my holdings' (64)
XIX.	Feud-end—(OUT)—	The 3 Frost (*Three Around the Old Gentleman*) (37–9)
XXIII.	Funeral and games	'Peter's not friendly' (55)
XXIV.	Priam and Achilles	'Henry's Confession' (76) 'Pulling' (unpublished) and 'Seedy Henry' (77)

There is clearly much that is *a posteriori* about these approximations, and despite his efforts to categorise the Songs, the importance of the *Iliad* to Berryman's sense of structure remained a matter of example rather than of strict equivalence. The Achilles theme did remain with Berryman for some years, however, until Song 320, which (it is interesting to know) was probably the last of *The Dream Songs* to have been written—in 1968.

Although it might be possible to criticise Berryman on the grounds that he often seemed to be cutting and assembling the Songs according to one and then another epic format, what must be seen as more consequential are his efforts to remain fluid and flexible, to discover an artistic sequence into which the Songs might naturally fall. He needed to avoid the absolutist and the categorical. The internal demands of the poem, while they would not permit him to order the individual Songs *seriatim*, were not such as to allow of any similarly easy option.

Next in importance to Berryman's decision to devise dialogues between Henry and his friend as a nexus of the plot, his desire to construe the poem by analogy with more than one epic format was fundamental. The work was to find its own integrity. The configuration of Mr Bones and his friend, which may be seen as a device similar to that of ego and id, or of *alazon* and *eiron*, is essentially a device of episodes and eventualities. More important to structure was Berryman's feeling for the larger movements and design of his work. Individual poems might share characteristics of temperament, psychology, and social exchange, and indeed individual poems might have won the appearance of design—simply by virtue of mass and accumulation. Berryman often feared losing control of the poem by heaping up more and more occasional verses. 'Be very careful,' he remarked, 'how I Henrify *poems*—NEVER try to pull into series. Lean the other way.' It was not enough for each Song to look and sound right, with Henry's characteristic tricks and tone, since there remained the danger of (to use Berryman's own phrase) bringing any poem into line stylistically.

As early as November 1958, Berryman had wondered how seriously to take the Songs. The subject was clearly 'a man vibrating with *emotion*'.[78] What emotion? was a real question. Hatred, at imposition and insult. Fear, and anxiety. Remorse, love, a contempt for life. Doubt, especially of immortality. Grief at the loss of his father, for whom he wrote the following fragment: 'I am older than my father, Henry wept.' Finally there was, as he called it, 'rage' towards his mother. All of these emotions were relevant and indispensable: Henry is a complicated personality whose every trait and action might be articulated. Moods and behaviour patterns, particularly sullenness and weakness, prevail in the poem. The plot, the narrative, is constituted by the ways in which Henry's nature tackles the occasions of his experience, the contingencies of Berryman's own life. So too, the unity of the poem inheres in its construction as a serial, not as a series.

Berryman was tireless in seeking out all possible archetypes of his poem, to give it the credentials that he felt it needed. It was hard for him to realise that its very resistance to conventional epic overgrowth was a source not of weakness, but of strength. Rather, the integrity of the form can be found expressed by the substance of its parts. It is possible to disfavour many individual Songs, but it cannot be disputed that Berryman tried to coordinate the whole set. In October 1961, he indulged in salutary self-mockery in this unpublished note to the poem:

> The manuscript—of this pseudo-poem or epic—was found in an abandoned keyhole and transmitted to me by enemies, anxious to thwart my lawful work. It is doubtful whether its author—of whom nothing is known, except that he claims (in 67) to be a human being, and male—gave it a final form; in 89 at any rate a variant reading survives which calls Satan not 'Lord of Matter' but 'Lord of Matters,' and the order of the Songs is sometimes far from clear. But this hardly matters, the work being *so* patriotic that it can hope for no hearing in the present stage of our national destiny (see 48). The indifferent reader will be relieved to learn that I have let loose here only a fraction of the manuscript. The stupid notes seem to be a product of the labour of the poet's grandson (whose armpits can even sometimes be smelt in the chaotic originals)—later put to death under Kennedy III, for damned good reason. Who Henry was, or is, has proved undiscoverable by the social scientists. It is hoped, tho', that he knew Russian, and certain that he claimed to be a minstrel. R.I.P.
>
> J.B.

In 1965 Berryman had stated that 77 *Dream Songs* was about 'the turbulence of the modern world, and memory, and wants',[79] but such a statement of theme is so general as probably to be incontrovertible and quite unhelpful. As Jack Barbera has pointed out (with reference to a further outline in which Berryman characterised the themes of that volume as loss, death, and terror), 'the thematic groupings of the first three Books are not mutually exclusive'.[80] It was Berryman's intention from an early stage to publish a second and final volume of the Songs. Even in September 1962, when he sent the first batch of 75 Songs to his publisher, he disclosed that 150 more were 'finished'.[81] In fact, the prodigality of his writing embarrassed him from a comparatively early stage. Early in 1963, for instance, he sent Allen Tate a copy of Dream Song 70, dubbing it 'Dream Song 70015',[82] although the joke may have been a response to the fact that Tate tended to dislike the form and style of the Songs. In answer to a reproof from Tate, Berryman wrote in June 1963:

> Of course I am wild to be done and move on. I don't write these

damned things willingly, you know. Each one takes me by the throat. I've vowed 100 times: never again. So I stall one, for hours, days, weeks; then I've had it. I figure a few more months or years will see the poem through.[83]

The truth is that Berryman had begun to find the poems a customary and convenient outlet; from 1964 onwards they assume more of the qualities of a diary. By July 1966, when he was ready to take the Songs to Dublin for a year on a Guggenheim Fellcwship, he told his friends:

> It's not less than 259 Songs, of which only ten have been published and 15 are brandnew, besides 35 unfinisht and scores of fragments—I feel dazed: since the 2nd (final) volume will only contain 84 Songs, you can see that I have my work cut out.[84]

On his departure for Dublin, Berryman believed that he had written all the Songs he needed, and that his task was to arrange and structure them in the four Books that were to conclude the work. By about October 1965, for example, he reported to his ex-wife Ann that he had 'composed the whole of Book VII—eleven Songs'.[85] In the event, because of the length of his stay in Dublin (otherwise unoccupied), and because he had become habituated to writing the Songs, the number of sections in the final Book mounted apace.

Like that of *77 Dream Songs*, the structural principle of the second volume is vague, but it seems to be the case that he saw Books V, VI, and VII as being conditioned by Henry's death in the fourteen Songs of Book IV (the *Opus posthumous* sequence). Jack Barbera has drawn on Berryman's work notes to show that the basic principle of organisation of Books V and VI is outlined as 'a succession of states from recovery, to rage, to loss, to contempt'.[86] In a loose sense of order, we can see that in Book V Henry is recovering in hospital from his death, and that he then re-encounters the balefulness of the world in Book VI, which includes many of his deeply personal, elegiac Songs, especially those—numbers 146 to 159—for his friend Delmore Schwartz. Anne B. Warner argues interestingly that

> The final impact of these elegies about friends comes with the sense of Henry's total isolation in Book VI, which contains the low point, the 'way down note' Henry speaks of in his elegy for

Roethke. Book VI portrays the darkest period in *The Dream Songs*, the point from which Henry moves eastward toward rebirth.[87]

In that scheme, therefore, Book VII represents Henry's geographical departure for a new land of possible fulfilment, and may be seen to correspond more overtly to the classic voyage of adventure in works such as the *Odyssey*, the *Télémaque*, and the *Lusiads*. It must be said, however, that the narrative of *His Toy, His Dream, His Rest* is more apparent than real. Book IV does not really function as the *point d'appui* that it may appear to be. To take just one example, Berryman originally numbered Song 128 among the *Opus posthumous* sequence while in the completed volume it figures among the recovery group of Book V. Similarly, many of the Songs in Books V, VI, and VII are really interchangeable with those in other books, for both subject and theme. Berryman's manuscript drafts and notes give evidence of his confusion as to thematic groupings: at least twelve Songs which now figure in Book VI, for example, were originally designated for Book V. Other examples of Berryman's woolly sense of demarcation may be seen from the facts that Song 210 (Book VI) was originally assigned to Book III, that Song 300 (Book VII) was categorised indiscretely as 'V or VI', and that Song 379 (late in Book VII) was, in the first place, assigned indecisively with the abbreviation 'beg. VI?' The narrative movement of the second volume continues to be as hazy as in the first, despite fulfilling the general outline of another loose work note (probably dating from late in 1966) which indicates that Book V represents 'hospital', Book VI, the hero 'stunted' in Minneapolis, and the final Book, a grand release summed up in the word 'Out!'

Perhaps the most important feature of the weakness of Berryman's design is that he had written the final Song, number 385, at the latest by early May 1965,[88] a time when he expected to finish the poem within a year. Accordingly, a reading of the narrative or metaphysical structure of the poem can rely very little on the evidence of that concluding Song, since it was designated as the poem's closure long before very many of the Songs of Books V, VI, and VII had been written. Since the poem was artificially predetermined, and since most of the Songs in the last Book resulted from Berryman's removal to Dublin, Song 385 cannot be said to be the necessary and inevitable conclusion of the emotional and incidental course of events which intervened. It is no more than Berryman's rudimentary shot at narrative completion, to convey the effect of a trajectory reaching its target. The weakness of the plan lies less in that simple predetermination, however, than in the fact that, because Berryman indulged the habit of writing Songs so steadily during the academic year 1966–7, he allowed himself no alternative but to make Book VII expansible to an almost indefinite degree. The seven-book structure was designed originally to create an equal balance about the artificial fulcrum of the *Opus posthumous* sequence. It is clear, that is to say, that the total of 161 Songs might have retained numerical symmetry by having seven Songs in Book IV followed by a further seventy-seven Songs to match the first volume. Berryman's failure to apprehend a distinct narrative structure led him to lack restraint in writing more and more Songs, and consequently to overbalance the second volume. Of Book VII at least, then, it seems not unfair to say that its structural possibilities are limited only to those of reasonable containment. Like the earlier books, it lacks significant progression.

What my argument points to is not that the final published sequence is ill-organised and unsuccessful as a poem of epic dimensions and some pretensions to the genre, but that *The Dream Songs* needs to be judged in terms less of received generic categories than of its own identity. It is possible that Berryman himself did not comprehend the nature of his finished work. It is likely that he thought it a disappointment for not matching the epic paradigms which he had applied to it. It is equally relevant to see that when Berryman shrugged off questions about the poem's structure, he was actually making a boast of what he would rather have considered a deficiency. His pronouncement that the plot was designed in terms of the personality of Henry is acute but retrospective. Very few of the Songs were actually written with a view to pertinency, but Berryman did stop at frequent intervals to reassess the course of his materials with a view to shape and sequence: with a view, that is, to a conventional narrative structure. The actual process of composition was desultory. Each Song may relate to any other Song, but not by way of sequence, story, or progress. Under those circumstances, it seems reasonable to infer that Berryman did not indeed understand the character which *The Dream Songs* had attained. He lacked a true perspective because of reviewing his composition so often in accordance with epic models. In the event, Song 385 should be read properly as irresolute, as not finding any conclusive answer to the questions which are thematic in the work as a whole, and accordingly as of a kind with what may be called (without detriment) the aggregation of the volume.

Berryman was acutely aware of the moral responsibility of being a creative artist, especially one whose work involved a vast amount of self-exploitation. For example, Song 271 begins by suggesting some reasons for his writing:

> to waken ancient longings, to remind (of childness),
> to make laugh, and to hurt,
> is and was all he ever intended.

The manuscript preserves a three-line fragment (neglected probably for no other reason than that Berryman lost sight of it, or was unable to fit it to a complete Song) which tells more of his purposes:

> He lied, a little, just now: he meant more.
> To solve the problems, and reform hisself,
> also was his desire.

An important aspect of Berryman's moral responsibility (which includes the need for solution and reform) inheres in his sense of his relation to Henry, his persona in *The Dream Songs*. He knew that his working brief was to depersonalise himself, to comprehend, to contain, and to resolve.

> Henry both is and is not me, obviously. We touch at certain points. But I am an actual human being; he is nothing but a series of conceptions—my conceptions . . . He only does what I make him do.[89]

Elsewhere he added, 'I feel entirely sympathetic to him. He doesn't enjoy my advantages of supervision; he just has vision.'[90] The emergence of whatever structure *The Dream Songs* possess was dependent on Berryman's own developing ability to define his relationship to his persona. To order Henry's adventures was a mode of coming to terms with all that was contingent in his own life, to resolve the irregularity of his own fortunes. Each of the Songs, which often rely wholly for subject or theme on whatever happened to Berryman himself, is an interpretation of experience.

> Now Henry is a man with, God knows, many faults, but among them is not self-understanding. He believes in his enterprise. He is suffering and suffering heavily and has to. That can't be helped.[91]

In his discussion of Lowell's 'Skunk Hour', Berryman insisted that 'the speaker [of a poem] can never be the actual writer . . . The necessity for the artist of selection opens inevitably an abyss between his person and his persona . . . The persona looks across at the person and then sets about its own work.'[92] That definition of persona to person is exactly the relation in which Henry stands to Berryman himself. In another place, he was categorical: 'Out of these possibilities of I which I have given a new identity to, Henry, I let some flower.'[93] Such a formulation of his artistic strategy—which implied the absolute necessity of artistic design and moral control—represents a hard-won achievement for Berryman.

Since Berryman's death, Douglas Dunn has usefully suggested[94] that an analogue for *The Dream Songs* might be found in *Don Juan*, a work of which Jerome McGann observed:

> Coleridge postulates exactly what *Don Juan* refuses to postulate. According to Coleridge, the purpose of a narrative is to convert a series into a whole. But Byron meant to sail directly into that wind, and to say, as it were: the purpose of his narrative is to convert the world (i.e. the human world) into a series. Everything that is the case is taken for granted, not in the order of form, but in the form of experience.[95]

Berryman's awareness in writing *The Dream Songs* may be seen to have developed to that point when he could concede that his weakness as a Coleridgean formulist gave him his strength as a Byronic pragmatist. The act of composing Henry was an act of selection and arrangement. His deep fears for the arbitrariness of Henry's thoughts and deeds stemmed from the feeling that the order of experience was a gaffe in the order of art. In his discussion of Byron's poem, Jerome McGann has taken care to differentiate the importance of preliminary designs, which are constantly cancelled and revised during the composition of the poem, from predesignated 'forms' and 'structures'.[96] Like *Don Juan*, *The Dream Songs* needs to be seen as neither finished nor integral in a pure way. Like Byron's designs, the weakness of Berryman's designs became a condition of artistic success; working intentions gave way to the order of the poem itself. The distinction which I am making here is not fanciful, for it is essential to appreciate the steps of Berryman's design; without those designs the poem would not now be constituted in the form and order which are the realisation and solution—that is to say, the surrender—of those very designs.

If *The Dream Songs* is an epic, Berryman actually travesties epic expectations. Yet he is not unaware of his position: he tries to distract critics from the structural deficiencies of the work by setting them to chase a hare, the mysterious identities of Henry and his friend. Berryman's epic is decidedly a reflection of an unheroic age. Its hero is unheroic in all postures. His adventures are not necessarily encountered during geographical journeys, but are better seen as incursions into psychological depths. He is morbidly self-centred (though not complacent), a man for whom all times provide occasions of concern, regret, and reproach. The ground of those occasions is always the thought of death. His basic preoccupations seem to be lust, lament, catechetics, and family consolation. He himself is recriminatory, commiserative, vagrant, and regressive: a composite, in sum, of passive or even negative qualities.

Like its hero, *The Dream Songs* is, curiously, best defined by what it is not. It is a poem virtually without linear progression; cumulative, but without significant addition. Individual Songs seem often indeterminate in meaning, and sometimes of little consequence to any larger profession or showing. The various Songs are brought into a relation with each other by being concentred on the personality of Henry. They are faceted in his consciousness; each Song is a function of his mind. It is remarkable that in a poem of such length there is really only one character, no heroine, and little overt conflict. The most pervasive features of Henry are his isolation and his egotism. What *The Dream Songs* does achieve is the effort to quiz the laws of Henry's being. At root, the themes of the Songs are loss and *ubi sunt*, which are of course two faces of the same theme. The work explores the stock—the spectrum—of Henry's fears and concerns. *The Dream Songs* is Berryman's own system of defence and aid against a threatening world; its efficacy is that of having held language to his trials. Thrilled and scared, Berryman observes and records one man's world: that man, Henry, himself. The poem may consist of variations on obsessive themes, but those themes are radically inexhaustible. It is a work fundamentally concerned with ontological uncertainties. The quest for values is shaped by a matrix of attitudes and insights. To study himself and insinuate his destiny: that is Henry's design.

In a late Dream Song written after *His Toy, His Dream, His Rest*, Berryman indicates that he needed to withdraw from his persona after the completion of *The Dream Songs*, that ultimately Henry could not

personate the wholeness of being human, and that from then on (as in
Love and Fame) he needed to face the moral responsibility of his life
without intermediary:

> A human personality, that's impossible.
> The lines of nature & of will, that's impossible.
> I give the whole thing up.
> Only there resides a living voice
> which if we can make we make it out of choice
> not giving the whole thing up.[97]

4. *Love & Fame* and Berryman's Luck

Berryman described the subject of *Love & Fame* as 'solely and simply myself. Nothing else. A subject on which I am an expert . . . so I wiped out all the disguises and went to work.'[1] This is a clear statement of autobiographical intention; the poet has purged himself of earlier personae or masks, whether the poet–lover in *Berryman's Sonnets* and *Homage to Mistress Bradstreet* or 'Henry' in *The Dream Songs*—'all the disguises'. Since the word 'disguises' suggests deception, it is reasonable to infer that *Love & Fame* would present the poet *in propria persona* speaking of a self formerly guarded or travestied. Berryman regarded the 'collection of lyrics' which constitute the volume as being unified 'because most of the poems are autobiographical, based on the historical personality of the poet'.[2] By 'historical' he meant a real, physical, space-time identity, not a fiction, except that the phrase 'based on' cautions us against reading the facts of the poems as forensic. Earlier Berryman had seemed to belie that statement with the words, 'I am not writing an autobiography-in-verse, my friends' (in the poem 'Message'),[3] but he was more exactly disclaiming the possibility of total reconstruction. There seemed to him no hope of giving an account of the empirical truths either of character or of event, especially when the story was the partial one which makes up Parts I and II of *Love & Fame*—the six-year span from the ages of eighteen to twenty-four, covering the period of his education at Columbia College, New York, and Clare College, Cambridge. 'It's not my life,' he averred cannily. 'That's occluded and lost.'[4]

The structural principle of the sequence would appear to be simple; it functions by assessing the youth driven to two parallel ends—the pursuit of a series of girls (love as lust) and of fame both through scholarship and through poetry. It would appear further that the polemics of the sequence are conscious and deliberate, and work to demonstrate that the youth was misdirected when viewed in the light

of the metaphysical and spiritual revelation which is the referent of
Part IV of *Love & Fame*. Berryman accordingly does severe justice to
his former self, the late adolescent of limited outlook and achievement. J. M. Linebarger says that in these poems Berryman 'has
entirely mastered the reticence about himself that obscured some
early poems and that led him to assume the mask of Henry'.[5]
Linebarger laments too the lack of aesthetic distance involved in
Berryman's 'descent into embarrassing self-revelation'.[6] I think that
an important distinction is in question here, however, for Berryman
lacks reticence only with regard to the surface detail, the gossipy or
simply anecdotal subject matter of the poems. What is strikingly
absent is the appearance of inwardness, perhaps because, as John
Bayley has suggested, the sentiments have been 'cauterised by
contrivance':[7] "Such a poetry has nothing of the *accidental* and
inadvertent in it, no trace of genuine impurity".[8]

Berryman sees himself when young as a type of the lords who
'turn sonnet' in *Love's Labour's Lost* (I. ii. 173): temperament and
circumstances drove him as much to expressions of love as to loving.

> My love confused confused with after loves
> not ever over time did I outgrow.
> Solemn, alone my Muse grew taller.
> Rejection slips developed signatures.[9]

The view may be condescending, but the sanctions which Berryman
directs against his younger self do often reflect on himself at the time
of writing.

The concensus of critical opinion has run to the view expressed by
J. D. McClatchy: 'The naked trial of *Love & Fame*, its flattened style
and obsessive details, make it the most exposed and intimate
confessional collection—which is perhaps one factor contributing to
the general puzzlement and disappointment which surrounded its
publication.'[10] Even a more affirmative critic such as Peter Stitt has
felt impelled to acknowledge the technical paucity of the more
overtly autobiographical sections of the volume: 'The quality of the
verse parallels this movement: the poems grow in power and
technical mastery from the early ones, which are *prosaic, intentionally
almost bad* [my italics], to the last eleven, which comprise a virtual
tour de force.'[11]

One of the most sustained criticisms of the volume is by Ernest
C. Stefanik, who argues well for the case that the volume involves

'a conscious disintegration and re-integration of personality'.[12]
But his argument leads toward a statement about structure
which is certainly over-schematic and in some ways slavish to
Berryman: 'It proceeds from exuberance of language and
scurrilous details to elegance of style and homage to the
Lord. . . . John Berryman's pilgrimage is from unconsciousness to
heightened awareness, from objective thinking to subjective faith.'[13]
Stefanik seems undecided, however, about the very tone and thrust of
the autobiographical passages of the sequence; his statements that
'Berryman exposes the past with the objectivity and candor of a
disinterested observer'[14] and that 'the self-revelations are made by
steady, harrowing degrees'[15] comport uneasily with the proposition
that the poem is 'one written apparently in the immediacy of crisis—
confusion, torment, and anguish; guilt, purgation, and epiphany'.[16]
Even more uncritically, it would seem, he accepts the premise that
the first two parts of *Love & Fame* are "self-parading"[17] and that the
first three sections of *Love & Fame* constitute the poet's confession,[18]
while suspending his task by claiming of the fourth and final part that
'no critical judgment is possible'.[19]

Another critic, Jonathan Galassi, sees no irony, self-criticism, or
any other more positive form of self-apprehension, behind what he
styles 'the histrionic self-advertisement of *Love & Fame*'.

> *Love and Fame* is devoted like all Berryman's last work to the
> phantasies or delusions which dominated the poet's life . . . a
> passion for literary renown and an insatiable sexual urge inform
> this obsessive, regretful recollection of Berryman's youth
> . . . *Love and Fame* is an attempt at writing properly about the
> poet's own personality without the mediating device of an alter-
> ego . . . raw, unilateral self-scrutiny . . . the 'I' of these guilt-
> motivated recollections is often hysterically one-dimensional,
> hollow, and unreal. . . . In *Love and Fame*, the poet has blurred the
> distinctions we normally expect form, persona, and tone to make
> between what the writer feels and what he chooses to express.
> . . . Each poem is a new, uncorrected edition of the self, incom-
> plete and failed because unchallenged and unamplified by another
> point of view.[20]

I have extrapolated what I take to be the burden of Galassi's
argument, not because it marks an extreme point of view, but because
it is all too representative. For many critics, it appears, Berryman

accomplished in *Love & Fame* little more than an act of personal catharsis—'an attempt to neutralise his obsessions' by glorifying them'[21]—which is beneath art.

Going beyond Stefanik's argument that one should perceive the thrust of the narrative line in the sequence, and that (for that purpose) 'the reader must first understand how the poems are brought into relation with one another',[22] it strikes me as equally important to discriminate the extent to which Berryman does actually contrive lyrics of a sufficient internal irony, and create a tension between subject and form. This is to acknowledge the act of imagination and crafting at work in the lyrics of the volume, and not merely to take their measure as artless and irresponsible acts of self-exploitation. The structure of *Love & Fame* was in no way predetermined but corresponds to a radical change in Berryman's outlook which took place during the period of composition. For that reason, the ironic structure of the work should be regarded as adventitious, not as prescriptive. It is well to bear in mind that the title *Love & Fame* is announced in the last poem of Part III of the book,[23] which was written before the 'Addresses to the Lord' (Part IV) had even been conceived.

   The lyrics of *Love & Fame* may perhaps be belittled for not fulfilling conventional expectations, for their loose anti-categorical prosody or their lax conversational idiom, even for the jargon (in 'Drunks', for instance) of phrases such as 'crawling with' and 'she turned out to have nothing on'.[24] Certain critics[25] have exaggerated the scatalogical interest to which the poems apparently appeal, and have undertaken the possibly fallacious procedure of levelling moral judgements at imaginative work. They are beguiled by the flagrant anecdotes, and fail to perceive the form of the poems. Tastelessness should be viewed, however, as a decoy for the psychological and emotional meaning which can be construed from the total form of each lyric. On the face of it, most of them make apparently inconsequential shifts between constituent statements: the meaning must be derived from the relatedness of those statements. The weakest poems in the book (such as 'In & Out')[26] are those where the shifts are arbitrary and capricious, without serving a perceptible pattern. Berryman was himself well aware of the *forma* which the details of each poem were designed to fulfil. Reviewing the poem 'Transit', for instance, he could find little sense of cogency and wrote 'mere damned rambling' on the manuscript; similarly, he thought that 'A Huddle of Need' was 'poor', and 'Of Suicide', 'disordered'.[27] On the other hand, when studying the galley-proofs for the volume, he remarked 'a treat' against 'Drunks' in the list of contents.

The poem 'Friendless'[28] may be satisfactorily interpreted by paying high regard to points of strategic irony and structural meaning. The simple sense progression alone of the poem seems to yield little more than random reflections and historical recollections.[29]

> Friendless in Clare, except Brian Boydell
> a Dubliner with no hair
> an expressive tenor speaking voice
> who introduced me to the music of Peter Warlock
>
> who had just knocked himself off, fearing the return
> of his other personality, Philip Heseltine.

The poem situates the 'expressive' speaking voice of Brian Boydell against the 'voice of a lost soul moving', Philip Heseltine (who took the name Peter Warlock).[30] As Berryman understood it, the fictive Warlock killed himself because of a schizoid division from his real self. To that apparently disinterested observation Berryman juxtaposes his recollection that, when asked to read some modern American poetry to his fellow undergraduates, he discovered that the distinctive poetic voices of Stevens and Hart Crane did not register with the English ear. Worse: he remembers too that even W. B. Yeats signified so little to his contemporaries that they were unable to spell his name correctly.

> The Dilettante Society here in Clare
> asked me to lecture to them on Yeats
> and misspelt his name on the invitations.[31]

So precarious is self-identification, so unstable is fame, that the poet may well fear for his lack of personal voice or creative voice—for what he calls 'failure, or, worse, insignificance'—in the face of such object lessons in lost self-recognition and lost creative significance. The words 'voice' and 'fear' figure twice each in the poem, not necessarily as discrete: the one voice seems mostly to be direct speech, the other imaginative self-expression; the one fear is for sanity; the other, that of Berryman's anticipated failure to fulfil his vocation as poet. Berryman sees himself ironically in a context which condemns acknowledged masters—Stevens, Crane, and Yeats—to incomprehension and neglect, and the success of a composer like Heseltine to the schism between his achievement and his real self. The bafflement which Berryman's contemporaries evince before the work of Stevens and Crane stands in adroit relation to his own failure to comprehend his burdensome sense of himself: that helplessness is signified by the plangent use of epanaphora in the last stanza:

> I gorge on Peek Freans and brood.
> I don't do a damned thing but read and write.
> I wish I were back in New York!
> I feel old, but I don't understand.

Similarly, the following poem, 'Monkhood',[32] is divided into two almost equal parts of five stanzas each; the first half appears to focus attention on Berryman's friend Patrick Barton, the second on Berryman himself. Berryman draws a terse portrait of his eccentric 'companion'[33] which seems little related to the almost exclusive self-appraisal of the second half of the poem. The point is that Barton's eccentricity is used to define the poet's own relative normality: 'And I think in my unwilling monkhood *I* have problems!'

Accordingly, in the second half, he sees himself as an object of attention and analysis, as defined either by himself, 'I knew I wasn't with it yet', or by others, 'Did even Eileen ever understand me sharper?' He recalls that another friend, Delmore Schwartz, had a 'gentle heart and high understanding of both the strengths and cripplings of men', but, in context, the praise is ironically self-gratifying, for it was the perceptive Schwartz who ('to my *pleasure* one day') imputed 'Satanic pride' to Berryman. The midpoint of the poem functions as an artistic and psychological axis about which Berryman balances two apparently contrasted modes of self-identification. In the first, Berryman reflects himself by association with the spectacle of a wayward friend; in the second, he expatiates more directly upon his own complex and unclassifiable behaviour, as the absorbing subject of speculation and self-inquiry.

> Will I ever write properly, with passion and exactness,
> of the damned strange demeanours of my flagrant heart?
> and be by anyone anywhere undertaken?
> one *more* unanswerable question.

It is tactically appropriate that the poem modulates from historic present tense (the first five stanzas) through simple past tense (the next fourteen lines), and then back into a present tense (the last seven lines) which has canny reference to both historic and present predicaments. One meaning that emerges in the poem is that, *mutatis mutandis*, Berryman's understanding of himself remains partial and undeveloped, despite the strictly limited decisiveness about his younger self shown, for example, in four statements which parallel the final stanza of 'Friendless', 'I never went . . . I knew I wasn't with it' (ll. 21−25).

Since both 'Friendless' and 'Monkhood' take personal isolation and literary unfulfilment for theme, it is important to observe that the syntax of the first line of 'Monkhood' collapses two discrete and non-sequential ideas into one. The statement that 'I don't show my work to anybody' does not *require* the phrase 'I am quite alone'. In view of the fact that 'Monkhood' proceeds to enlarge on a particular friendship, there seems to be an internal contradiction not unlike the contradiction in 'Friendless' which holds that the poet is friendless (a word, strictly speaking, absolute and unqualifiable) 'except for Brian Boydell'. It should be understood that Berryman identified his failure as a poet with personal isolation; friendships such as those with Boydell or Barton did not signify on a level of permanent validity to him. They did not have access to what Berryman considered his real being, his creativity.

J. M. Linebarger has pointed out that *Love & Fame* 'is more limited than *The Dream Songs* in the kinds and intensity of its emotions'.[34] It may be that the fault, if it is one, is incurred because the basis of the lyrics is conceptual rather than perceptual. If they lack inwardness, that is to say, the poems lack vigour. The poet seems to coin what he calls 'fragrant scenes',[35] and responds to them (if at all) in a patronising or judgemental capacity. If such a view is taken, Berryman's vision of his younger self must be regarded as simplistic, involving his conscious mind much more than emotional empathy— largely because of the general law that 'memory is dissociated from the feelings that the original experience engendered'.[36]

An instance of such a dissociation from original experience may be found in the schematic poem 'Down & Back'.[37] As the title suggests, the poet's observations are held to correlate with an emotional graph which begins in suspense, finds its nadir in one mode (sex), and its consequent zenith in another (scholarship). The poem is equally divided into two halves of twenty-four lines each (a count which

takes the half-lines 28 and 29 as equal units, as Berryman clearly
intended), the descent of the first half culminating in the line 'It was
then I think I flunked my 18th Century', and resurgence charted in
the second half. This swing from sexual frustration (the first five
stanzas) results by implication in examination failure (stanza 6), for
which Berryman compensates by earning academic acclaim. Such a
swing is a simplistic structural device for the polemical purposes of the
poem, with which the facts of the matter do not correspond so nicely.
A number of falsehoods or just misrememberings were to
Berryman's purpose in the poem, one of them being crucial.

As 'Down & Back' states, Berryman studied so ill during the
summer of 1934 that he failed an examination and consequently lost
his scholarship, which then *de facto* prevented his return to college—
purely for financial reasons. In truth, Dean Hawkes wrote cordially at
the beginning of October to grant him leave of absence: 'I regret to
learn that you are obliged to drop out of college for a little while. I
enclose a leave of absence as you request and hope that we may see
you back in school before long.'[38] The last twelve lines of the poem
return to verisimilitude, including the facts that Berryman kept what
he calls 'an encyclopedic notebook' and that he made 'an abridgement
of Locke's essay' (which was even more concise than the 'hundred
pages' he recalls),[39] but their effectiveness as a dénouement relies
heavily on the earlier implication that he had been rusticated, as he
euphemistically phrased it for the purposes of dramatic effect in these
lines:

> The Dean was nice
> but thought the College & I should part company
> at least for a term, to give me 'time to think'
> & regroup my forces (if I'd any left).

—when his family's indigence alone had kept him from school. The
Dean in fact granted him a year's leave of absence, but Berryman was
able to return to college the next spring when his stepfather managed
to make some money on the stock exchange. The poem gives the
situation a more heroic cast than it actually took, being more precise
as to artistic design than as to emotional rehearsal. Berryman's
reconstitution of historical fact is climaxed with a sense of elation in
the last two lines of the poem:

> My scholarship was restored, the Prodigal Son
> welcomed with crimson joy.

Far from being shameless and lacking reticence, the sentiment of the poem is as little self-purgation as it is *mauvaise honte*.

In other lyrics in Parts I and II of *Love & Fame* Berryman is equally ambiguous, as in 'Views of Myself'[40] where (through double irony) his present self seems as arrogant as his past:

> I stand ashamed of myself;
> yes, but I stand. Take my vices alike
>
> with some my virtues, if you can find any.
> I stick up like Coriolanus with my scars
> for mob inspection.

Such a rationale for exposing his personal history contains a large proportion of continuing self-gratification. Similarly, 'Images of Elspeth'[41] moves from the callow memory that he had been driven 'wild' by the girl's disclosure that she possessed photographs of herself in the nude, to the final line in which the poet continues to share that sense of ingenuous titillation: 'wishing I could lay my old hands somewhere on those snapshots.' A similar effect is betrayed through the use of the historic present tense in the poem 'Anyway',[42] which conveys the sense of immediacy of anticipation, of participation, or in the last stanza of 'Olympus', where, moved by the reflected glory of Mark Van Doren and Richard Blackmur, Berryman concludes:

> I have travelled in some high company since
> less dizzily.
> I have had some rare girls since but never one so philosophical
> as that same Spring (my last Spring there) Jean Bennett.[43]

The parallelism of 'high company' and 'rare girls' (Fame and Love respectively) is telling, for the poet concedes that they marked the limit of his impressionability and sexual involvement—'since' when, all else has seemed 'less'. More recent achievements have actually been as prestigious, but he himself (with a tenor that must be interpreted as wistful or envious) has lacked the capacity for surrender that he enjoyed in his last spring at Columbia. Similarly, in 'Tea', Berryman both relishes and regrets the reminiscence that

> By six-fifteen she had promised to stop seeing 'the other man'.
> I may have heard better news but I don't know when.[44]

In fact, many levels of significance are in play in the lyrics of *Love &*
Fame, since the irony inherent in Berryman's mode of narration
works at the expense not only of the *jeune premier* but also of the poet
who unwittingly discloses his current weaknesses and predilections.
'Similar to the point of view of the Sonnets,' J. M. Linebarger says,
'this double view achieved by a man analyzing an earlier self is one of
the pleasures of *Love & Fame*.'[45] The book is not an autobiography-
in-verse only in the sense that, as Berryman himself admitted, it is not
at the service of the truth of experiences. In 'Message',[46] he supplied
the phrase which begins the second stanza—'Impressions, structures,
tales'—after rejecting a draft version, 'Impressions, facts'. The change
implicitly concedes the truth that he was not attempting
verisimilitude.

A statement which has been taken as crucial to an understanding of
the overall structure of *Love & Fame* is Berryman's own
'Afterword'[47] to the first English edition. Written in June 1971, at a
time when Berryman chose to suppress a number of poems in the
volume, including 'Thank You, Christine' and 'To B—E—',[48] the
'Afterword' was, Berryman believed, an attempt ('little as I like to
show my hand') to answer the 'uncomprehending' reception accor-
ded the book by critics:

> It is—however uneven—a whole, each of the four movements
> criticizing backward the preceding, until Part IV wipes out
> altogether all earlier presentations of the 'love' and 'fame' of the
> ironic title. . . . But the attack on these two notions begins in the
> opening poem.[49]

There is a sleight involved in the passage—whether a delusion, a
rationalisation, or an untruth—which is radical. By arguing for the
unity of the book, and by stating that the metaphysical–spiritual
resolution of Part IV ('Addresses to the Lord') is implicit even in the
first poem of Part I—and hence, we must infer, in the succeeding
poems of Parts I and II—Berryman tries to persuade both himself and
his audience that the teleological development of the plot was
predetermined, and not a matter of hindsight. R. Patrick Wilson
bases a short article unquestioningly on that proposition: '. . . the
'stern religion' of the Addresses quenches the 'unwilling flame' of lust
and pride. Berryman seems to be confessing his sins (rather than

bragging about them) so that he might in good conscience begin his prayers.'[50]

The actual state of affairs differs markedly from such a view. In February and March 1970, Berryman had not yet experienced a moment of divine intervention in his life, and clearly relished the telling of the secular, lubricious autobiography of Parts I and II. The poems validated his present proud ambitions, and originally contained other stanzas of contemporaneous significance. As J. M. Linebarger says, many of the poems in *Love & Fame* achieve 'a delightful humor and irony by presenting the younger Berryman through the eyes of the older one'.[51] But certain of the poems show an older Berryman who is surely unregenerate, and as arrogant, as ambitious, as self-exalting, as the younger. It cannot be said that in such poems Berryman is simply lamenting his misspent youth. Stanza 13 of 'Shirley & Auden'[52] was substituted at a late stage of composition for stanzas which included these lines:

> Great now my power, which also I husband now
> although I stake my life on one image.
> I count on flowering into age.
> (I'm 55) unlike my superiors Schubert
>
> but Goya whose horror I almost emulate
> and if K leaves me I could surely rival
> Beethoven and his bangs
> and deaf his final ecstasies
>
> the most *promising* artist perhaps who has laboured:[53]

Taken in conjunction with line 64 of the published version—'I wonder if Shakespeare trotted to the jostle of his death'—it is evident that Berryman was proud of the implicit over-ambitious comparison.

By the time he came to write Part IV of the book—in a spirit of 'grave piety'[54]—he hoped that it might function as a palinode to the earlier poems, as Joel Conarroe observes in a judicious essay: 'My own sense is that the book can most helpfully be analysed in terms of its two halves, the second representing a total repudiation of the values inherent in the two sections that make up the first.'[55] In such a scheme, Part III of the volume may be seen to mark a transitional phase in Berryman's actual life, and consequently in the structure of the volume, ending no later than the first day of May 1970. It rehearses his sense of situation during the time he was undergoing treatment for alcoholism at St Mary's Hospital, a period when he was, though haggard, yet unreclaimed. It was only after many weeks that Berryman arrived at his wish to obviate or negate the swaggering mood among the earlier poems, when he reviewed unbound page proofs and wrote 'v. unpleasant! What ever made me think it anything else?' by the poem 'Thank you, Christine', and 'UGH' and 'disgusting' by 'To B——E——'.[56] Berryman's 'Afterword' must accordingly have been conditioned by self-saving hindsight. This might have been discerned earlier, but it has been difficult for critics to perceive anything more than that the devotional sequence at the end of the book was expected to lend an ironic colouring to the earlier, more 'scurrilously' autobiographical poems: such simple, declarative lyrics seemed not otherwise sophisticated enough in themselves to suggest the play of a strong internal irony for which I have argued. The alternative to recognising and analysing the irony at work in those poems akin to 'Friendless' is to interpret them as modes of naive wilfulness. In fact, they are lyrics not of artless candour, but of disingenuous and successful craft.

The different parts of *Love & Fame* correspond to the changes in Berryman's own spiritual development during the early months of 1970, and not to the plotting of a sequence of lyrics with a foregone thematic conclusion. It is certainly ironic that the volume may be judged very favourably on Berryman's own terms, as 'a whole, each of the four movements criticizing backward the preceding, until Part IV wipes out altogether all earlier presentations of the "love" and "fame" of the ironic title',[57] since its eventual and real success was contingent upon the luck of Berryman's real life.

5. Notes and Commentary on *The Dream Songs*

Numbers to *The Dream Songs* are given in the left-hand margin of the page, followed by line numbers in parentheses and quotations from the Song in question, both in italics.

On 2 January 1955 Berryman wrote for a friend a sonnet which includes these lines:

> I'm
> All over again my father, partners in time . . .
> This apple is delicious. My fears hide.

Though first thinking of the sequence as *The Apple Songs*, Berryman seems to have invented the title of *The Dream Songs* on 21 August 1955, while on his way to have a picnic by the River Apple in Wisconsin.

*   *   *

The work began with three lines written in 1947 (at a time when Berryman had no idea at all how the whole scheme would shape up):

> The jolly old man is a silly old dumb,
> with a mean face, humped, who kills dead.
> There is a tall girl who loves only him.

It was only on 13 August 1955 that these lines expanded to become the original Dream Song, which was later published in *The Noble Savage* (no. 1 (March 1960), p. 119), though not included in the canon of *The Dream Songs*.

*   *   *

The day before his son was born, Berryman wondered (Unpub. DS, folder 1) if *The Dream Songs* might 'precisely end with *one on this*' subject—his child—a figure of what he elsewhere called "beauty, slowness" (Unpub. DS, folder 2). It is not difficult to determine that the last of the sequence, number 385—'My daughter's heavier'— stands as the fulfilment of that wish, even though the child was of a different sex and born to a different marriage.

*   *   *

In a note of 28 July 1959, Berryman categorised *Homage to Mistress Bradstreet* as 'mother', *The Dream Songs* as 'father (and wife and son)' (Unpub. DS, folder 16).

*   *   *

For an interesting and informative discussion of the epigraphs to both *77 Dream Songs* and *His Toy, His Dream, His Rest*, see *Berryman's Baedeker: The Epigraphs to The Dream Songs*, by Susan G. Berndt (Derry, Pennsylvania: The Rook Society, 1976

Berryman's sense of being a prophet unheeded in his own country prompted him in January 1959 to choose for the second epigraph a text from *Lamentations* (3:63) ending 'I am their musick'. He associated that text with *Jeremiah* 20:7:

> You have seduced me, yahweh, and I have let myself be seduced: you have overpowered me: you were the stronger.
> I am a daily laughing-stock,
> everybody's butt   (Jerusalem Bible)

The images of seduction and fight illustrate Yahweh's power over His prophet. Gary Q. Arpin has explained what appear to be the specifically religious implications of the epigraph:

> The references to Lamentations serve—and perhaps this is their most important function—to indicate the relationship between the poet and his world and the poet and his audience. Henry's suffering is meant to embody ours. . . . In *The Dream Songs*, Henry suffers not as Job—an individual bearing great personal pain—but as Jeremiah—an individual bearing our general pain, for what

reasons he knows not. ("'I Am Their Musick": Lamentations and *The Dream Songs*"', *John Berryman Studies*, vol. 1, no. 1 (January 1975), pp. 5–6.)

But it must be said that Berryman did see Henry as a type of Job, and does express personal suffering in *The Dream Songs*. He construed the verses from *Jeremiah*, and so from *Lamentations* (the context of his epigraph), as irreligious, imaging not only the people's scorn but also (as what he called, in loose notes dating from 1960, the 'nexus of contempt and desire') a feeling that might be reciprocated between Henry himself and another person—as of lust. Explicitly, that is to say, Berryman related the epigraph from *Lamentations* to Song 69, 'Love her he doesn't', (ll. 13–18). Mrs Boogry, who is the object of Henry's lust, is far from being the subject of his love. The irony is self-accusatory: the poet–prophet, as an exponent of his art, may deserve better from his country, but the poet as an individual person may also merit contempt.

1. On 29 March 1971, Berryman wrote: 'I've always supposed Dream Song 1 to be about his father's suicide, exposing him to the insolence of the world ('they tho't they could do it" images the long interdepartmental war against Humanities here, etc. etc.)—(letter to Peter Stitt, carbon copy in JBP). At that late date, he decided too that the poem concerned the Fall, in terms both of a birth-trauma and of expulsion from Eden. In such terms, the poem may usefully be glossed by Berryman's observation, in conversation with William Heyen: 'Isn't it true that the three of us sitting here, began with a great loss, from the controlled environment of the womb? After my son was born, I wrote him a little poem that started: "Feel for your bad fall how could I fail, / poor Paul, who had it so good'.' I have many objections to Freud's findings, but he was right about the importance of the womb.' (William Heyen, 'John Berryman: A Memoir and an Interview', *The Ohio Review*, vol. xv, no. 2 (Winter 1974), p. 60.)

   See discussion above for further observations on Dream Song 1.

2. Written on Thanksgiving Day, 1962, in Boston, where

Berryman was giving a poetry reading; revised on 16 September 1962. The first stanza refers to the fact that, on Election Day, all bars are closed. The Song is dedicated to 'Daddy' Rice (Thomas Dartmouth Rice), who began the tradition of negro minstrel shows; Berryman's source for information on Rice and the minstrel show tradition was Carl Wittke, *Tambo and Bones* (Durham, N. Carolina, 1930). See also Berryman's letter to Van Meter Ames: 'Of course I saw vaudeville, in Oklahoma and Tampa and Loew's State (the capital!), though I admit I never saw genuine minstrels' (14 September 1963; Van Meter Ames).

3. The first stanza, and the title of the Song—'A Stimulant for an Old Beast', derive from Berryman's own journal of 1948. On Friday 7 May of that year he had become very excited by a phrase in one of Swinburne's letters that referred to the Marquis de Sade as 'a stimulant for an old beast'. On 1 January 1948, Berryman had attended a party where a woman had announced to him that she ached to tell Delmore Schwartz, 'My psychiatrist can lick your psychiatrist' (l. 6). Much later, in 1955, he had noted that a girl named Susan referred to herself as 'not so young but not so very old' (l. 2). The disgust with Rilke expressed in the last stanza of the poem may be glossed by a letter that Berryman drafted in 1955:

> I am down on Rilke and the hieratic boys just now. I don't deny his sensitivity and his marvellous melody, or Valery's vivacity—incomparable exc w Stendhal's whom he passionately admired. But it is necessary to get down into the arena and kick around. Yeats was prepared to do this, and so I respect him more and even forgive his vulgar posturing. Of course the point is that the others were not *capable* of doing this. Take that rigmarole on solitude you quoted. Yes, it is stunning, and what is it based on? an elaborate and painfully self-satisfied *fear of life*. I like him when he was writing out of his active grief and awe, not these damned letters, these lay-sermons he sprayed around Europe instead of sleeping with people like a wicked but actual man. Love affairs on paper; ugh. The contemptible fear of writing poetry that many good men suffer from comes from these babies too.

. . . Valery? silent 25 years, so when Rilke hears about
this he is profoundly encouraged, having been silent for only
10 years. The hell with it. Not that it was deliberate in them,
and I feel with their suffering. . . . I'll tell you the truth: there
is something neauseating about Rilke, in-human, unmanly,
woman-mimicking. I don't mean homosexual, Whitman
and Auden say are quite different, and Marlowe, and one
doesn't object to them at all. Toadyish . . . I don't know
how to put it . . . but when the cult is over, I don't know
how the future will like it either. I *admit* he is a wonderful
poet. Yes! yes! he is. (16 April 1955; unsent.)

Other references in the poem include those to the relatively
short life-expectancy of meso-endomorphs, in the phrase
'Thick chests quit' (l. 10), and to the Czechoslovakian prime
minister Klement Gottwald.

   A Communist, Gottwald (d. 1953) was Czech premier from
1946; in 1948, after becoming president, he subserved Soviet
interests, and was responsible for the 'deviationist trials' in
which several of his former colleagues were executed. In his
diary ('XIX') for Wednesday, 24 March 1948 (the day after
writing the first stanza of *Homage to Mistress Bradstreet*),
Berryman include the remark: 'On with Gottwald, stanzas of
Masaryk himself . . .' Jan G. Masaryk, to whom the entry
refers, was a statesman who became head of the Czech
delegation to the UN Assembly in 1946. He strove for a
rapprochement between East and West, but, disillusioned,
committed suicide in March 1948; he is commonly held to have
been a victim of Communism.

4. Written in the Gaslight Restaurant, Minneapolis.

5. (*l. 15*) *Mr. Heartbreak*.
   At his reading in Spoleto, Italy, Berryman disclosed that 'the
French is Crèvecoeur': i.e. Michel Guillaume St Jean de
Crèvecoeur, *Letters from an American Farmer* (London: Thomas
Davies; Lockyer Davis, 1782).
(*ll. 17–18*) The witch Camacha of Montilla was able 'to cause the
living or the dead to appear in a mirror or upon the fingernail of

a newborn child'. (Miguel de Cervantes, 'The Colloquy of the
Dogs', *Three Exemplary Novels*, trans. Samuel Putnam
(London: Cassell, 1952) p. 182.)

In manuscript versions, the poem is entitled 'A Trail to the
Hill-Fire'.

At Spoleto, Berryman said that the poem was about 'a trip
from New York to New Delhi' (presumably that made by
Berryman in the summer of 1957), and that the 'Mountain'
(l. 11) is the great peninsula in Northeastern Greece.

6. A poem of the historical consciousness in a resentful aspect:
Berryman deplored his father for an act of self-destruction that,
as he often believed, had blighted his own life. A passion to
understand why his father deserted him through suicide infested
Berryman's mind, and underlies this Song. The poem takes a
view of time quite like that of Dream Song 11 (discussed in
Chapter 3), as J. M. Linebarger's analysis confirms: 'throughout
the slow time from that day to this, the stone capital at Wells has
continued to exist, ready to tease us out of thought' ('Dream
Song 6: "A Capital at Wells"', *John Berryman Studies*, vol. 11,
no. 1 (Winter 1976), p. 37). The Song does more: it tends to
fulfil Berryman's wish, as he expressed it at about this time, to
write a Song 'about my ancestor and *my* enemies' (Unpub. DS,
folder 16). He believed that he was descended from Ethan
Allen, the Vermont rebel against the British in the American
War of Independence, identified with Allen for his rebelliousness, and found one of Allen's assertions apt to his own emotion:
'I am a hardy mountaineer and scorn to be intimidated by
threats. If they fright me, they must absolutely produce some of
their tremendous fire, and give me a sensitive scorching.'
(Stewart H. Holbrook, *Ethan Allen*, (New York: Macmillan,
1940), p. 223; cited in Unpub. DS, folder 16.) The background
to Berryman's particular feeling was a state of academic
interdepartmental rivalry at the University of Minnesota which
threatened and eventually succeeded in diminishing his own
department. His experience of university politics found a
precedent in the political rebellion of his 'ancestor'. (Yet the
animus behind the poem also marked the honoured forebear: in
drafts for the poem, Berryman originally termed Allen, not a
'calling' man, but 'savage' and 'staggering'.) In 1940 Berryman

had addressed Allen in 'A Point of Age' (now most readily available in *Short Poems* (New York: Farrar, Straus and Giroux, 1967), p. 8):

> Ethan Allen, father, in the rebel wood
> Teach trust and disobedience to the son
> Who neither obeys nor can disobey One

—a passage which alludes to Antony's speech upbraiding Cleopatra (*Antony and Cleopatra*, IX, xiii, 42–3):

> The shirt of Nessus is upon me: teach me,
> Alcides, thou mine ancestor, thy rage

Antony curses the woman for being the death of him, and compares himself to Heracles, who was also killed by his wife acting from love and jealousy. A key point for Berryman, moreover, was that both Antony (through Octavia) and Heracles (through Iole) were unfaithful in love. Accordingly, as Berryman phrased it in the unpublished manuscript of *St. Pancras Braser*, 'Heracles deserted Antony who loved him; ah but *both* were unfaithful, like my father and me, and the fireshirt was the punishment'. (ibid., folder 4). A vivid mingling of themes takes place in Dream Song 6: Berryman's resentment of his personal academic difficulties, the rage that he felt towards his own father, and his own nuptial unfaithfulness. Guilt and righteousness are in a way conflated, without excluding each other.

The other crucial reference in the Song is the phrase 'Day was killing Porter' (l. 11). Henry Porter (fl. 1596–9), an English dramatist who wrote a play called *The Two Angry Women of Abingdon*, was killed, as Berryman understood it, by one John Day (ibid., folder 10). In a note of 26 June 1955, Berryman identified himself with Henry Porter (especially as being involved with two angry women, his mother—angry at her husband's alleged unfaithfulness, and at his suicide—and his own wife, angry at his own infidelity). In this view, it was logical for Berryman to wonder whether John Day, who killed "Henry" Porter, might not be seen as an image of 'JAS?'—his own father, John Allyn Smith.

The story of Abelard, to which the Song also alludes (l. 17), and his mutilation at the hands of Heloise's uncle, is well known. Line 13: Aeneas Sylvius (1404–64) was elected to the papacy after a fierce conflict in the conclave of Cardinals. They are important to the poem because—along with Keats and Milton (also referred to), Day, Porter, and Berryman himself as 'Henry'—they are all poets who suffered or caused agonising obstruction to life-work or even (as in Porter's case) to life itself.

7. ' "The Prisoner of Shark Island"
           with Paul Muni'
     Berryman first saw the film on 10 October 1936; in a letter to Mark Van Doren of that date, he enclosed a poem of which this is the first stanza:

> This night I have seen a film
> That would have startled Henry James
> Out of his massive calm
> Of discipline or sent Donne
> Into tortuous passion, and all names
> Of crafty men flooded with the sun.

Shortly afterwards, he saw Clark Gable and Jean Harlow in *Wife or Secretary*, and was so thrilled at discovering the possibilities of film that he told Mark Van Doren it would soon emerge as an art in our day to parallel the play in Shakespeare's. (Letter to MVD, 27 October 1936; Columbia University Library.) Within a few months he wrote to Robert Penn Warren that 'competent recognition, in *The Southern Review*, of the film as a formidable or legitimate art-form would, it seems to me, be worth any trouble or breach of policy.' (Letter to RPW, 4 February 1937; carbon copy in JBP.)

(*l. 2*) *Mr. Deeds' tuba*
     Mr. Deeds Goes to Town, starring Gary Cooper, was directed by Frank Capra in 1936.

(*1.3*) *the race in Ben Hur*
     Probably seen by JB in 1926.

(*l. 14*) *William S*
     William S. Hart appeared as the good-bad-man in thirteen films between 1914, when he starred in *Two Gun Hicks*, and 1922, when (by then a wealthy man) he retired from the screen.

On the MS. of the Song, Berryman notes: '*Amer prose and style of* [lines] 7 and 9 *shd be* rebuked by Chin. traditionalism of 8.'

9. The poem alludes to the Humphrey Bogart film *High Sierra* (1941). See J. M. Linebarger, *John Berryman* (New York: Twayne, 1974), pp. 110−11.

12. Written after seeing *La Sorcière*, a film starring Marina Vlady and Maurice Ronet; directed by André Michel, 1955.

13. At one time, Berryman fancied that he might write notes to the Songs, as the following to line 8, '*Let's investigate that*': 'This line is dedicated to the social scientists, in particular an intelligent one who once remarkt: "If I can't feed it into an IBM machine, it doesn't exist".' (Unpub. DS, folder 2; note dated 24 November 1958). (One of Berryman's friends had just turned his hand to empirical social research, dealing, for example, with questionnaire studies.)

> *My lass is braking.*
> *My ass is aching.*   (ll. 11−12)

Social and scientific research is satirised by alusion to the story of a man from Hamburg in Germany (although Berryman always associated the story with Unter den Linden) who sat contemplating his navel; eventually, unable to resist his enquiring mentality, he applied a screwdriver to the object of his gaze, whereupon his 'ass fell off!' (Berryman alludes to the story in a dream-association in *St. Pancras Braser*, folder 10: 'speech on navel (in another favourite story—Anthony Clark's originally)—in Unter den Linden—inserted screwdriver—ass fell off—"my brass is aching" (fame, him).' This cryptic reference is confirmed by Anthony Clark, letter to Haffenden, 22 March 1975: 'The Auden joke about the navel, salt, and eating celery in bed was relatively contemporary, and the screwdriver story—which I suppose the 60's hasn't helped—came from a great Jewish source and was not very new then, in 1955; I *think* it was newer in 1947 and I related it then.' Cf. a

Dream Song fragment, Unpub. DS, folder 2: 'Things get into one's navel. I just had a stern feel, /and look, in mine.')

The very idea of Henry being a 'human American' is mocked by association with the story of a German whose investigativ. mind makes a machine of him. Berryman diminished his original phrase 'my ass is breaking' to the doggerel of the finished version in order to enforce the imprecation. In addition to swingeing national traits and conduct, the Song expresses Berryman's disrespect for any scientific research that could prove reductive.

15. Based on an anecdote related by Saul Bellow. On 14 August 1962, Berryman sent Bellow a copy of the Song with this inscription: 'For Saul—excusez mon vol—but I warned you 10 years ago that if by some point you hadn't used this, I would.' (Chicago University Library.)

16. (*l. 14*) *in Sealdah Station*
During his reading at Spoleto, Berryman observed (with reference to Song 16) that Henry is 'a man without tolerance', and described Sealdah as the 'terrible station in Calcutta where refugees from East Pakistan are repatriated'. Berryman himself witnessed the ghastliness of Sealdah Station (which accommodated between 4,000 and 5,000 of the desperately poor) on Sunday, 25 August 1957 (Diary, JBP).

17. (*ll. 16–18*) See Linebarger, *John Berryman*, p. 102. At Spoleto, Berryman described the Song as a 'conversation between Henry and the devil'.

18. See Jo Porterfield, 'Berryman's "A Strut for Roethke"', *The Explicator* vol. XXXII (December 1973), item 25.

19. (*l. 14*) For a while in the 1950s, Berryman possessed a mirror formerly owned by a murderer named Axelrod who was gaoled in Stillwater Prison, Minnesota.

20. (*ll. 16—18*) St Paul's *Epistle to the Romans* 5:20.

22. 'Of 1826' laments the reduction of the ideals of Republic to automatism, and stands (according to Berryman himself) "properly at the climax of this theme'— that of Henry's ambivalent view of his homeland, which is both 'patriotic' and 'anti-U.S.' (Unpub. DS, folder 2). A note on the manuscript reads: 'the Beckett made it poss.'

(*l. 10*) *blackt-out*: 'shuddering' (MS.).

23. (*l. 17*) *Clauswitz*

Carl von Clausewitz, *On war*.

(*l. 18*) (*O Adlai mine*).

Adlai Stevenson.

In a letter to Edward Hoagland, Berryman mentions that he is about to record some poems at the Library of Congress: 'One I'm going to read is a savage nursery rime abt the State Dept, Eisenhower, etc which I wrote in Italy last Fall . . . but actually nobody will pay any attention or I'm afraid they won't' (21 February). In the event, Berryman did not read the poem at the Library of Congress on 24 February 1958, but he repaired the omission on 23 October 1962 at the National Poetry Festival. At Spoleto in 1957, he commented: 'I would like you to understand that this is not a political poem. I am not responsible for Henry's reprehensible opinions.'

Revised on 18 November 1958, 'The Lay of Ike' (originally entitled 'Doloneia') is a mordant satire directed against General Eisenhower. The middle stanza impugns Eisenhower for nominating Admiral Lewis Lichtenstein Strauss (a name which, Berryman knew, rhymes with 'laws') as chairman of the Atomic Energy Commission in 1953. Upon his appointment, Strauss initiated proceedings which resulted in the travestied investigation of J. Robert Oppenheimer as a security risk. The lawyer engaged by Strauss was Roger Robb, 'a man best known as the lawyer for Senator Joseph R. McCarthy's chief journalistic incense-swinger, Fulton Lewis, Jr.' (Joseph and Stewart Alsop, *We Accuse: The Story of the Miscarriage of American Justice in the Case of J. Robert Oppenheimer* (New York: Simon and Schuster, 1954), p. 7; Berryman owned a copy of this work and used it as his source of information.) Berryman also ridicules Eisenhower's ineptness as a military tactician, taking his text, as J. M. Linebarger has pointed out (*John Berryman*, p. 90), from Montgomery's claim that Eisenhower mismanaged the D-Day Invasion of Europe in 1944. Eisenhower's sins as a tactician are seen by Berryman to parallel those of Dolon in the *Iliad*, Book XI, where Hektor calls for a Trojan to reconnoitre the Grecian lines. Acting out of 'pride and excitement' (Robert Fitzgerald, *Homer: The Iliad* (New York: Doubleday-Anchor, 1974), p. 239), Dolon volunteers in return for the promise of Achilles' horses and chariot as his reward. A wretched tactician, Dolon is surprised by Diomedes and Odysseus and captured after a cowardly chase. He then betrays information which enables the two Greeks to slaughter a Thracian group. For his pains, Dolon is slain by Diomedes. Berryman's equation of Eisenhower and Dolon is accordingly severe, and before long he regarded the title he had first proposed for the poem as perhaps too explicit.

24. (*ll. 1–6*) In the summer of 1957, Berryman gave twenty-four lectures during a tour of India under the auspices of USIS. Howard Munford, who shared the platforms with Berryman, recalls:

> The Indians were obsessed with public address systems. We found outselves invariably speaking into a microphone, even in small rooms with a few people, and frequently it squealed or distorted our voices.

It was probably at Ahmedabad on 2 September (Berryman Diary) that, as Munford recalls,

> . . . flocks of large black birds circled around in front of the open windows facing the platform. In response to some insistent questions from the audience, we had to keep on talking and explaining for a period long beyond what we had expected. . . .

(Howard Munford, letter to Haffenden, 29 January 1973, pp. 3, 1.) Berryman called the procedure 'competing with the fans, the crows' (letter to J. Alister Cameron, 30 November 1957; in possession of Cameron).

(*ll. 7–11*)

> Berryman, one evening, had given what I had considered to be a brilliant discussion of some recent achievements of American poetry and then a stunning line-by-line analysis of an Eliot poem. The Chairman of the evening, an elderly and distinguished Professor of English, rose to his feet to give the official summing up and vote of thanks and proceeded to say: 'America has never produced any important poetry. American poetry has no words of power, no words of passion, no words of beauty, and no words of real poetry.' I looked across at John. His face was a fiery red and his temples throbbing, but, as he later said, 'I'm a real pro, Howard, and I never lose my temper before an audience,' and he never did. (Munford, p. 2.)

Berryman himself wrote later that 'the "summing-up" after the lecture . . . might likely old boy make yr blood boil' (letter to Cameron).

> This was the summer of Little Rock, as I recall. At any rate, the American racial situation was very much in the news. Although we did not get many questions on this from the floor, everywhere else, at social gatherings or in private conversations, we were called upon to explain or justify 'race bigotry', and this by the most color-conscious people in the world. An American Black is given a dreadful time in India. John bit his tongue and was polite on this score. (Munford, p. 3.)

(*ll. 12–14*) In mid-August Berryman and Munford took a break from their teaching:

> In Benares . . . we had an affable and intelligent guide. John was enthralled with the thousands of pilgrims, the holy men, the turmoil of the streets, the colorful bazaars, the beggars and the lepers. The first morning we hired two boatmen to row us down the Ganges by the burning ghats

and the bathing places. A gigantic copper-red sun rose as we floated by the pilgrims washing away their sins in the holy river, men greeting the sun with a deep salaam, holy men in contorted postures of worship, smoke drifting from the ghats. John . . . said later that the whole Indian venture was worth that experience in Benares. (Munford, p. 3.)

(*l. 17*)

The missionaries, Mr and Mrs K. F. Weller, took Berryman to visit the Cuttack Leprosarium, which housed 490 lepers, on 8 August (Berryman Diary). Berryman was shaken by what he saw (Notebook '1'), and very moved by the beauty of the salaams with which he was greeted. He memorialised one moment in this unpublished verse-fragment:

'Young Lady's Song at Cuttack'

My heavy hair
    I am beautiful
        I am not blind
It had my left foot wholly, and besides
throws out a semi-foot off to the side,
and the visitors look.
        All the others smile,
I am about to.   (Notebook, 'Calcutta 2 August', n.
                    pag.)

25. On the MS., Berryman commented: '*no more*; this is the END', a remark dated *c.* 19 January 1963.

31. (*ll. 1–3*) Berryman was introduced to hatha-yoga by a man named Datta on 28 August 1957. '. . . a Calcutta banker instructed me a little in Yoga. I achieved the free lotos position at the 1st try.' (JB, letter to his mother, 11 September 1957: Mrs Jill Berryman.) See also:

Severance was not very good at Natha (?) and yoga. He had mastered lobhastana and [*indecipherable*], but the instructions of his guru, a banker in Calcutta, went largely neglected. ('Author's Notes', *Recovery*, London, 1973, p. 238. The

word that the editor has transcribed as 'Natha (?) and yoga'
actually reads 'hatha-yoga'.)

A 'tatami' is a prayer-mat.

(*l.* 5) *parnel*
a priest's mistress.

33. The source of this Song is Plutarch's *Life of Alexander*. During a
supper to which Alexander has invited Cleitus, certain guests
sing songs ridiculing the Macedonians. Emboldened by drink,
Cleitus objects, whereupon Alexander (also drunk, a fact to
which Plutarch attributes the ensuing tragedy) loses his temper
and throws an apple at Cleitus. He then looks about for his
sword, which a guard has prudently concealed. Cleitus is
pushed out of the hall by his friends, but he rushes back in by
another door. Alexander seizes a spear and impales him.
Instantly overwhelmed with remorse, Alexander offers to kill
himself, but is restrained and carried by force to his chamber
(where Callisthenes flatters him and quiets his distress).

The fact that Berryman calls Alexander's weapon a 'spear-ax'
and then simply an 'ax' is significant: he uses the word 'ax' as a
'major triad' (see votes to Song 46 below for the loose use of this
phrase) in Songs 95:14, 271:16, 352:12, and 384:13, 17, in
contexts which associate murderous impulses and love. In Song
33, Berryman is registering the relationship of Alexander to
Cleitus as an analogue of that between himself and his father. By
calling Alexander 'the boy-god', he draws attention, not to
Alexander's youthfulness (he was in fact twenty-eight at the
time of the incident), but to his own age—eleven—at the time
of his father's suicide. The phrase 'Pluckt out' is perhaps
intended to convey overtones of Oedipus' action on learning of
Laius' murderer. The sly phrase 'As if an end' signifies that for
Berryman death does not finish anything—least of all guilt.
Finally, the last sentence—'Weeping & blood/wound round his
one friend'—is not true of Alexander; nowhere in Plutarch is
there the suggestion that Cleitus is even a particularly close
friend of Alexander's, let alone his 'one' friend. It may be
inferred instead that Henry images himself when young as
killing the very man to whom he was 'one friend'—his father.
The first manuscript draft of the poem had a different final

sentence: 'All the blood/covered the men like a coat.'
Berryman forsook the convenience of the rhyme 'throat-coat'
in order to introduce the 'one friend' motif. Berryman's
description of Alexander as 'A baby' who is readily led away
(whereas in fact Alexander was carried by force to his chamber)
would seem to support this reading. See also: ' . . . part of the
Song's interest is that it reveals one of Henry's concerns, fitting
in with a larger motif of anger and guilt toward a father figure.'
(Jack Vincent Barbara, 'Shape and Flow in *The Dream Songs*',
Twentieth Century Literature, vol. 22, no. 2 (May 1976), p. 155.)

34. A Song addressed to Robert Fitzgerald, with whom Berryman
taught for eight weeks at the School of Letters, Bloomington,
Indiana, at the time—the summer of 1961—when Hemingway
committed suicide. Fitzgerald was sharing a taxi with
Berryman when they heard the news of that death—'in the taxi
too, sick—' (l. 15)—and although they did not then know *how*
Hemingway had killed himself Berryman responded: 'The
poor son of a bitch blew his fucking head off.' (Interview with
Robert Fitzgerald, April 1974.) The first line of the poem
originally read, 'I have a tale to say', which Berryman then
changed for a direct address to Fitzgerald: 'My mother has your
shotgun' (maintaining the Hemingway-suicide theme). In the
Autumn of 1953, Berryman had gone to the airport to see off
Fitzgerald and his family, who were leaving for Italy. Fitzgerald
had hoped to take a shotgun with him, but failed at the last
minute to acquire a permit to export the weapon; accordingly,
he left it in Berryman's keeping. Berryman then gave it to his
mother to look after, and the gun eventually ended in the
custody of Berryman's brother. The middle stanza of the poem
alludes to the suicide of Berryman's own father on 26 June
1926, at the age of forty—'he verbed for forty years . . .' (l. 10).
See also Song 235:1−7.

35. (*l. 5*) *One professor's wife is Mary*
Mary Hughes, wife of Daniel Hughes, who was Berryman's
colleague at Brown University, Providence, Rhode Island,
during the academic year 1962−63.

37. See Haffenden, 'A Year on the East Coast: John Berryman 1962–63', *Twentieth Century Literature* Vol. XXII, no. 2 (May 1976), pp. 134–5, for the background to Songs 37 and 38. *stoic deity* (l. 17): 'idiotic deity' (MS).

40. See Haffenden (as note to Song 37 above), pp. 140–1.

41. This Song incorporates the very essence of what Henry considers inimical—God's indifference to Man's fate and the inhuman treatment of the Warsaw ghettos—and alludes to Paul Célan's poem 'Todesfuge' in the phrase 'Death is a German expert' (l. 1)—'Der Tod ist ein Meister aus Deutschland'.

45. (*l. 13*) *a wrong opinion, 'Epileptic'*.
Berryman began suffering from what were taken to be epileptic attacks late in 1939, while teaching at Wayne University, Detroit, Michigan. After tests early in 1940, Berryman's doctor, Eugene Shafarman, diagnosed the complaint as epilepsy.

> 'Gene believed it was petit mal epilepsy, but didn't want to give him medication for it, because, he said, one might control the epilepsy but might also run the risk of curing him of being a poet.' (Letter, Florence Miller to Haffenden, 11 February 1976.)

E. M. Halliday (interview, 3 July 1975) witnessed at least one 'attack' and is convinced that it was epilepsy. Jean Lanier (interview, 3 September 1974) overheard what she took to be convulsions (but not epileptic) with unidentifiable noises lasting for about forty-five minutes.

46. (*l. 1*)
The line alludes to the following dream recorded by Wilhelm Stekel:

> 'I find myself upon the street. A great panic rules there.

The people are in flight, are hurrying; they press into the
street cars; in short there is a turmoil. Some one is trying to
explain to me the mechanism of what is happening . . . '

In view of Berryman's device in *The Dream Songs* of employing
a voiced dialogue between Henry and his friend, it is interesting
that Dr Stekel interprets what he calls 'This beautiful dream' in
these terms:

> . . . represents a flight from the analysis. The highly in-
> telligent patient wants to escape his own thoughts . . .
>   He feels in life the disharmony in his thought and would
> gladly come to a unity of feeling and idea. He is always
> hearing a second voice, and this speaks contrary to the first.
> He is a typical doubter . . . The lower voices out of the
> harmony of thought make themselves heard in the doubter
> and often drown out the upper notes. The counterpoint is
> often too obtrusive, so that hate manifests itself with love,
> scorn with appreciation, defiance with submission. (Wilhelm
> Stekel, *Sadism and Masochism*, English version by Louise
> Brink (London: The Bodley Head, 1935), vol. I, p. 11.)

In Song 46, which is characterised by blasphemy, 'I am', the
first words, probably allude to the pronouncement, 'I am that I
am'—*Ehyeh asher ehyeh* (Exodus 3:14), an utterance which
denotes the highest existence. In Song 85 ('Op. posth. no. 8')
(ll. 14–18), Henry reports his physical dismantlement. For
Henry, being ('I am') means simply having a body. God is
complete and sufficient to himself, unconditional; in Song 141,
(ll. 16–18), Henry asserts the blasphemous view of selfishness
and self-interest.

Finally, in Song 320, Henry wakes from a paranoid dream
with the words:
' "I am—" cried Henry, / waking sweated & sordid' (ll. 17–
18).

The phrase 'I am' may be regarded, for the sake of convenience, as a "major triad" in Songs 46, 85, 141, and 320. I
borrow the term from one of Berryman's favourite texts,
Archbishop Carrington's *According to Mark* (Cambridge
University Press, 1960), where it is used to account for "a

threefold repetition, at intervals in the narrative, of a word or phrase which draws attention to some theme of high significance." (p. 6) It is clear from Berryman's Introduction to Thomas Nashe's *The Unfortunate Traveller* (New York: G. P. Putnam's Sons, 1960, pp. 7–28) that he thinks of triads, as does Archbishop Carrington, not in terms of an Hegelian dialectic, but in terms of related groups of three. For Carrington, the symbols, phrases and images of the Gospel are structured towards neatness of form, relation and interrelation. The words 'new', 'house', and 'cup', for example, and the phrases 'thy way', 'three days', and 'right hand', are all motifs repeated three times. Although Berryman does not necessarily limit himself to repetition in groups of three, he did use the same technique to bind some of the Songs (not in proximate clusters, but spaced widely about the work).

Even a partial concordance to *The Dream Songs* reveals a number of words and phrases—such as 'survive' and 'ax'—which function as triadic—in this sense, as leitmotifs—and accordingly as a structural device binding the poem. J. M. Linebarger (who also observes the feature) calls the device one of 'interlocking phrases and images', but he feels that they are 'insufficient in themselves to structure *The Dream Songs*'. Nevertheless, he does allow for the possibility that the Songs might contain 'a thematic coherence' ('Dream Song 6', p. 84).

Do, ut des. (l. 18)
In Chapter III, 'The Theory of Resistance', Stekel explains:

> Now experience shows that this transference very soon becomes the source of resistance. Love is only a seeking for love in return, *'Do, ut des'* ('I give, that thou shalt give'). If the patient notices that love is not given in return or that it has not reached that degree which he expected, defiance enters in place of the love, which in turn manifests itself as active resistance. Adler has remarked that the parapathic reacts with obstinacy or with obedience. Often both forms of reaction are combined to make the picture still more confused. An intense, unyielding stubbornness hides behind an apparent obedience . . . (p. 46.)

A note on the manuscript (dated 1 December 1958), which Berryman originally entitled 'SEVEN', observes: 'first one,

perhaps, all year, written at home: I can only write in solitude
(= bars)'.

48. The first stanza revolves around the word 'yelled' (l. 1), which
refers to what Berryman has called 'the most terrible pronouncement' (letter to A. Alvarez, n.d., quoted in letter to
Haffenden, 1972) of the Little Apocalypse (Mark 13). St Mark's
Gospel deals in that chapter with the distress that is to befall
Judea before the arrival of the Son of Man in power and glory.
It presents a vision of the end of the world, with the reward of
eternal life for God's chosen. Song 48 hinges on the fact that
Christ spoke Aramaic (l. 3), and yet this pronouncement comes
to us in Greek via the Gospels. Berryman's deduction is
sweeping: 'Greek—on the concensus of scholarly opinion—he
did not know—so we're dealing w fictions' (letter to Alvarez).
The second stanza of the Song draws on Archbishop
Carrington's analysis of the Second Seed Parable (*According to
Mark* (Cambridge, 1960), pp. 112–13), which Henry finds
'troublesome' precisely because it is so highly artificial that the
referent must be mythical, not a real man (in the person of
Christ) who rises from the dead. The notion troubles 'imaginary Jews' (l. 12) because Henry as Berryman is 'The
Imaginary Jew' of Berryman's early, famous story (now
available in his *Recovery* (London: Faber & Faber, 1973), pp.
243–62, and in *The Freedom of the Poet* (New York: Farrar,
Strans & Giroux, 1976; London: Faber & Faber, 1977), pp.
359–66).) In that place, Berryman had to assume a fiction in
order to undercut the irrationality of racial prejudice; now it
becomes a question of the irrationality of death-with-
resurrection. As long as the tale remains a parable, Henry may
tolerate it; as soon as it purports to be, not just liturgical but
historical and forensic, Henry has no time for it.

Since Berryman drafted Song 48 on a carbon copy of Song
74 ('Henry hates the world'), it should probably be read in
conjunction with what was chronologically the earlier Song. In
line 16, the pronoun 'He' may refer either to Henry or to
Christ; if to the latter, it is particularly interesting to note the
draft variants of the verb 'sybilled' in that line: 'chattered',
'whispered', 'murmured', and 'bleated'.

53. Written just ten days before 'The Lay of Ike' (Song 23).
(*l. 2*) *Sparine for Pelides*

Berryman considered that the name Pelides too obviously denoted Achilles, son of Peleus (cf. Song 14:11–12) (Unpub. DS., folder 16.) The title 'Pelides' is actually uncommon; Byron uses it in *Don Juan*, IV, 104, l.8). Sparine is a tranquillizer.

(*ll. 9–12*) Saul Bellow is the novelist, as he confirms for me in a letter, 16 September 1972.

54. (*ll. 16–18*) Issa's mother died when he was three; his father married again to a tough-fibred woman who tormented Issa. In 1776, at the age of fourteen, Issa left home. According to Lewis Mackenzie, it seems

> . . . that to the years immediately following his mother's death Issa traced in himself that awareness of the essential loneliness of men and women and of the limitation of human relationships which pervades many of his verses. (*The Autumn Wind*, Selection from the poems of Issa, trans. and intro. by Lewis Mackenzie, London: John Murray, 1957, p. 11.)

Substituting father for mother in that quotation, the same could be said of Berryman. 'Issa chronicled the circumstances of his father's death in a pathetic short journal, called *Chichi no Shuen Nikki*' (ibid., p. 33). In a letter to Edward Hoagland, Berryman remarked:
'Tell you a v. good poem—Issa's self-portrait: . . .

> 'Even considered
> in the most favourable light,
> he looks cold.'   (21 February 1958; Edward
> Hoagland.)

55. In a filmed interview for BBC television in 1967, Berryman described the Song as being like the graveyard scene in *Ulysses*, where, prompted by the words 'I am the resurrection and the light', Bloom utters his thoughts about an afterlife. He is averse to the notion of resurrection since the thought of physical corruption strikes him as too conclusive. So, for different reasons, it is conclusive for Henry. Song 288 (ll. 7—8) alludes again to Ulysses. Although Henry opposes the dogma of Christ's Resurrection, he is yet wary of what he calls 'a coda of blaming' (194:12). He feels immersed in an existentialist dilemma (347:7—10).

For Kierkegaard, whom Berryman studied, not just to live, but to be a Christian, is to suffer. He makes it clear that, for him in serving an Absolute absolutely, suffering is unavoidable in this world which is a conditioned world. Kierkegaard explains the paradox: 'Suffering depends on the fact that God and man are qualitatively different, and that the clash of time and eternity in time is bound to cause suffering.' (Soren Kierkegaard, *The Last Years: Journals 1853—1855*, ed. and trans. by Ronald Gregor Smith (London: Fontana Library, 1968), p. 255). He also isolates the paradox by which, for the Christian, grace is known negatively—since it brings suffering. 'Christianity', he explains, 'is sheer grace, and suffering for a few years in this life is infinite, infinite grace' (ibid., p. 279). Henry verges towards the same belief in Songs 113 (ll. 1—3) and 194 (ll. 1—3) but his nuance is invariably ironic, for he severely questions the same paradox elsewhere, as in Song 256 (ll. 16—17) or in 266 (l. 10).

Similarly, when Henry speaks of death—and consequent nothingness—he often does so in terms of a refuge from the horrors of Hell (239:14—16).

In general, the balance of Henry's thoughts on the matter is weighted in favour of death being literally a dead end, or at least a condition in which one simply dreams the past forever (123:11) (Cf. 140:14, 146:6, and 195:17—18).

One of the main reasons why Henry desires obsessively to know about the afterlife is because of guilt, his fear of punishment. He asserts almost desperately that he will not believe in Hell, and sues above all for a continuance of his life, as in Song 266 (ll. 11—18)

56. The first stanza alludes to Origen's doctrine of *apocatastasis*, a notion in which Berryman took evident delight: he told A. Alvarez that Origen was 'non-sainted not so much for his self-castration, in my opinion, as for his interpretation of Apocotastasis [sic], intolerable to the Church: everybody's

freed, even Satan repents: all Bad Guys become GOOD GUYS, much too Christian for the Church' (letter, n.d.). The doctrine holds that at the end of time everything and every person will be re-established in Christ. It was condemned by the Fifth General Council of the Church not only because of the philosophical principle that evil must eventually disappear altogether, but because it adopts the Orphic doctrine of the pre-existence of the soul (taken up by Plato and given expression in *Meno*), and because it avows Pythagoras' teaching of metempsychosis. The latter point is crucial, since it gives cause for hope even to a non-believer such as Berryman: Origen asserts that there must be more than one existence. Eventually the soul will return to the purely spiritual state which it enjoyed before coming to the body. Berryman embraces Origen's doctrine with fervid delight: it provides both an absolution from the fear of death and a heart-warming rationale for the life of Art. For a discussion of the Song as a whole, see Barbera, 'Under the Influence', p. 147.

59. Song originally entitled 'The Death of the Bells'.
(*l. 1*) *the Giralda*
   On Thursday, 12 December 1957, John and Ann Berryman climbed to the top of the Giralda, the great bell-tower of Seville Cathedral. The tower (originally Moorish) was built *c.* A.D. 1000 after the design of Geber, the inventor of algebra. The belfry was added in 1568 by Francisco Ruiz. Berryman sketched a fragment of verse probing the underside of the Spanish national character:

> And so it may be the patios and the gardens dreams
> under the Giralda, and all's well,
> and it may not be;
> but   I see blood on the palms
> and oranges more like blood in the   leaves

> The   governless   blood   of   Spain   runs   upland   and
> waits.   (Berryman notebook '4' (headed: 'my swing Prado
> Sev').

He associates the Giralda with another bell-tower, 'Great John's

belfry' (l. 4) in the Cathedral of St Mikhail the Archangel in the
Kremlin, where 'Brother Jonas (formerly Ivan the Terrible)'
(l. 15) is buried. The bells bespeak the continuing guilt of
repressiveness smirching Russian history down through
'Brother Josef' (Stalin) (l. 16) to Krushchev (l. 10), whom
Berryman sarcastically suggests should be anointed,

(*l. 11*) *poor evil Kadar*

After the Hungarian revolt of 1956, Janos Kadar (b. 1912)
became first secretary of the Socialist Workers' Party, and
Prime Minister. His government abetted the Russians in
crushing the revolt, and subsequently imposed a repressive
regime which Berryman laments in this Song (first drafted in
April 1958).

66. For annotation, see Barbera, 'Shape and Flow in *The* Dream
Songs', p. 161, n. 2.

68. The artists mentioned in this Song were star performers during
the zenith of the blues in America, the 1920s. The Blues, a
subdued, personal music, its intonation undoubtedly Black,
reflects the influence of a deep-rooted racial musical instinct.

Miss Bessie (l. 2) (Smith), a powerful contralto, sang with
simple, rhythmic phrasing. She sang (in Wilder Hobson's
terms) 'with her whole body' (*American Jazz Music*, London:
J. M. Dent & Son, 1941, p. 144). Frederic Ramsey jun. and
Charles Edward Smith explain further that 'Bessie Smith was
the depressed, mournful type; her blues were eloquent masterpieces of human misery bordering on the spirituals. She was
blues personified.' (*Jazzmen*, London: Sidgwick & Jackson,
1957, p. 115.)

(*l. 14*) *Pinetop he hit some chords*

Pine Top Smith, famous for his 'boogie-woogie' style,
played the piano with zest and simplicity.

Mackie Jarrell informs me:

> The Charlie [l. 15] . . . may be Charlie Parker, but I've
> always thought that he is Charlie Green, trombonist and one
> of Bessie Smith's 'Blue Boys'. He played trombone in her
> recordings of 'Empty Bed Blues', [l. 15] . . . of 'Yellow Dog
> Blues' [l. 8], and in the wonderful 'Trombone Cholly',

which exhibits his virtuosity. I seem to remember that she and Green lived together . . . 'Empty Bed Blues' . . . is unusual largely for being more raucous than she usually was, and exceptionally bawdy for the times. (letter, 5 November 1972, p. 2.)

(*l. 17*) *sick-house's white birds'*
Bessie Smith was finally reduced to poverty and alcoholism, as Robert Goffin explains:

As if to justify the dramatic portent of the blues, Bessie Smith, once rich as Croesus, returned eventually to poverty. Desperate, embittered, soddened by gin, she heard the graveyard blues echo a last chorus for her in 1937 when she was injured in an automobile accident in Tennessee and carried bleeding to the hospital. (*Jazz*, London, 1946, p. 240.)

As Berryman's lines indicate, she was refused admission to a hospital for whites.
Similarly, Pine Top Smith died a violent death—'shot down in a brawl over "some ol' gal in a cheap West Side dance hall"' (*Jazzmen*, p. 187). Other examples of violent deaths and killings accumulate throughout *The Dream Songs*: the motif stems from Berryman's obsession with his father's suicide. He acknowledges that 'I scrounge ensamples violent by choice' (190:13).

70. (*l. 18*) *the blue father*: 'Allyn' (MS.) [John Allyn Smith, Berryman's father].

71. (*l. 1—4*)

'He went out to the street and down to the market place . . . He walked to the stands covered with tooled leather-work, over to the story-teller's corner. An ancient man kept his audience spellbound beyond the filth and the noise that surrounded them.' (D. Mackenzie, *Moment of Danger* (London, 1959), p. 95.)

72. (*ll. 3–4, 9*) From December 1963 until c. June the following year Berryman and his family lived just across the street from the Supreme Court Building in Washington, D.C. Cf. Song 200.

73. Berryman visited the Ryoan-ji Temple and Garden on 12 July 1957 (Diary). Founded by Hosokawa in 1450, the temple consists of a vast, serene compound extending towards the western foot of Mount Kinugasa and commanding a magnificent view of Mount Otokoyama beyond Yodo River in the distance to the south. The garden provides the focal point, the quintessence of the Zen sect of Buddhism. Berryman wrote later, 'The Ryoan-ji garden—sand, fifteen stones—is a work devoted wholly to thought (tumbling Zen thought, it's true), and purely symbolic.' ('Thursday Out', *The Noble Savage*, No. 3 (May 1961), pp. 190–1.) Shortly after his visit he described it as 'the most perfect and satisfying garden even in Japan' (Letter, JB to Dr and Mrs A. Boyd Thomes, 15 July 1957: A. Boyd Thomes). He observed that he had been dazed with attention: 'I have never been so happy in my life as here in Kyoto . . . ' (ibid.). As Song 73 suggests, Berryman found himself entirely in harmony with the sublime serenity of the philosophy expressed by the garden, and marvelled at its immutability— the ultimate artifact.

It is significant that Berryman should say of himself that 'I do survive beside the garden' (l. 6): the word 'survive' stands in direct relation to the last two words of the poem, 'thought die'. He often employs the verb 'survive' (frequently in association with a pun on the word 'vivid'), not in the sense of remaining alive after an onslaught or disaster, but in a sense combining mute relief with what amounts to surprise when he sees that everyone else appears to be dying—especially his friends (cf. 358:13). Similarly, if the act of surviving includes a feeling of bitterness, so the act of thinking connotes the ultimate thought of death—'thinky death' (10:9); 'dreadful thought' (138:2); 'Henry's mind grew blacker the more he thought' (147:1). Song 182 states that Henry 'sprayed thought like surf' (182:9), where the word 'surf' may be referred to the phrase 'the surf of death' in line 14 of an early poem, Song of the Man Forsaken and Obsessed' (*Homage to Mistress Bradstreet and Other Poems*,

London: Faber & Faber, 1959, p. 83). Finally, Song 75 refers to
a book as a thing made by 'thoughtful / surviving Henry'
(ll. 13 – 14).

76. Second stanza drafted separately on 1 September 1956, and later
incorporated in the Song.

97. (*l. 17*)   *Yo-bad yóm i-oowaled bo*   *v'ha'l lail awmer h're gawber!*
    From the *Poem of Job*, meaning: 'Let the day perish wherein I
was born, And the night wherein it was said: "A man-child is
brought forth"' (trans. V. E. Reichert).
    Berryman was fascinated by the Book of Job, and first began
to learn Hebrew in 1954: 'my Hebrew effort Peret and
Bargebecher (?)' (*Recovery*, p. 241). The name should be
transcribed 'Peretz Bargebuhr', as, earlier in the novel,
'Severance's Journal' notes:

> . . . studies with Peretz Bargebuhr (write—still alive?) re-
> gular O.T. stint daily, at last, this year (till lately) unique
> devotion to *Job*—text, Stevenson's Schweik lectures, trans-
> lation fooled with for sixteen years.
>   People often think I *look* Jewish—resentment, liking.
>   (Ibid., pp. 73 – 4)

Frederick P. Bargebuhr tried to teach Berryman Hebrew at
Iowa late in 1954:

> As to his participation in my Hebrew course, I failed . . . and,
> maybe due to feeling overly sworn in on my teaching
> methods, felt that his 'tourist approach' to learning a
> language upset my principles and that I had to cater to the
> regular student with regular methods. (Letter, Bargebuhr to
> Haffenden, 27 July 1973.)

Berryman wrote to Saul Bellow about his translation of *Job*:

> . . . I finally got my tone and rhythm right and did the first
> nine lines . . . behind the celebratory night—not in front of
> it—hangs the cursed night of conception. Here they go:

> Perish the day's fire into which I was born, and that
> night's joy crying 'A boy!'

Letter, *c.*1 December 1956; Chicago University Library.
Cf. ll. 1–2 of Song 136.

98. (*l. 1*) *I met a junior*
Paul Petrie, who was poet in residence at the University of
Rhode Island, where Berryman gave a poetry reading in 1963.

101. (*l. 4*) *Betty & Douglas, and Don*
Donald and Elizabeth Mackie were close friends of the
Berrymans' at Princeton, New Jersey, from 1948 to 1953;
Douglas is their son.

102. (*l. 8*) *Lippmann*
Walter Lippmann (b. 1889), a major American pundit. His
best-known works are *The Public Philosophy* (London: Hamish
Hamilton, 1955), which was criticised for its natural-law
theory, and *Public Opinion* (London: G. Allen & Unwin 1922),
which seemed to imply that ordinary citizens could no longer
apply rational judgement to public issues. Although Lippmann
doubted the possibility of democratic government, he was
opposed to government by an elite.

113. Amy Vladeck, Riva Freifeld, and Valerie Trueblood, who are
named in this Song, were all students of Berryman's at Brown
University, Providence, Rhode Island, during the academic
year 1962–3.

115. The first lines of the Song draw on a letter written by a former
student of Berryman's while she was working in a bakery
during the summer of 1963 (JBP).

126. The title of the Song, 'A Thurn', is a neologism.

129. The Song commemorates a boyhood friend of Berryman's, *F.J.* (l. 3), (Callahan), and is elucidated by this passage from *Recovery* (p. 179):

> Himself as pallbearer for his little-older hero, F. J. Callahan, surreptitiously touching the dead hand in the funeral parlor, running screaming night after night to Mother in the living room, crossing the street and then re-crossing it to avoid that fearful building, on his way across town . . .

and by this unpublished verse-fragment:

> . . . . the dead friend's hand at ten he toucht, as cork yieldless, odd-textured, with nobody looking.
> (Unpub. DS, folder 1)

132. (*ll. 6—7*) *I am the only other*

> *and I say go to bed!*

A. E. Housman's 'Fragment of an English Opera' relates the dialogue in which mother and father try to persuade an exasperating daughter to go to bed; the daughter insists significantly on casting doubts on their parenthood:

> *Daughter:* Are you my mother?
> *Mother:* You have no other:
>   You go to bed.   (Laurence Housman,
>   *A.E.H.* (London: Cape, 1937), p. 242.)

Cf. Song 298 (ll. 3—4).

135. (*l. 7*) *Speck*

Richard Benjamin Speck, who committed mass murder on 14 July 1966.

(ll. 10—12, 15—18). '. . . . even Time magazine . . . they did a cover story on him called 'The Madman on the Tower', and that was very moving to me' ('An Interview with John Berryman', *The Harvard Advocate*, p. 9.) In August 1966 Charles Joseph Whitman mounted the tower of the University of Texas and shot down forty-four people, killing thirteen.

Time reports Whitman's father as saying, 'I'm a fanatic about guns . . . I raised my boys to know how to handle guns.' (*Time*, 12 August 1966, p. 21.) Although Berryman seems to suggest that Whitman was driven by the pain of a tumour, *Time* dismisses the notion: 'An autopsy showed that Whitman had a pecan-sized brain tumor, or astrocytoma, in the hypothalamus region, but Pathologist Coleman de Chenar said that it was "certainly not the cause of the headaches" and "could not have had any influence on his psychic behavior."'

145. (*l. 4*) *as bad as Whitman on his tower*
    A reference to Berryman's own father at the point of suicide. Before his trip to the tower, Charles Whitman wrote: 'I've been having fears and violent impulses. I've had some tremendous headaches. I am prepared to die. (*Time*, p. 22.)
(*ll. 5–12*) Berryman never knew the exact circumstances of his father's death; in 'A Florida Story', he wrote: 'If you argue against the fact that my father tried to drown himself and me, failed, and shot himself dead, lying like an eagle across the concrete stoop at dawn . . . you get nowhere. Where I got.' ('Unpublished Fiction', JBP, n.d.) For a fuller appreciation of Berryman's painfully mixed feelings for his father, it is important to compare specific references in other Songs: notably, 'your stance on the sand' (42:15; 76:7–11; 154:6–14; and 384:7–9).
    For Berryman's association of the word 'freezing' (145:9) with death, cf. 79:17–18 and 127:1–2.

149. (*l. 11*) *I got him out of a police-station once, in Washington*
    See Haffenden, 'A Year on the East Coast: John Berryman 1962–63', *Twentieth Century Literature* vol. 22, no. 2 (May 1976), p. 138.

153. (*ll. 13–15*) The friend is Howard Nemerov, who declares (in a context presuming that the poet is more blessed than the saint) that 'In a glum and prosy, unglamorous manner, I continue to believe the same, remaining of the opinion that Mozart's life and work express a purer and more efficacious benevolence to mankind than the life and work of God.' (*Journal of the Fictive Life* (New Brunswick: Rutgers University Press, 1965), p. 12; cited in letter from Nemerov, 5 May 1972.) In the light of such an allusion, it can be seen that Henry is discrediting God, whose career he calls 'that worst' in 335:16.

(*l. 1*) *god who has wrecked this generation.* (*l. 1*)

Archbishop Carrington points out that the phrase 'this generation' (as Jesus uses it in Mark 8) refers to *Numbers*—where none of 'that generation' following Moses would see the Holy Land. According to Carrington, the phrase is a triad (see notes to Song 46 above), and dramatises the sense of conflict with the indifferent, unresponsive Israel of Jesus's day (*According to Mark*, p. 165). Berryman's use of the phrase must be seen as painfully ironic.

Likewise, Song 13 states outspokenly that God is Henry's enemy (l. 13), and, in Song 314, Henry asks: 'Were there any other gods he could defy, / he wondered, or re-arrange?' (l. 18)

The only positive version of God that Henry overtures is the wholly secular variety that he drives from Freud. In *The Ego and the Id* Freud propounds the view that the ego-ideal—as a substitute for the longing for a father—contains the germ from which all religions have evolved, and continues:

'Religion, morality, and a social sense—the chief elements of what is highest in man—were originally one and the same thing. According to the hypothesis which I have put forward in *Totem und Tabu* they were acquired phylogenetically out of the father-complex: religion and moral restraint by the actual process of mastering the Oedipus complex itself, and social feeling from the necessity for overcoming the rivalry that then remained between the members of the younger generation.' (Trans. Joan Riviere, London: L & V Woolf; Institute of Psycho-Analysis, 1927, pp. 49–50.)

Berryman gives this idea poetic expression in Song 26 (ll. 12–13) where the phrase 'others, my God, my God' should perhaps be construed as appositional.

154. (ll. 13–19) As note to Song 149, pp. 144–5.

167. (*ll. 8—19*)

> 'If the Postmaster-general would kindly keep his deep thoughts to himself and just have letters delivered as rapidly as occurs in civilized countries it wd be agreeable to me. I remember when, in a southwestern town a third of a century ago, there were three mails a day.' (Letter, JB to Saul Bellow, 27 June 1960; Chicago University Library.)

180, 181. See 'Trial of a Young Poet: The Case of Joseph Brodsky', *Encounter* vol. 23, no. 3 (1964), pp. 84—91.

185. (*ll. 11—12*)   '*His Majesty,*
          the body.'
Gustav Janouch, *Conversations with Kafka* (New York: Frederick A. Praeger, 1953), p. 27. See also Song 247:6.

186. A Song addressed to Berryman's third wife, Kate. 'His Honor' (l. 7) is Judge Theodore Knutson, who performed their wedding ceremony. 'Erie Plaza' (l. 10) was the address of their apartment from 1961 until 1965.

188. (*l. 11*) *Miss Cienfuegos*
In the summer of 1964, Berryman flew from Washington to give a poetry reading in California; after collapsing in his motel, he was looked after by Miss Cienfuegos.

189. (*l. 16*) *Bhuvaneswar Dog*
The name Berryman gave to a dog acquired in the summer of 1963.

192. (*l. 5*) *Kierkegardian leap*
'For an eternal decision in time is the most intensive intensity, the most intensive leap.' (Soren Kierkegaard, *The Last Years: Journals 1853—1855* (London: Fontana, 1968), p. 127.)

193. (*ll. 1–2*) Yvor Winters died on 26 January 1968. 'Henry's friend' is Arthur Naftalin, then Mayor of Minneapolis, who (in late February 1968) underwent a throat operation.

> 'Naftalin is one of the best city managers in the United States,' Berryman remarks, 'and he has no more power than I have. Unless there is a heavy reform in the city charter, we will continue wasting the talents of one of the most able men in American politics.' (Minnesota *Alumni News*, February 1968, p. 17.)

See also Song 213:15–19.

195. (*l. 12*)   *reality is*
For some reason, the published text omits the next word of the manuscript, 'feasts', rhyming with 'priests' in l. 9.

200. (*ll. 15–18*)   Henry decries the liturgical constructions of Christianity, not the fact that Christ died, nor the manner in which he died.

In a late poem, 'The Search', Berryman disclosed the sources for his study of Christ (*Love & Fame*, p. 59).

In his interview with *The Paris Review*, he mentioned that the narrative of *The Dream Songs* developed 'partly out of my readings in theology and that sort of thing, taking place during thirteen years' (op. cit., p. 191), so the matter clearly requires attention. What the scholars whom Berryman mentions have in common is the conviction that the person of Christ is absolutely central in any study of the Gospels, and that one must discriminate firmly between Christ as he really was, what he did and what he said, and Christ as he has been recorded, even misrepresented, for the purposes of dogma. Guignebert, to whom Berryman paid most heed, is tendentious and de-flationary, and concludes that, 'So far as history is concerned, he is not the incarnate Logos, nor the Son who is consubstantial with the Father, but only a Jewish prophet.' (Charles Guignebert, *Jesus*, trans. S. H. Cooke (London: Kegan Paul & Co., 1935), p. 405.)

Henry's object, as here in Song 200, is to disavow a belief in the Resurrection, and hence in a personal resurrection for all individuals. The thought of an afterlife inspires mankind with crippling anxiety, so Henry feels that to explode the concept is to leave one free for the business of living. But he derives little satisfaction from his nihilism, a death to life, and it is on that ground that his heroic tussle takes place.

Henry's friend—whom Berryman calls a 'Job's comforter' (Kostelanetz, 'Conversation with Berryman' p. 346)—may speak for the Old Testament's view of God, as against Henry himself who, like Guignebert, is avid to deracinate the myth of Christ.

204. (*l. 16*) *my gramophone*
   Bought from the celebrated musicologist B. H. Haggin in 1942; Berryman sold the machine in the late 1960s.

208. (*ll. 4, 9–11*) See *T.L.S.*, 30 September 1965, pp. 870, 857.

216. (*ll. 16–17*) *Powers,*
the feted traitor
   See Linebarger, *John Berryman*, pp. 87–8.

225. '*Pereant qui ante nos nostra dixerunt*'
   See Jack V. Barbera, "Under the Influence", pp. 60 and 65, no. 4.

229. (*ll. 7–9*) See my discussion of 'Scholars at the Orchid Pavilion' below.

231. (*ll. 13–15*) These lines commemorate the vexed summer of 1961 before Berryman's marriage to Kate Donahue: the father (l. 14) is Kate's father; the 'Jesuit' (l. 15), a priest who counselled against the marriage (since Kate was a practising Catholic engaged to a divorcee), which took place on 1 September that year.

234. (*ll. 1–5*) In 'The Search' (*Love & Fame*, p. 59), Berryman has two lines to the effect that, for him,

> The Miracles were a stumbling block;
> until I read Karl Heim, trained in natural science

Heim's opinion is that 'In the Bible, the miracles wrought by God never stand in opposition to laws of nature or to a causal nexus', and that, 'It is not possible, on the biblical view, to find in miracle an experimental proof of God's existence.' (*The Transformation of the Scientific World View* trans. Neville H. Smith (London: SCM Press 1953), pp. 189, 191.) Berryman allows that Jesus was an enthusiast, even a holy man or prophet (Guignebert insists that Jesus did not want his miracles advertised), but his case rests on what he hopes is persuasive evidence that Christ was not God.

237. See Linebarger, *John Berryman*, p. 159, n. 17.

238. (*l. 7*) Goya's last etchings were completed in 1819, when he was seventy years old: deaf, isolated, and disillusioned. Entitled *Proverbios*, they were originally called *Suenos* (Dreams): their hallucinatory inspiration is evident. The fantastic and mysterious is uppermost in Goya's vision: gigantic or grotesque beings with deformed faces figure largely, as well as manikin-like masked forms, the types of tormented dreams. Unreason and paranoia is rife. Huxley has written that the figures in these etchings 'are inexpressibly horrible, with the horror of mindlessness and animality and spiritual darkness.' (Quoted in Enrique L. Ferrari, *Goya: Complete Etchings, Aquatints, and Lithographs*, trans. Raymond Rudorff, London Thames & Hudson, 1962, p. xxvi.) The utter pessimism that Goya expresses extends to his view of the supernatural. The series conveys the impression of darkness, night, gigantic forms, distorted shapes, flight, emptiness, fear, panic. Apart from groups of etchings devoted to Woman and libidinousness, politics, and flying, perhaps the most striking of the etchings are those which express Goya's notions of religion and death. Evidently it is these to which Berryman refers. In the etching called 'Exhortations', a man is bizarrely confronted with a choice between world and religion; in 'Loyalty', an old man is benighted for the same reason. In another *Proverb* a ghost arises from a decaying body, but is barred from entering the realm of darkness by other spirits. The meaning of such etchings is ambiguous, but, in his admirable definitive edition of the etchings, Enrique Ferrari refers to another drawing in the Prado:

> 'Showing winged beings tugging at the iron ring on a tomb as if anxious to discover its secrets: '*They say nothing!*' Those from beyond have nothing to tell us. What frightens the spirit arising from the grave is this same nothing, contradicting all the illusions it cherished during life. (Ibid, p. xxix.)

Nothing could represent more forcefully Berryman's negative vision of God.

240. (*l. 14*) Nancy Jewell and Blair Torrey were among Berryman's students during a summer school at the Bread Loaf School of English, Vermont, in 1962. Recalling the examination period at the end of the session, Nancy Jewell Aldrich writes:

> Jonathan Aldrich and I were in the room, for different exams, at a time when Berryman was proctor, sitting on the stage . . . in front of us . . . He seemed hard at work on something himself, and it turned out to be Dream Song 240 . . . in which I am mentioned . . . He had commented often on my eyes, and their imperfection, saying they are (and it is true) not level, one droops. He inscribed my copy of HOMAGE TO MISTRESS BRADSTREET: 'For Miss Jewell, possessed as she is of, by, and with one pair of rare eyes.' (Letter, 2 December 1974.)

241. (*ll. 1—6*) Berryman's father joined the Oklahoma National Guard in the early 1920s. By 8 July 1924 he was Captain of Battery E, 160th Field Artillery. (A Notebook, with this information on the cover, survives in the John Berryman

Papers, 'Personal Papers', Box 1.) One of Berryman's keenest memories was of a visit one rainy day to Fort Sill, where he saw men with field-glasses, his father in puttees moving away to give orders, the firing of French 75s, and of 110s, and the coming and going of guns. (Impressions recorded *passim* in manuscripts relating to the unpublished work *St. Pancras Braser.*)

244. (*l. 1*) *Calamity Jane*
Martha Cannary (1 May 1852?—1 August 1903) is better known as 'Calamity Jane'; see entry under Martha Cannary Burk, *Notable American Women 1607–1950* (Cambridge, Mass., 1971), p. 267: 'In 1941 a diary and wedding certificate purporting to prove that Jane had been married to Wild Bill Hickok were produced by a Mrs. Jane Hickok McCormick, who claimed to be their daughter, but these documents have not been generally accepted.'

245. (*l. 13*) *the Harlem vicer*
Probably Adam Clayton Powell jun. (1908–1972), pastor of the Abyssinian Baptist Church, New York City, who led boycotts and marches against stores and businesses that discriminated on a basis of colour.

250. (*l. 5*) *Seconal*
The trade name of seco-barbital.

252. (*l. 11*) *Old Ben in Paris*
Banjamin Franklin (1706–90), who was recognised as American minister by France in 1778; he was responsible for drawing France into the American War of Independence.

262. A Song addressed to the late Randall Jarrell.

267. (*l. 1*) *Louis*
Louis MacNeice, whom Berryman visited in London in 1953.

276, 277, 278. Addressed to Berryman's friends and colleagues, the Rosses and the Siegelmans, who left Minneapolis for California in 1965.

282. (*l. 11*) *labile*
For Berryman's earlier use of the word, see Joseph Warren Beach, *Obsessive Images*, ed. by William Van O'Connor (Minneapolis: University of Minnesota Press, 1960).

283. (*l. 16*) *my loved Basque friend*
See 'Anyway', 'First Night at Sea', and 'London', in *Love & Fame*, pp. 43—5.

285. See Denis Donoghue, 'Berryman's Long Dream', *Art International*, 20 March 1969, p. 63.

293. (*ll. 16—17*) The 'Little Baby' is Berryman's daughter Martha; Diana, the daughter of Kate Berryman's friend, Eugenia Foster. 'The Beast' is the nickname given to the boy who lived next door to them in Lansdowne Park, Ballsbridge, Dublin. 'Mir' is the family name for Berryman's mother.

295. (*ll. 1—3, 11—14*) In September 1966, Berryman wrote from Dublin to Maris Thomes in Minneapolis, asking her to investigate his bank's failure to transfer credit to his bank in Ballsbridge when he had cabled that request on 9 September (letter, 19 September 1966; Maris Thomes). She responded on 23 September:

> When I went to see Mr. Stotesberry with my sword and coat of mail I was greeted by welcoming smiles and sighs of relief, because they had been waiting for their next clue—and I was it. [Berryman's telegram had been mistranscribed and needed to be clarified.]
> . . .
> I have filled my wild flower garden at the river with peat

moss and leaf-mold, both acid and neutral. Into soft, dark, wet little holes I have put various secret roots and bulbs. Next spring strange plants are supposed to emerge—wild ginger, bloodroot . . . and blueheads . . . and pearly everlasting. (JBP)

297. (*l. 2*) *His old friend*
William Meredith.

304. (*ll. 13–15*)

Joke: apparently, along w. Johnson's other economies, putting out lights: there are no airmail stamps in the White House! We rec'd an invitation to a reception there, wh. came by ordinary mail and took *weeks*, into Oct. (p.m. Sept 2, reception 8th) I wrote without irony, regretting and explaining that I had not boycotted the affair, hating his conduct of the war but thinking like Bellow that he was doing his best. Mrs. Johnson wrote me, concluding 'It was a lovely evening.' (Letter, JB to Maris Thomes, 15 November 1966; Maris Thomes.)

306. (*l. 5*) *His housemother Miss Dulon*
Clara Christiane Dulon, an affiliate of the Order of St Anne, was housemother at Berryman's preparatory school, South Kent.

311. (*ll. 13–18*) Jean Bennett Lanier, the subject of the last line of 'Olympus', *Love & Fame*, p. 28. See also: 'Weirdness: my ex-fiancee of 1936 telephoned day before yesterday and came for a drink w. her new husband.' (Letter, JB to Valerie Trueblood, October 1966; Valerie Trueblood.) See also Song 337, lines 1–8.

318. (*l. 14*) *Miss Carver*
Catherine Carver, an editor at OUP.

320. Berryman jockeys with Heinrich von Kleist's *Penthesilea*, a dramatic version of Achilles' association with Penthesilea.

A study of Kleist is helpful to our understanding of Berryman's work. All forms of reality were suspect and untrustworthy to Kleist; he believed in the primacy of the inner world and the unreality of life's *Schattenspiel*. Possessed by what amounted to an obsession with his *Innere Welt*, he often seemed to lose contact with reality. The chief characters of his plays are the product of his dreams. Walter Silz says of *Penthesilea* that it makes a fairy tale credible: 'The landscapes and events of *Penthesilea* are entirely 'internal' and visionary; its key line is *War je ein Traum so bunt, als was hier wahr ist?*' (l. 986) (Walter Silz, *Heinrich von Kleist*: Studies in his Works and Literary Characters (Philadelphia: Univ. of Pennsylvania Press, 1961), p. 266. Other points in my commentary draw on Silz's work.)

Kleist began life as an eudemonist, believing in divine benevolence, but his natural propensities were discouraged by such works as Kant's *Critique of Pure Reason*, which asserted that man should not worry about abstract principles, but base his life on doing his duty. Kant's scepticism affected him deeply; his dramas are born of despair. Unlike Kant's, the cast of his mind was emotional rather than logical. Gradually he found that he could rest no faith in a cosmic order of harmony, and came to see human suffering as the product of intervention by a superior power. By the same token, man cannot be held responsible: Kleist's pessimism shows little self-criticism. According to E. L. Stahl, it must be inferred that, at his most pessimistic, Kleist identifies God with whatever is fatal or accidental in life.

It is impossible to overestimate the strength of appeal that Kleist exercised for Berryman: *The Dream Songs* partake to a large extent of those aspects of Kleist's world-view which I have laid out. The love-conflict of Kleist's drama *Penthesilea* is motivated by the heroine's defiance of God; Berryman pursues the same theme.

Penthesilea is queen of the Amazons, a race whose very existence depends on their decision that sex should be entirely arbitrary; they wed no man whom they have not conquered in battle. Penthesilea's mother prophesies that she will wed Achilles, an utterance which deprives the god of his prerogative:

. . . der Gott,
Begehrt er ihver, ruft sie würdig auf,
Durch seiner grossen Oberpriestrin Mund.   (Cited in E. L.
Stahl, *Heinrich von Kleist's Dramas* (Oxford: Basil Blackwell,
1948), p. 82.)

Her mother's prophecy plants the seed of an obsession in
Penthesilea's mind: she goes out of her way to continue the
battle and enslave Achilles. At the crucial moment in this
exploit, however, she is suddenly and unaccountably overcome
by weakness and captured by Achilles. Stahl explains the crux:
'The external motivation of the tragedy is hardly prominent in
the first draft of the work . . . Kleist worked into his play the
theme of Penthesilea's conflict against a superior external
power . . .' (ibid., p. 79). The point of the emendation is that
Penthesilea is not destroyed by her own passion, but by the
angry violence of the gods. Achilles shortly releases her in order
for her to win him—as she desires—in battle. The result is that
she kills him 'in a transport of fury and savagery, a debased form
of the love which she still feels for him' (ibid., p. 88). Song 320
may be appropriately associated with Song 244, written some
twelve years earlier (at the end of 1956): Berryman noted on the
MS.: 'women at war = error').

Berryman does little to change this theme in Song 320, except
to personalise the myth in the figure of Henry. Henry sees
himself as Achilles, a vision, it is important to notice, in a dream:
at the end he wakes 'sweating and sordid'. He registers the fact
that an unseen intruder is female and threatening, and makes a
mental inventory of all the women who might fulfil the role: his
mother, a whore, some 'foe', and finally a list of unnamed
sexual conquests whom he dismisses one by one—'not her, nor
her, nor her'. His unconscious sense of guilt then settles on the
ultimate female avenger, Penthesilea. Yet Penthesilea is the very
woman who did not succumb to her own mortal passion, but to
the wrath of the gods. To Henry Penthesilea is Woman,
avenging all those women who have ever been inveigled and
misused by him.

It is ironic to observe that Kleist's Penthesilea is unforgiving
because she fails to understand Achilles' courteous and heroic
action in releasing her (he would make an honest woman of her
by permitting her to conquer him properly), whereas Henry

projects his own guilt-feelings in the person of Penthesilea, who will wreak a much-deserved retribution upon him. The climax of Berryman's reading of the myth is that, whereas for Kleist it is Penthesilea who is destroyed by the gods, Henry (at the moment of losing his nerve) attempts to declare his identity—as God or godlike. His abortive announcement, 'I am—', is (as I showed in notes to Song 46 above) a profane allusion to the Absolute Being of God in *Exodus*. Henry is accordingly denying God, to a certain extent as a result of his love-life. To deny God is, in a sense important to Berryman, to become one's own god.

It is interesting to know that this Song—or section—stood last in the order of composition of *The Dream Songs*, as a manuscript note records: '9 March '68—*end!*'

325. A Song addressed to Berryman's friend Bob Lundegaard, who had recently suffered a bereavement. See also notes to 'Interstitial Office' (*Delusions Etc.*, p. 8) below.

327. (*l. 16*) *I took one once to forty-three structures*

Cf. 'Berryman, after he had been psychoanalyzed, for years made an elaborate, systematic practice of analyzing his dreams by himself. "It's not something you can do without training," he says, "any more than you can play the piano without practising scales. One dream I had turned out to have 38 structures—not levels, structures.' (Jane Howard, 'Whiskey and Ink, Whiskey and Ink', *Life*, LXIII (21 July 1967).

329. A Song entitled 'Drugs too, man?' in manuscript.

348. (*ll. 16–18*) On Good Friday, 4 April 1958, Cheryl Turner stabbed and killed her mother's belligerent lover, Johnny Stompanato, who had formerly been a bodyguard to the mobster Mickey Cohen. (See Joe Morella and Edward Z. Epstein, *Lana*, (London: W. H. Allen, 1972).)

351. (*l. 3*) *his demon lover*
An allusion to Adrienne Rich's poem 'The Demon Lover':
Berryman's first draft manuscript is written on the back of a
copy of the poem.

354. (*l. 18*) '*Tetelestai*'

John tells how on the Cross one last saying is breathed
from the lips of Jesus: 'Tetelestai.' The evangelist, perhaps
without knowing it, thus expresses a great truth. . . . This
means: It is finished. Indeed everything seemed
finished. . . . But . . . also means: 'All is accomplished.'
The work of Jesus was finished. The faith which he had been
able to plant in the hearts of a few men, feeble and hesitating
as it was, had roots which were too deep to be ever
eradicated. Nothing was finished; in reality, everything had
just begun. (M. Goguel, *The Life of Jesus*, trans. Olive Wyon
(London: G. Allen & Unwin, 1933), pp. 585–6.

356. Numbered 160, and entitled 'His Final Sing', in manuscript.

360. (*l. 8*) *the most beautiful woman*
Valerie Trueblood.

361. See Patricia A. Brenner, *John Berryman's Dream Songs*
(Introduction, n. 15), pp. 195–6.

369. (*l. 4*) *Tricky Dick the coach*
Richard M. Cuyler, co-founder of Berryman's preparatory
school, South Kent, Connecticut.

376. (*ll. 11–13*)

'Christian died in Penn Station—Erich Kahler saw him an
hour before—very "tired", and *anxious to get back to*

Princeton, but never made it. My own fear (I took the nom-de-plume "John Christian" once).' (An unsent draft letter—concerning an analysis of one of his dreams—from JB to Fr. William F. Lynch, 11 August 1955; JBP.)

385. See 'A Symposium on the Last Dream Song', ed, Gary Q. Arpin, *John Berryman Studies* vol. III, nos. 1–2 (Winter-Spring 1977).

(For additional notes on Songs 76, 149, and 312, see Richard Ellmann and Robert O'Clair, *The Norton Anthology of Modern Poetry* (New York: W. W. Norton, 1973), pp. 898–9.)

6. Notes and Commentary on *Delusions, Etc.*

The title to each poem is given in quotation marks, preceded by a page number referring to the first English edition of the volume (London: Faber and Faber, 1972). Line numbers and quotations to which specific comments refer are in italics. Where variant readings of some interest or significance occur in Berryman's draft manuscripts (John Berryman Papers, Manuscripts Division, University of Minnesota Libraries), I cite them in quotation marks after a colon following either the quotation from the text (word or phrase in italics) or the line reference. In addition, to avoid confusion, I have followed variants with the abbreviation 'MS.' in parenthesis. Where there is more than one variant, a further colon denotes that the following phrase or line is another (not necessarily second or later) variant; the sign 'MS.' is then placed at the end of all variants.

As well as studying the manuscript drafts of *Delusions, Etc.*, I have had the benefit while compiling these notes of access to Berryman's Library, which is still lodged in his house on Arthur Avenue, Minneapolis, Minnesota.

Epigraphs
We have piped vnto you, and ye haue not danced:
wee haue mourned vnto you, and ye haue not lamented.
    These words from St Matthew's Gospel (11:17) are addressed to the Jews who will not yield to God's suasion. Cf.

Like petulant children who will play none of the games suggested (in this case they refuse to play either at weddings or at funerals), the Jews reject all God's advances whether through the stern penance of John or through the gentle courtesy of Jesus. In spite of this, God's wise design carries through, independently of anything extrinsic to itself, and so its success is its own vindication. (Jerusalem Bible, footnote to p. 33.)

'On parle toujours de 'l'art réligieux' L'art est réligieux.'

'The intent of the book is indicated in one of its five epigraphs, a quotation from the French critic Claudel.' (Peter Stitt, 'Berryman's Last Poems', *Concerning Poetry* vol. 6 (Spring 1973), p. 9.

And indeed if Eugéne Irténev was mentally deranged everyone is in the same case; the most mentally deranged people are certainly those who see in others indications of insanity they do not notice in themselves.
From Tolstoy's story 'The Devil', in *The Kreutzer Sonata, The Devil, and Other Tales* (OUP, 1940), pp. 292–3. The significance of the story's ending is pointed up by R. F. Christian:

The tragedy, which Tolstoy resolves variously in the different endings (in one the man commits suicide, in the other he kills his wife), stems solely from the husband Irténev's lapse before marriage—an affair described with typically Tolstoyan reticence, which eschews naturalistic detail, and leaves everything to the imagination. Happily married, he fears that his self-control will fail him against his will and his better judgment. His wife is good, kind and loving, but she is not realised as a person. His former mistress, the potential threat to Irténev's fidelity, is hardly less nebulous. Irténev monopolises the story. The woman are merely A and B, the necessary bases of the triangle of which he is the apex. (*Tolstoy, A Critical Introduction* (CUP, 1969), p. 234.)

Berryman's epigraph is the first ending to the story, where Irténev shoots himself because of fears for his sexual weakness. In the alternative ending he shoots Stepanida, his wife, and waits for justice. He spends nine months in prison, a month in a monastery, and returns home an enfeebled, irresponsible drunkard. Berryman was perhaps rather reluctant to allow the full significance of Tolstoy's story to stand as epigraph to his own often obsessive and dire self-revelations among the poems of *Delusions, Etc.*; in one manuscript he noted the potent question, '? kill 3rd Epigr.'
'Than longen folke to goon on piligrimages'
From the 'Prologue' to Chaucer's *Canterbury Tales* (l. 12).

p. 1. 'Opus Dei'

The 'Opus Dei' or Divine Office signifies certain prayers to be recited at fixed hours of the day and night by monks, priests, and others of a religious vocation. It consists normally of certain prayers in the Breviary. The Office was standardised during the fifth century, to consist of a nocturnal Office, Vigils or Matins, and seven Offices of the day, Lauds, Prime, Terce, Sext, None, Vespers, and Complin. In general the task of the Opus Dei is to praise and accord honour to God. Berryman's own notes towards his sequence modelled on the Divine Office contain indications of his understanding of its purport and of his own intentions for the poems:

> awe gratitude acceptance petitionary surrendered rejoicing colours in each! birds, plants   esp. endurance, care for others (Paul and Martha [Berryman's children])   courage   rebellion   error-sin   fatigue of day— your greybeard pilgrim *illness* (mortal)

p. 3. 'Lauds' (poem revised 21 February 1971)

The character of 'Lauds' in the Divine Office is to praise God; its name being derived from the three last psalms in the Office (cxlviii, cxlix, cl). The hymns of Lauds are designed to celebrate the break of day, and to commemorate the Resurrection of Christ and the spiritual light he introduces to the world. Among his manuscript notes, Berryman indicated what the Office meant to him. He understood it to be read at midnight or later, to praise God, and, for his own purposes in the poem, to announce 'awe' (as of what he called the 'old, vast', the astronomical amazements of the first stanza), and to show gratitude (as for the 'new, tiny' hat received as a Christmas present). The third stanza was in fact written at Christmas 1970, two months before the poem received final shape.

(l.1) Let us rejoice on our cots

A reference to the verse 'Let the saints be joyful with glory: let them rejoice in their beds,' Psalm 149, from *The Book of Psalms*, from the version of Miles Coverdale as published in the 'Great Bible' of 1539 (The Haymarket Press, 1930). On the end-boards of his own copy, Berryman noted that Lauds always included Psalms 148 to 150. In Psalm 148 he marked the line, 'Praise him, all ye heavens: and ye waters that are above the heavens.'

(*l. 2*) *the Local Group*
  i.e. the local group of Alcoholics Anonymous.

(*l. 4*) *parsecs-off*
  A parsec is a unit of measure used for interstellar distances.

(*l. 4*) *Hale reflector*
  George Ellery Hale (1868– 1938) was an American astronomer. In 1904 he established the Mount Wilson observatory in California, where his greatest achievement was the installation of a 100-in. reflecting telescope. In 1928, after his retirement, he worked towards the building of a great 200-in. reflecting telescope.

(*l. 8*) *this glow*: 'glowing stove' (MS.)
  An important feature of 'Lauds' is that, while God is referred to as 'He', 'His', or 'Him' in the first stanzas, the poet grows in confidence and gratitude enough to use the more intimate address in the second person, 'Your Benevolence' and 'You'.

p. 4. **'Matins'** (January–February 1971)
  Matins originally signified *Aurora*, the sun-rise. It is often considered the most important Office of the day, and includes psalms and readings, litanies or supplications, and prayers for all and sundry. The psalms used run in a series from i to cviii (Berryman referred himself in a note to Psalm 100). The Lessons are crucial to this Office, and consist of readings from the Bible, from the Church Fathers, or from legends of the martyrs or of the other saints. On some days the Office is concluded with the recitation or singing of the canticle Te Deum (see Berryman's reference to 'Handel's Te Deum' (l. 22), which in draft manuscripts he called 'gay'). The Office is celebrated, as Berryman understood it, at 3 or 4 a.m. His notes for the poem devise that it should begin with a 'complaint' against the night, continue with 'my long absence' (i.e. his apostasy since childhood—'past forty years / lost to (as now I see) Your sorrowing / I strayed abhorrent, blazing with my Self'), and then draw on to the poet's 'reception-achievement', his return to the Church. He

chooses also to acknowledge what he calls 'Your forbearance' and, in consequence, his own 'jubilant' feelings. This strategy reverses the address in the previous poem, and shifts from what is now the over-familiar 'Your' and 'You' to the third-person reverence of a phrase like 'He is our overlord.' (In a draft version, for example, the word 'some' in l. 6 originally read 'You'.)

(*l. 10*) *in vincible ignorance*

The phrase is Aquinas's, who deals with the questions of ignorance and moral responsibility in the *Summa Theologiae*. In article ii of Pars I–II, quaestio 76, 'De Causis peccati in speciali', he draws the distinction between invincible and vincible ignorance: 'Ex quo patet quod nulla ignorantia invincibilis est peccatum; ignorantia autem vincibilis est peccatum, si sit earum quae aliquis scire tenetur, no autem si sit eorum quae quis scire non tenetur.' (S. Thomas de Aquino, *Ordinis Praedicatorum, Summa Theologia*, editit Commissio Piana (Ottawa: Harpell's Press, 1953).) Berryman marked in Psalm 95 of *The Book of Psalms* the following verses:

> Today if ye will hear his voice, harden not your hearts: as in the provocation, and as in the day of temptation in the wilderness;
> When your fathers tempted me: proved me, and saw my works. Forty years long was I grieved with this generation, and said: It is a people that do err in their hearts, for they have not known my ways;
> Unto whom I sware in my wrath: that they should not enter into my rest.

(Ed. cit. in note to l. 1 of 'Lauds' above.) Berryman commented in the margin 'Hm. Then: "in vincible ignorance" no?'—punning on the belief that ignorance can indeed be conquered even after, as in his own case, forty years.

(*l. 14*) *Daddy's cowardice*

A reference to his father's suicide when Berryman himself was eleven years of age.

(*l. 21*) *scotographer*

Scotography signifies Radiography, the production of images on sensitised plates by means of the Rontgen rays. In view of Berryman's phrase 'holding up yet with crimson flags the Sun' in the penultimate line of the poem, it is perhaps relevant that a radiograph is an instrument for measuring and recording the duration and intensity of sunshine.

(*ll. 25–8*) allude to the following quotations:

> Slowly as the sun rotates, it still does so in a remarkable manner: it spins faster at the equator than at the poles, so that its surface must be in a state of shear—that is, some parts of the surface must be continually slipping past others. (p. 12)

> *The Wolf-Rayet Stars*—One of the most spectacular stars in the sky lies in the constellation of the Great Dog. . . . It is perhaps as luminous as Alnitam, but may well have twice the surface temperature. Its spectrum gives evidence of a huge and brilliant chromosphere, for bright-line radiations outweigh all other atomic lines. The spectroscope gives evidence of violent motion, with showers of atoms spurting rapidly at speeds of several thousand miles a second. Matter is pouring either inward or outward in tremendous quantities and at immense velocity. Some of the atoms, which lie between us and the star, are certainly spurting upward from the surface. But when we recall the motions of solar prominences, we recognize the possibility that atoms may be cascading downward as well as upward. This star (a representative of a small and fascinating group, the so-called Wolf-Rayet stars) is evidently in a state of crisis. Even a star like Rigel, with its limited future, is likely to last longer without drastic change. (p. 24) (Cecilia Payne-Gaposchkin, Phillips Astronomer, Harvard University, *Stars in the Making*, (New York, 1959).

By likening himself to the sun or to a Wolf-Rayet star in its irregular constitution and behaviour, Berryman also manages to compare himself wittily to the much more radiant and absolute command of the transcendent Sun, his 'Dear', Jesus Christ. One draft version of the poem demonstrates that Berryman arrived at the exaltation of the participle 'mounting' in the last line of the poem after listing words like 'brandnew', 'pristine', 'redhot', 'zero', and 'crescent'.

p. 6. **'Prime'** (mid-February, 1971)

Prime (*prima hora*) is celebrated towards 6 a.m. The Office ended with a prayer for the work the monks were about to undertake. Prime therefore consecrated the work of the day: cf. Berryman's 'doubt, fear', as he calls it in a manuscript: 'What fits me today / which work I can? I've to poor minimum / pared my commitments; still I'm sure to err/grievous & frequent before Evensong.' In a manuscript draft there followed originally these lines:

> I'm too tired, Master, to perform. My blood's
> thin and [word illegible] my delinquent belly,
> eyeballs throbbing, recollection skids.

Not only is he physically incapable, he is also, the poem says, fearful of the day of reckoning. This eschatological terror is relieved by what he called (in drafts) 'examples to *join*', that is to say, martyrs like Saint Julian who gave themselves up for their theological beliefs. Such a conclusion to the poem is in line with the historical development of the Office of Prime, which came to include a reading of the martyrology, the necrology, and a prayer for the dead.

(*l. 11*) *Claudel*

Paul Claudel (1868–1955), a French poet, dramatist and diplomat, was converted to Roman Catholicism shortly after 1886. He served as French ambassador to a number of countries and wrote extensively, his works including the popular *L'Annonce faite à Marie* (1912) and *Le Soulier de Satin*. Claudel, whom Berryman dubs 'old' because he attained eighty-seven years, was recognised as the greatest French Catholic writer of his time. In 1959 Berryman translated Claudel's dramatic cantata 'The Way of the Cross' for the Minneapolis Symphony Orchestra; a performance on 6 February was conducted by Antal Dorati, to a setting by the conductor himself.

(*l. 20*) *post-Lupercal*

The pagan feast of Lupercalia, a fertility rite celebrated on 15 February. The following phrase 'sure The Baby was my valentine' (St Valentine's Day being 14 February) refers to the conception of his child, Sarah, born later this year.

(l. 22) here disabled, still
>   originally read 'this disabled dawn', a phrase which, discountenancing the weather, assumed more subtlety in the concessive meaning of the published version.

(l. 25) blue trumps, hazy, vainless glory
>   A phrase which originally was less ambiguous: 'far trumpets of glory'. The epithets 'blue', 'hazy', and 'vainless' tend to adulterate their subject, glory. Although, as he says, the poet does 'take heart' upon his return of faith, the tenor of this poem is less enthusiastic than in 'Lauds' or 'Matins', more formal and ego-centred and ironic: his self-characterisation as limping along behind 'humming' (implying a certain casualness) illustrates this half-hearted modus, as does the irony of the concluding litany which gives thanks that martyrs must suffer and die to prove themselves His.

p. 8. 'Interstitial Office' (variously 'Interstitial Hour') (written 8 a.m., 19 January 1971)

>   Berryman seems to have invented this Office for the sake of giving utterance to a sudden upheaval of indignation. The subject of the poem is a miscarriage of justice which, for the poet, reflects directly on God's justice. Berryman's source is an article, 'Draft-Raid Defendants Convicted', by Bob Lundegaard, in *The Minneapolis Tribune*, Tuesday, 19 January 1971, from which I extract:

>>   Francis X. Kroncke and Michael Therriault were convicted Monday by a federal court jury of attempting interference with the draft for raiding the Little Falls, Minn., draft office last July.
>>   The verdict by the jury of seven women and five men brought to a close the third and last trial of the Minnesota Eight. Of the other six defendants, five were convicted and the sixth has offered to plead guilty.
>>   Judge Philip Neville, in his instructions to the jury, threw out virtually the entire defense contention that the attempt to destroy draft files was justified.
>>   . . .
>>   When the verdicts were read, several of the women on the jury blinked back tears.

Therriault had printed several signs and propped them on the defense table for the jurors to read. 'We Love You,' said one.

. . .

'We felt we had no alternative, since all their evidence was stricken,' said another juror, Edward Oswald.

. . .

Kroncke, who acted as his own attorney . . . said that 'in a certain sense, I'm glad to be here. Twenty-six years of my life are right here in this courtroom.

I hope you glimpse the fact that men sometimes make laws that usurp God's power, and I hope you'll try in your own way today to speak peace. God guide you.'

Prosecutor Thor Anderson, an assistant U.S. attorney, accused Kroncke of attempting to rationalise his crime by writing a paper on radical theology 'to weasel his way out of it.'

Bob Lundegaard, who reported this piece for the newspaper, was a friend of Berryman's and discussed the case with him, which accounts for the additional personal detail of ll. 17– 18. On a draft of the poem, Berryman noted: 'Keep the *helpless* jurors to the fore.'

p. 9.   **'Tierce'** (February 1971?)

Terce (Berryman's spelling is now anomalous), celebrated at 9 a.m., comprises, with Sext and None, one of the so-called 'little hours'. Church Fathers and liturgists considered that Christ was condemned to death at this hour. Nine o'clock was also the hour at which the Holy Ghost descended on the Apostles at Pentecost. Berryman's poem again advances causes for questioning God's providence and love and for withholding his own love, since, as one phrase indicates, 'the Enemy's paratus' (an obscure phrase mixing modern phonetic elision and Latin: the slangy pomp of the phrase is clarified by a draft version which reads "the Enemy is ready"). The central grievance of l. 11, 'his envenomed & most insolent missive', refers to a letter addressed to Berryman by Allen Tate on 21 January 1971, which rebuked Berryman for the quality of his book *Love & Fame*, for the obscurantism of a novel idiom, and for his condescending to his superiors. Berryman took the message badly and returned an answer on 12 April: 'You hurt me.' Berryman's exasperation at being obliged to utter forgiveness was emphasised in draft versions by an underlining of the phrase 'too much' in l.15, followed by an exclamation mark.

Two other stanzas were drafted but omitted from the published version:

> I seem to hear Retreat blast thro' blue air
> back to an unassailable redoubt,
> even old Nile-sounds, where 'tears' and 'men' sound the same
> and 'not to be' and 'be complete' are one.
>
> Ugh. What the *hell* quail I perplexed about?
> Christ Jesus. Gethsemani and Calvary
> and the Emmaus road, hardly propose
> (someone was saying) most of us are lost.

The latter stanza is obscure, but signifies that the Gospels detailing Christ's ministry, crucifixion and resurrection, must all stand to prove something of an afterlife and, accordingly, of the possibility of redemption.

p. 13. 'Vespers' (24 March 1971)

Vespers is celebrated at 6 p.m., the evening hour. Berryman moves in the poem from self-accusation, through doubt and distrust of God, to a concluding sense of obeisance aroused by the witness of the Old Testament.

(*l. 2*) *slimed*: 'corrupted' (MS.)

(*l. 3*) *feared*: 'Loved' (MS.)

(*l. 4*) *leaned forward toward &*: 'anticipated' (MS.)

(*l. 7*) *top*: 'make' (MS.)

(*l. 8*) *paracme*

A point or period at which the prime is past; the point when the crisis of a fever is past.

The poet describes himself as vain and lustful, and deserving of contempt 'verging on horror' because, even though he has passed his paracme—the mid-point of his crisis, secondarily of his mental and physical energy to sin—he is still 'greeding', still solicitous of occasions of sin.

(*l. 13*) *addition to Deuteronomy 6*

What Berryman believes to be an interpolation in Deuteronomy is the injunction to love God unreservedly, as glossed by Black's *Bible Dictionary* (London: A. & C. Black, 1954, p. 135): 'The love and service of Yahweh and of one's fellow men is the supreme demand, together with the undivided loyalty of all to the one and only God of Israel' (Deut. 6:4–9).

The poet's response is to escape or excuse himself, but that resource is balked by the realisation that some individuals do attain devoutness.

(*l. 17*) *I flinch from some horrible saints*

indicates that such exemplars cause the poet considerable unease. A draft manuscript of l. 17 names the paragons he had in mind: "Dan Berrigan seems to, and Teilhade Simone Weil.'

Often, after ancient custom, Vespers ends with a lection or reading from the Old or New Testament: so the poet resigns his own capacity for the proof of God to the evidence of the Old Testament:

(*l. 29*) *Solomon's cherubim 'their faces were inward'.*

2 Chronicles 5 describes Solomon's bringing the ark of the covenant of the Lord out of the city of David, which is Zion. The ark of the covenant is set in the most holy place, the inner sanctuary of the house, 'underneath the wings of the cherubim. For the cherubim spread out their wings over the place of the ark, so that the cherubim made a covering.' As the priests attend to celebrate praise and thanks giving, 'the house, the house of the Lord, was filled with a cloud, so that the priests could not stand to minister because of the cloud; for the glory of the Lord filled the house of God' (*The Oxford Annotated Bible with the Apocrypha*, Revised Standard Edition (New York: OUP, 1965), p. 534.) The poet rests his own case on the forensic reliability of this miraculous manifestation.

p. 15. 'Compline' (? 10 February, 1971)

Compline is the Office of bedtime, a prayer before sleep,

often to include the confession and absolution of faults. The
Roman Compline includes the response *In manus tuas,
Domine* and the evangelical canticle Nunc Dimittis.

(*ll. 7–8*) Josiah (Heb. 'God-healed') succeeded to the kingdom of
Judah at the age of eight and reigned 640–09 B.C. After he
had reigned for eighteen years, Josiah was suddenly shown a
newly-discovered book of the law. Hilkiah, the high priest,
showed the book to Shaphan the secretary, who read it to the
king. 'And when the king heard the words of the book of the
law, he rent his clothes' (2 Kings 22:11). The prophetess
Huldah disclosed that Judah would be destroyed; but, she
added,

> as to the king of Judah, who sent you to inquire of the Lord,
> thus shall you say to him, Thus says the Lord, the God of
> Israel: Regarding the words which you have heard,
> because your heart was penitent, and you humbled
> yourself before the Lord, when you heard how I spoke
> against this place, and against its inhabitants, that they
> should become a desolation and a curse, and you have rent
> your clothes and wept before me, I also have heard you,
> says the Lord. Therefore, behold, I will gather you to your
> fathers, and you shall be gathered to your grave in peace,
> and your eyes shall not see all the evil which I will bring
> upon this place. (2 Kings 22:18–20)

Josiah then instituted sweeping reforms, directed chiefly
against heathen altars and cult objects.

(*l. 15*) '*l'affabilité, l'humilité*'

The Jesuit's mode of converting North American Indians is
exemplified in the 'Divers Sentimens': 'Pour convertir les
Sauvages, il n'y faut pas tant de science que de bonté et vertu
bien solide. Les quatre Elemens d'vn homme Apostolique en
la Nouuelle France sont l'affabilité, l'Humilité, la Patience et
vne Charité genereuse.' (Quoted in Francis Parkman, *The
Jesuits in North America in the Seventeenth Century*, London,
1894, footnote 1 to p. 134.)

(*l. 25*) *the Kingdom here here now*

> Life, by which eternal life is meant, is a word which
> looks forward to the eternal destinies, but not to a

combustion of the universe or an end of historical time. This eternal destiny is something which one enters into *here and now*, and it is the same with the Kingdom of God; and such entry is for little children and those who like them. [Berryman's underlining] (Philip Carrington, *According to Mark* (Cambridge, 1960), p. 212.)

On the end-board of his copy of this book, Berryman wrote simply: "212 the Kingdom!"

(*ll. 33–6*) A reference to Origen's teaching that God's patient love will eventually induce everyone to reciprocate love, and 'at last even his enemy death will be overcome'. (Jean Daniélou, *Origen*, trans. Walter Mitchell (London & New York: Sheed & Ward, 1955), p. 287.) This principle, which Origen called apocatastasis, relied on the belief that eventually all intransigent creatures would submit to God of their own free will: ' . . . the hostile purpose and will which proceeded not from God but from itself will come to an end' (*Origen on First Principles*, trans. G. W. Butterworth (London: S.P.C.K., 1936), p. 250). In a footnote, Butterworth explains further: 'Origen's reference here is to the devil, though this is concealed by Rufinus. See Theophilus Alex. *Ep. pasch.* Gr. Frag. 16 (in *Doctrina patrem* ed. Diekamp, p. 180, 12): 'He has dared to pay great honour to the devil, saying that when he is freed from all sin he will be restored to his ancient rank, and that the kingdom of Christ will come to an end and that Jesus will then together with the devil be reigned over by God.' (Ibid., p. 251.)

Berryman situates this serious programme in a context that betrays poor logic and facetiousness. What does emerge, however, is a sense less of facetiousness than of celebration. Cf. ll. 1–6 Dream Song 56, written on Labour Day 1961, some ten years before 'Vespers'. In drafts for the poem, Berryman insisted upon the richness of temporal experience, in tune with what he called 'Carrington's marvellous comforting gloss of *Mark* 10'—the kingdom of God being here and now, as alluded to in ll. 25–6 above. He decided that the following items should feature in the poem: 'colours   *shapes   smells feels   tastes*   "sour"   spice   aroma   horse-radish   oxblood   scallion   "wild little resiny after-tastes"' (According to Berryman's notes, the latter phrase derived from a columnist for *The Minneapolis Tribune*, Will

Jones, who would often report on a new restaurant or dish.)
    Several fragments survive among drafts for the poem,
characteristic examples being:

> How do I dare to be happy, so deserveless,
> and among the American maniacs half one
> helping to wipe out people or distort
> their beings and destroy Your air and sea?

and:

> I have seen death, and it is drawing nearer,
> and I must lie down now, my offices done
> for today only, but I will see too other.

p. 19. 'Washington in Love'
    For complete draft version of the poem, see *Henry's Fate &
other Poems, 1967–72,* ed. John Haffenden, pp. 74–9.

p. 20. 'Beethoven Triumphant'
    The first stanza does not figure in early drafts for the poem. In
conjunction with the last phrase of the poem, 'I hear your
thighs' the notion that Beethoven was 'Chary with his loins
womanward', implies a correlation between the composer's
sexual abstinence and his prodigious musical creativity—'he
begot us an enigma'. The couplet that begins stanza 19 is a
muted, more delicate version of a draft,

> Did you ever sleep with a woman? a man? an animal?
> sometimes I wake and wonder. Musical thighs

—the last two words of which Berryman then transposed to the
more rhetorical context of stanza 20.
    The details of the poem may be checked against Alexander
Thayer's *The Life of Beethoven* and Anton Felix Schindler's *Life*
and *Beethoven as I knew him* (ed. Donald W. MacArdle and
trans. Constance S. Jolly (London: Faber & Faber, 1966)).
Other references will be taken up in the following notes.
(*l.* 5) Ferdinand Ries (1801–5) observed in connection with

Beethoven's deafness that 'When he did not understand something he usually blamed the absent-mindedness to which he really was subject in the highest degree.' (*Beethoven, Impressions by his contemporaries*, ed. O. J. Sonneck (New York: Dover Publications, 1967), p. 56.)

(*ll. 7–8*) Berryman mistook the page reference in his source here: the quotation should in fact be ascribed to Rossini, who described a gala dinner at the palace of Prince Metternich:

> After dinner, the evening ended with a reception which assembled in the Metternich salons the foremost names of Viennese society. There was also a concert. On the program figured one of the most recently published Trios of Beethoven . . . always *he*, he everywhere, as one says of Napoleon. (Ibid., p. 120.)

Rossini's entry, written in 1822, is preceded in the book by some pages by Russell; Berryman, in checking the quotation, simply flipped over too many pages and lit on the wrong name.

(*l. 18*) 'that show him at his unrivalled (exc. by Mozart and Schubert) middle best.' (MS.)

(*l. 20*) 'How in whatever attic he must have been pleased.' (MS.)

(*ll. 26–7*) Ferdinand Ries described Beethoven's awkwardness: 'No furniture was safe from him; least of all a valuable piece; all was over-turned, dirtied and destroyed' (Ibid., p. 58).

Stanza 11 was substituted for an earlier draft (significant chiefly for Berryman's sympathetic identification in the third line):

> Blacks militant! the Chinese! were not your thing.
> You apologised, and did it again.
> O had your father stayed with you, would you have suffered so?
> And with your notes in your head, fumbling, what did you *read*?

(*l. 55*) An obscure phrase dislocated from an earlier draft which at least gave it context:

> You probably never read the *Timaeus*.
> Ah you'd have liked it: it's Plato's responsio

to Opus 95, 'the Serious'
and the Heiligerdankgesang, Op. 132.

(*l. 59*) 'one note hovering, as it must' (MS.)
    The word 'hovering' was a leitmotif in Berryman's work, suggestive of hallucinatory fears (cf. 'Compassion waves you past, you hoverers, /Forms brutal, beating eyes', in 'The Song of the Bridegroom' and *passim*). Compare also l. 78 of the poem, which suggests psychological terror: in an earlier draft version the line read less portentously: 'There are things cannot be fixed by you.' The poet states that he often uses music as a sop to anxieties, but there remain 'Things' which are not appeased by that form of escapism.

(*l. 100*) *our chief prose-writer*
    i.e. Edmund Wilson. Cf. an earlier draft: 'the best prose-writer in America /(except maybe Saul and Mailer) /at his home on the Cape'.

(*l. 103*) *Neither of us laughed*: 'I shivered and almost laughed.' (MS.)

(*l. 104*) *I wish you'd caught*: I wish you could have heard Makeba and Bessie.' (MS.)

(*l. 107*) *the indignities you flew free from*: 'the indignities Hell's God took you off from!' (MS.)

(*l. 108*) *your self-abasements*: 'your self pardonings' (MS.)

(*l. 110*) Quoted from the Baron de Tremont in 1809:

> Does not our vanity count for something in all that makes us feel flattered by being well received and giving pleasure to some person of bad character, churlish and eccentric, rather than by one possessing all the qualities that amiability and amenity of manner are capable of suggesting?' (O. J. Sonneck, *Beethoven, Impressions*, p. 68.)

(*ll. 111–12*) Here Berryman again mistakes the context of his source; the Baron de Tremont was refused a letter of introduction, not by Beethoven (as the combination of 'For' and the colon at the end of the line suggest), but by Cherubine, who took the opportunity to dub Beethoven ungraciously:

> I asked Cherubine to give me a letter to him. "I will give you one to Haydn," he replied, "and that excellent man will make you welcome; but I will not write to Beethoven;

I should have to reproach myself that he refused to see some
one recommended by me; he is an unlicked bear!" (Ibid., p.
69.)

(*l. 114*) *under too nearly*: 'under all but perfect' (MS.)
(*ll. 97–8*)   *Musical thighs,*
         spared *deep age.*
The obscure discontinuity of these two phrases is elucidated by the total context of an earlier draft:

> Did you ever sleep with a woman?
> Sometimes I wake and wonder. Musical thighs,
>
> may be, spared that too you. The hells of our love,
> all the same, are in your movements, andante
> specially; some glass to read the soul
> prostrate some Genius willed you in youth.

Dislocations and impairments of logical sequence in other
lines and phrases may be accounted for by a similar revision of
early drafts. The substitution or omission of sequential lines in
those versions contributes to the effect of the poem as a
medley of reportage, metaphor, and moments of afflatus as
the poet recalls his favourite pieces of music.

p. 26. 'Your Birthday in Wisconsin You Are 140' (Tuesday
evening, 7 p.m., 1 December 1970)
Very shortly after Berryman wrote this poem to Emily
Dickinson, he read Albert J. Gelpi's *Emily Dickinson, The
Mind of the Poet* (Cambridge: Harvard UP, 1965).
(*ll. 3–4*)   *the 'pure and terrible' Congressman*
            your paralyzing papa
'Emily's measure of her father began and ended in awe: "His
heart is pure and terrible and I think no other like it exists."'
(Gelpi, p. 9.) Gelpi adds that Dickinson 'was, almost, the
incarnation of the Messiah whom she was defying more and
more in her heart' (Gelpi, p. 13).
(*ll. 4–5*) Berryman is slightly confused about the biographical facts
here. Emily Dickinson's two earliest readers were Benjamin
F. Newton who, as Gelpi explains, was the clerk in the law
office of Dickinson and Bowdoin during the early forties, and

Henry Vaughan Emmons, a student during the early fifties. Benjamin Newton died early, in 1853, when Emily herself was twenty-three years old. Leonard Humphrey was one of Emily's Amherst friends, but not as close as Benjamin Newton and Henry Emmons.

(*l. 6*) *Fantastic at 32 outpour*
     She wrote more than 360 poems in the year 1862.

(*l. 8*) It is assumed that the 'Master' to whom Emily Dickinson addressed many letters was the Reverend Charles Wadsworth of the Arch Street Presbyterian Church in Philadelphia, a married man whom she knew personally very little. They met at least as late as 1860. In 1862, he went to California for religious duty.

(*l. 9*) Emily opened a correspondence with Thomas Wentworth Higginson in April, 1862, the same month Wadsworth was departing for the West coast. She asked Higginson, 'But, will you be my Preceptor, Mr. Higginson?' (Quoted in Gelpi, p. 25.)

(*ll. 12–15*) In 1880, the relationship between Emily Dickinson and Judge Otis P. Lord, who was eighteen years her senior, 'deepened', according to Albert Gelpi, 'into genuine and shared love'. It is unlikely that Lord referred to Emily as 'cracked': Higginson, on the other hand, as Gelpi records, did not fully understand and appreciate 'his "half-cracked" and "eccentric poetess" in Amherst' (ibid., p. 28).

     The factual errors in Berryman's poem came about because he only read Gelpi's book very shortly after writing his address. For the facts, he was either misremembering or consulting a poor and bowdlerized biography or simply consulting carelessly. Like Ezra Pound, Berryman was not concerned with scholarly exactitudes when writing his poetry.

(*l. 16*) *I'm in W——*: 'Waukesha' (MS.)
     A fourth stanza was drafted for the poem:

> And all those strange years, since you sat alone
> (Miss Lyon asked the girls who at least desired
> to become Xtians to stand up), alone, – in quest.
> During the final summer of voyaging, to Mrs. Todd:
> 'I am glad you cherish the Sea. We correspond,
>   though I never met him.

The references here are to (1) Emily attended Mount Holyoke Female Seminary under its dynamic founder, Mary Lyon. Miss Lyon was zealous to save souls for Christ and on one occasion, in 1848, she 'asked those lost girls who at least desired to become Christians to stand up, Miss Dickinson was the only one to remain seated. "They thought it queer I didn't rise—I thought a lie would be queerer." ' (Gelpi, *Emily Dickinson*, p. 32.) (2) Emily Dickinson spent her life trying to resolve the antinomies represented by the heavenly goal of Christianity and the physical existence in a world of death: figuratively, it became her life voyage. 'During her last summer, at the end of the invisible voyage, she wrote to Mrs. Todd: "I am glad you cherish the Sea. We correspond, though I never met him." ' (Ibid., p. 34.)

p. 27. **'Drugs Alcohol Little Sister'** (6 January and 7 January, 1971)

A poem in celebration of Georg Trakl, born 3 February 1887 in Salzburg. See T. J. Casey, *Manshape that Shone, An Interpretation of Trakl* (Oxford, 1964): 'His drinking, "unsinning" and "vollkommen vervuckt", is the most constant theme in his own letters' (p. 6). Trakl's sister, to whom he was devoted, shot herself in 1917. During the First World War, Trakl served as a chemist with the Austrian Army in Galicia.

We are told that he was in sole medical charge of ninety seriously wounded soldiers in a barn outside which the bodies of deserters were hanging from the trees. He could do little to alleviate the suffering around him. One of the soldiers shot himself in Trakl's presence. What he here experienced, he said to Ficker, was "der Menscheit ganzer Jammer", and the effect on Trakl was similarly described by an eye-witness many years later, who speaks of Trakl's "Entsetzen" and "helle Verzweiflung". (Ibid., p. 9)

(l. 9) this schwartze Verwesung

A phrase—'black corruption'—often used in Trakl's own poems, as in 'Ruh und Schweigen' ('Rest and Silence'):

Night envelops the brow once more amid lunar stones;

> And a radiant youth
> The sister appears amid autumn and black corruption.

—and:

> All the roads lead to blackest carrion.
>
> > ('Grodek')   (Translations by
> > Michael Hamburger.)

p. 28. 'In memoriam (1914–1953)'

A poem about Dylan Thomas, who, as the first section records, Berryman discovered to be dead after a four-day coma in St Vincent's Hospital, New York, in November 1953. Cf. John Malcolm Brinnin's account in *Dylan Thomas in America* (London: J. M. Dent & Sons, 1956).

(*l. 10*) *I stopped panicked a nurse*

An early draft of the poem reads 'stopped outraged', an adjective perhaps more appropriate to Berryman's behaviour and feeling. John Malcolm Brinnin, whom Berryman encountered in the corridor, remembers the tone of his question, 'Where were you?', as aggressive. (Interview with John Malcolm Brinnin, September 1974.)

(*ll. 17–18*)   *born one day*
        before I surfaced

Berryman was born on 25 October 1914, Thomas on 27 October. Accordingly, Berryman himself was the older of the two poets—by two days. Berryman never knew that fact, so he is the butt of the joke recorded in the next lines.

(*ll. 26–8*)

> All I can say is that my mouth was dry and my heart was in my mouth. Thomas had very nearly succeeded in getting me drunk earlier in the day. He was full of scorn for Yeats, as he was for Eliot, Pound, Auden. He thought my admiration for Yeats was the funniest thing in that part of London. It wasn't until about three o'clock that I realized that he and I were drinking more than usual. I didn't drink much at that time; Thomas drank much more than I did. I had the sense to leave. I went back to my chambers, Cartwright Gardens, took a cold bath, and just made it for

the appointment. (Peter A. Stitt, 'The Art of Poetry XVI', *Paris Review* 14 (Winter 1972), p. 187 (an interview with John Berryman).)

This incident, and Berryman's meeting with W. B. Yeats, took place on 16 April 1937.

(*l. 33*) *Apart a dozen years*
   Berryman met Thomas again in Seattle in 1950, when he was lecturing at the University of Washington.

(*l. 37*) *one told me*
   Liz Reitell, a close friend of Dylan Thomas's.

(*l. 42*) *mid potpals' yapping*: 'while his friends yapped' (MS.)

(*ll. 45–8*) Thomas's letter (dated 11 May 1938) in fact reported that he and Caitlin were living in a fisherman's cottage, which was cheap and appeared romantic, and that he would have preferred a poet's cottage 'with Edna Millay on tap'. He also reported that James Laughlin IV (the publisher of *New Directions*) was about to visit for a few days, and parenthetically added an invitation to Berryman himself, concluding with a reminder to 'write sometime'. The letter is not that of an intimate, begins semi-formally with 'Dear John Berryman', and is signed 'Yours, Dylan T.' (John Berryman Papers).

p. 33. 'Gislebertus' Eve' (24 January 1971)
   The poem was written in one hour, 5–6 a.m. The epigraph is taken from Gustav Janouch, *Conversations with Kafka* (New York: Frederick A. Praeger. 1953), from which this is a fuller extract:

> 'Most men are not wicked,' said Franz Kafka, talking of Leonhard Frank's book *Man is Good*. 'Men become bad and guilty because they speak and act without foreseeing the results of their words and their deeds. They are sleep-walkers, not evildoers.' (pp. 58–9)

Berryman wrote a marginal comment, 'immense *responsibility*', by the passage in his copy of the volume.
   Cf. *Dream Song* number 185, ' "His Majesty, / the body." ', for which Berryman's source is p. 27 of the same work.

The sculpture of Eve figures over the north door of the
Cathedral of Saint-Lazare d'Autun, and dates from *c.* 1130.

(*l. 5*) *the austere Viennese*

Sigmund Freud.

(*l. 6*) *Bohr*

Niels Henrik David Bohr (1885–1962), Danish physicist,
born and educated in Copenhagen. He wrote many papers on
atomic structure, beginning with an explanation of the
spectrum of hydrogen by means of conflicting classical and
quantum ideas. He was awarded the Nobel Prize for Physics
in 1922, and worked on the Atomic Bomb in the USA.

(*l. 12*) *Ditheletic*

Ditheism defines a belief in two antagonistic forces, good
and evil, as in Manicheism. The notion opposes a belief in
monotheism.

Berryman is confused by the explanations of matter and
the universe offered by modern physics, propounding riddles
which seem insoluble. The universe resists absolute definition,
as Heisenberg's Principle of Indeterminacy, for example,
gives witness. The poem proposes an analogy with the myth
or fact of Eve's Original Sin, which science can likewise never
accredit. Cf. Dream Song 161, ll. 2–10.

p. 36. **'Tampa Stomp'**: variously, 'Tampa Blues' and 'Tampa Hoe
down' (MS.)

The location is Tampa, Florida, in the summer of 1926.
Berryman's mother and father had moved there from
Oklahoma in 1925, where they owned and worked in a
restaurant, together with Berryman's maternal grandmother.

(*ll. 1–4*) are taken from a letter written to Berryman by his mother at
Thanksgiving, 1970: 'The first signs of the death of the boom
came in the summer, early summer, and everything went like
snow in the sun: there was a miasma, a weight beyond
enduring, the city reeked of failure.' (p. 2)

(*ll. 11–12*)

By this time, Allyn had become infected with the disease of
the failing boom, so seriously affected that he finally agreed
to talk to doctors. During the free time he had on his hands,
he had met up with a Cuban woman who, it came out, had

been his mistress and whom he wanted to marry, he said.
(Ibid.)

p. 37. 'Old Man Goes South Again Alone' (Early December 1970–1 June 1971)

(l. 1) avocets
> One of the wading birds (*Grallatores*) allied to the Snipes and Stilts, distinguished by its flexible upturned beak.

(l. 4) albeit without the one
> Victoria Pope, a student whom Berryman had met after a poetry reading at Vassar College, New York. They subsequently became close friends. (Interview with Victoria Pope, May 1975; and letter, 8 March 1971: 'You never sent me a copy of the poem about me and Trinidad.')

p. 38. 'The Handshake, The Entrance'

(l. 1) Title and subsequent lines of a song originating in the Southlands of the USA, rediscovered and sung by John Jacob Niles (b. 1892, Louisville, Kentucky).

(l. 11) said goodbye to Sally
> Sarah Appleton, whom Berryman met in 1954 in Cambridge, Massachusetts.

p. 39. 'Lines to Mr. Frost' (12 March 1971)

(ll. 1–2) An allusion to Robert Frost's poem 'The Draft Horse', a poem in which the horse is 'deliberately stabbed' to death: the speaker assumes that 'the man himself' who performs this action has good reason, or that he is acting as the agent of 'someone he had to obey'. (*The Poetry of Robert Frost*, ed. Edward Connery Lathem (London: Cape 1971), pp. 443–4.)

> Robert Frost's 'The Draft Horse' . . . is a poem about the mystery of response to crisis, implying, I think, that the response of love can render evil impotent. Berryman makes a response to it . . . in his final collection. (William Meredith, 'In Loving Memory of the Late Author of "The Dream Songs",' Foreword to Richard J. Kelly, *John Berryman: A Checklist*, (Metuchen, N. J.: The Scarecrow Press Inc., 1972), p. xix.)

The occasion on which John and Kate Berryman chatted with Robert Frost took place in the summer of 1962, when Berryman was teaching at the Bread Loaf School of English, Vermont, not far distant from the Homer Noble Farm where Frost stayed. Cf. 'Three Around the Old Gentleman,' Nos. 37–9 of *The Dream Songs*.

p. 40. 'He Resigns' (4 August 1970)
The rhyme-words and sentence construction of the last three lines probably owe something to the final couplet of Yeats's poem 'The Circus Animals' Desertion':

> I must lie down where all the ladders start,
> In the foul rag-and-bone shop of the heart.

p. 41. 'No' (3 August 1970)

p. 42. 'The Form' (25–27 December 1970)
(*ll. 17–18*) A reference to Hendrik de Keyser's tomb of William the Silent in the Nieuwe Kerk at Delft (executed from 1614 to 1623), Fig. 413 in Erwin Panofsky, *Tomb Sculpture* (New York: H. N. Abrams, 1964). William the Silent is portrayed as he looked just after death, in a 'kind of dressing gown and nightcap' (p. 81n).

> Here the great liberator—represented . . . both *en transi* and enthroned, though both these effigies are on the same level—is protected by obelisks (symbols of the 'gloria dei principi'), glorified by Fame and extolled by four personifications borrowed, with minor changes, from Ripa's *Iconologia*: Justice, Fortitude (here also standing for Patience, since she holds a thorn in her right hand), Religion (with book and church model), and Liberty (Aurea Libertas) who carries a scepter and a hat because the Roman ritual of *manumissio* (the freeing of a slave) included the ceremonial covering of the future citizen's head with a hat or a cap (*pileus*). (p. 88)

(*l. 26*) *slid somewhere*: 'hovered before me' (MS.)

p. 44. 'Ecce Homo' (30 October 1970)

(*ll. 3–8*) A reference to a romanesque fresco dating from 1123, from the apse of S. Climent de Tahull, in the Museu d'Art de Catalunya. The fresco depicting the Pantocrator belongs to the Valley of the Bohi group of frescoes. 'Those of Sant Climent in Tahull, the masterpiece of romanesque art in Catalonia, mark the culmination of an amazing stylistic formula.' *Catalan Art from the Ninth to the Fifteenth Centuries*, compiled by Christian Zervos in 1936 (London and Toronto: William Heinemann 1937), p. 16. The Pantocrator is reproduced in plates lxviii–120 and lxix–121 of this work.

(*ll. 9–15*) A reference to the *Crucifixion* executed in painted and gilded wood in the second quarter of the twelfth century (Courajod Bequest, Louvre, Paris). It is reproduced in illustration 638, *Larousse Encyclopedia of Byzantine and Medieval Art*, ed. R. Huyghe (London: Paul Hamlyn, 1963). Berryman had his own photograph of this crucifixion framed in 1971.

p. 45. 'A Prayer After All' (27–28 December 1970)

p. 47. 'Back' ('? Back': MS.) (4–5 January 1971)

A draft fragment of the first two lines dates from 25 December 1970, according to a note page interleaved at pp. 45–6 of Berryman's copy of Sante de Sanctis, *Religious Conversion, a Bio-Psychological Study*, trans. Helen Augur (London: Kegan Paul & Co., 1927): 'I was out of yr Church for 43 yrs, my Dear. /I was grafted back in, sweating blood.'

Berryman seems to advance a syncretic account of his return to the Catholic Church. While it may be assumed that 'your ministers' in l. 3 refers to Catholic priests, his mention of 'the man in fury, /possessed' (ll. 5–6) arrogates to the poem a more ecstatic, pre-Christian rite. The poem concludes ambiguously with 'honour of the Mother' (l. 14), who may be the Virgin Mary, Mother of God, but is also another, alluded to in ll. 15–16, which refer to the hieroglyphic text discovered in the temple at Medinet Habu:

a small mound on the west bank of the Nile, near what was

once Thebes. Rameses II (ca. 1180) built this sanctuary and in hieroglyphics and pictorial carvings left on the walls and pillars a permanent record of all his undertakings. On this fragment an unidentified god from the underworld proffers life (the knotted loop with the cross) to a Pharaoh, recognizable by the 'uraeus' (the small serpent) on his forehead. The text is too fragmentary to admit of any precise translation. On the righthand side it says something about life, good fortune, and prosperity being given. To the left are two cartouches. In the right one is R' – mn – hpr, meaning 'Ra's coming to be is constant.' In the cartouche on the left is Dhwty [the god Thoth] – ms – nfr – hpr.s, that is to say, 'Thoth has caused her coming-to-be in beauty.' It is not clear, however, to whom these names are meant to refer. Above the right-hand cartouche can be seen the cane or reed-stem, the symbol of Upper Egypt, and the bee, symbol of Lower Egypt. (Jan H. Negenman, *New Atlas of the Bible*, ed. Harold H. Rowley (London: Collins, 1969), p. 30.)

p. 48. 'Hel*lo*'
(*l. 1*) Hel*lo there, Biscuit!*
  'Biscuit' was Berryman's pet name for his daughter Sarah, whose birth is commemorated by this poem.
(*l. 12*) *direction* and *velocity*
  A reference to what is called the Uncertainty Principle discovered by the physicist Werner Heisenberg (1901–76): a theory of quantum mechanics which (normally by way of analogy) has been a stimulus to a number of twentieth-century poets including William Carlos Williams and Charles Olson as well as Berryman. In brief, the principle has determined that it is impossible to measure exactly the properties of the physical world: one can measure *either* the direction *or* the velocity of a 'dynamic variable', but never both simultaneously. The notion has excited poets because it seems to destroy the possibility of verifying any so-called 'objective world', and to validate the subjective responses of a poem. Heisenberg's obituary in *The Times* (Monday, 2 February 1976) included this synopsis:

Perhaps his most far-reaching contribution to the further

understanding of quantum mechanics was the Uncertainty Principle which he identified as the epitome of quantum mechanics and the essential point at which it differs from classical mechanics. When a measurement is made of a dynamic variable, the observed system is necessarily disturbed; and it is a consequence of quantum mechanics that the greater the accuracy of the measurement, the greater is the disturbance to the system, that disturbance being in another, complementary variable to the one measured. This renders impossible the determination with complete precision of all the dynamic variables of a system; there is a minimum uncertainty in the information which can be derieved by making measurements on a physical system. This notion has had a profound impact on other fields than physics; through no fault of Heisenberg, this impact has often been misguided.

p. 51. 'Navajo Setting the Record Straight' (27 November 1970)
Poem draws almost entirely on an article by Henry P. Chapman, 'Powerful Medicine on the Reservation', (*Washington Post*, Sunday, 25 October 1970), Flff, which describes a five-day tour of the Navajo Nation under the direction of a 27-year-old Navajo driver. The following extracts gloss Berryman's borrowings:

A present from a girl friend, a royal blue mesh scarf twisted into a headband, kept his raven hair from flapping in the breeze.
He fitted our expectations of what a Navajo should look like as perfectly as molten silver fills a Navajo sand-cast mold. My wife, however, also anticipated a 'Flying Eagle,' or 'Red Cloud,' or 'One-Who-Talks-Thunder.' She'll never forgive 'Albert, no-middle-initial, Slinkey Jr.' for his un-TV-Indian name.

. . .

'. . . When I took my first sky-dive in the U.S. Navy, a Marine sarge told me to yell "Geronimo!" I said, "Hell, no! I'm going to shout a good old Navajo name—Albert, no-middle-initial, Slinkey Jr." . . . My sand-painter grand-father, Jeff King, "Warrior Who Went With a Crowd," served at Fort Wingate as a sergeant-major scout. He's buried with full military honors in Arlington.'

We arrived at Kayenta's 100-room Monument Valley (Ariz.) Holiday Inn, another Navajo-leased investment, with Albert explaining the Navajo myth. The first People emerged from the black world into the blue world, then into the yellow world and finally into the present white world through a giant reed. The hole, medicine men say, may be seen near Silverton, Colo.
. . . Every rock formation is a monument with an imaginative appellation—Totem Pole, Left and Right Mittens. . . .
. . .

Albert arranged a visit to the earth-covered log hogan of Mrs. Betty Cly. Around the interior log-faced walls were bedding, clothing, a mirror, eagle feathers, a drum, and a framed document of the Native American Church of North America, a religious organization whose rites of prayer and contemplation center around peyote. On a table, near a pot-bellied stove, a large flower pot contained two of the spineless peyote cactus plants.

(*l. 11*) *Yah-ah-teh*
means 'Go with joy.'
Rough drafts for the poem include the question, '(*were* the Navajo warlike?)', and these lines:

> You gave us whisky, we give you peyote,
> no sweat, we're inter-corrupted
>
> I don't have my native blood in me,
> it's all come recently, the 1750's
> and so on, but I'll underground his thought
> a little further:
>
> my people, too, wars of extermination
> waged, only we warred on enemies,
> bec. we hated them. Whites kill w. love
> being Christians, and that's well beyond

my seventh-grade education, and moreover
we massacred w. glee-you don't enjoy it
or say and think you don't, it's just yr duty
and doing yr duty fills you w. self-pity

p. 53. 'Henry's Understanding' (Sunday night, ?8 December 1968)

p. 53. 'Defensio in Extremis' (1/2 January 1971)
(*l. 1*) A line (cf. the poem 'Back') derived from Jan H. Negenman's *New Atlas of the Bible*, which glosses an illustration on p. 16 with these comments:

> A part of the second column of the Hymns of Thanksgiving from Qumran 1 QH 2:20–30). This scroll from the first cave is usually denoted by the Hebrew word Hodayoth. These songs are in general harder to understand than our psalms. They often contain more specific allusions to historical situations and events which are now obscure. Furthermore, they employ a variety of Biblical phrases and expressions to formulate their characteristic ideas. In the translation of the psalm the main Biblical turns of phrase are italicized.

This is an extract from the translation:

For it is *Thy favour that maintains me.*

I said: Mighty men have encamped against me,
surrounding me with all their instruments of war,
Arrows they let loose unceasingly
And javelins flashing like tree-devouring fire.
Like the thunder of mighty waters is the uproar of their clamour.
A tempestuous cloud-burst for the ruin of many.
To the very skies break through *outcry and roar,*
While their waves mount high.
And I, my heart *melted like water,* I clung to Thy Covenant.
But they, *their feet will be caught in the net they spread for me.*

(*l. 8*) X, Y and Z refer respectively to Mark Van Doren, Edmund Wilson, and John Crowe Ransom. (MS.)

p. 55. 'Damn You, Jim D., You Woke Me Up' (a poem written in ten minutes, at 4.20 a.m. on Friday, 2/3 October 1970. Within another five minutes, Berryman made thirteen revisions to complete the poem). 'Jim D' is the poet James Dickey.

p. 59. 'Somber Prayer': 'A Comparative Prayer' (MS.) (finished on 28 June 1970)
(*ll. 5—7*) refer to Uccello's painting 'The Flood and The Recession of the Flood', in the Convent of Santa Maria Novella, Chiostro Verde, Florence. (See Plates 27—28, John Pope-Hennessy, *The Complete Works of Uccello*, London: Phaidon Press, 1950.)

p. 60. 'Unknowable? perhaps not altogether' (8—9 October 1971)
(*l. 2*) . . . *I have lain skew over*: 'I have been wrong about' (MS.) For the word 'skew' here, cf. l. 28 of 'Matins'.

p. 61. 'Minnesota Thanksgiving' ('6th/7th Sun. aft. 4 p.m.' (MS))
(*l. 14*) conscience: 'awareness' (MS.) (The word 'conscience' as italicised by Berryman has the French significance)

p. 62. 'A Usual Prayer' (20 January 1971)
(*l. 16*) *and toughen me effective*: 'and assist me useful' (MS.)

p. 63. 'Overseas Prayer': 'Occasional Prayer' (MS.) (7 and 9 January 1971)
(*ll. 1—4*) In *New Atlas of the Bible*, Jan H. Negenman discusses (on p. 65) the city of Jerusalem:

There are references to it in the Egyptian execration texts of the 19th and 20th centuries B.C. There is mention of it again some centuries later in the Amarna period, when 'Abdu-Heba, the ruler of 'Urusalim,' as it was called at that time, sent a number of letters to the Pharaoh. One of them contains the following message:

> Say to the king, my Lord: thus speaks 'Abdu-Heba, the king's servant. At the feet of the king, my Lord, I fall seven and yet seven times. Behold what Milkilu [the ruler of Gezer] and Shuwardata [the ruler of Hebron] have done to the land of my lord the king. They have caused troops to march out from Gezer, Gath, and Keilah [a town between Hebron and Gezer]. They have occupied the country around Rubutu [possibly a town in central Palestine]; the king's land has gone over to the people of 'Apiru [semi-nomadic groups]. But now even a city of the country of Urusalim, called Bit-Lahmi [Bethlehem?], a city of the king, has gone over to the people of Keilah. Let the king listen to 'Abdu-Heba, his servant. Send his bowmen to win back the royal land for the king. But if no bowmen come, then the king's land will pass into the hands of the people of 'Apiru. This has happened at the command of Milkilu and of Shuwardata. Therefore, let my king have a care for his land.

Whether the ruler of Jerusalem was telling the truth is doubtful, for the man he accused, Shuwardata of Hebron, wrote to the Pharaoh making precisely the same accusation about 'Abdu-Heba. It is difficult to ascertain which of the two was telling the truth.

(l. 8) the blurred & breathless dead

> Then I addressed the blurred and breathless dead,
> vowing to slaughter my best heifer for them
> . . .
> Thus to assuage the nations of the dead
> I pledged these rites . . .   (*The Odyssey*, Book 11,
> trans. Robert Fitzgerald (New York, 1961), p. 198.)

(l. 9) The Valley of the Cheesemakers
Negenman, (*New Atlas of the Bible*) describes a picture of the

Ophel ('hump') of David, connected to Jerusalem:

> The tyropoeon or Valley of the Cheesemakers has more or
> less disappeared. In earlier times it ran from the small wood to
> the left of the Ophel towards the left-hand minaret. In the
> foreground are orchards surrounding the spring of Rogel. In
> former days the King's Garden probably stood there. (p. 66)

(*l. 14*) *not a very able father* (A manuscript interpolates—after the
word 'able'—the phrase, 'tho' of integrity'.)

(*l. 20*) *being all I ask*: 'being all I beg. . . .' (MS.)

In his copy of W. O. E. Oesterley and Theodore H. Robinson,
An Introduction to the Books of the Old Testament (London: SPCK,
1949), Berryman wrote 'cf. my "Overseas Prayer" ' in the
margin against a passage which describes the grouping of
psalms into categories, including '*pilgrim songs*, sung during
pilgrimages to the sanctuary in Jerusalem, either by the whole
company of pilgrims or by one of their number and, in all
probability, antiphonally (lxxxiv)' (p. 193).

p. 64. 'Amos' (revised 14 April 1971): 'The Ghost of Amos' (MS.)
A parody of the prophecy of Amos in the O.T., condemning
corruption and foretelling disruption.

In an earlier typescript, Berryman included two stanzas
before the published final stanza:

> For three insane things evil, and for four,
> baffle will I with victory Hanoi
> and gross pretenders, the black megaphone
> of doctrine over the tribes' hills saith the Lord.

> For three insane things evil, and for four,
> sustain alternately: topple will I puny and greedy Thieu
> the potent client—harrowing that people on,
> and I will have no pity, saith the Lord.

p. 65. 'Certainty Before Lunch' (April 1971)
See explication by John Haffenden, 'Berryman's "Certainty
Before Lunch" ', in *John Berryman Studies* vol. I, no. 3 (July,
1975), pp. 15—16.

p. 66. 'The Prayer of the Middle-Aged Man' (14 April 1971)
(*ll. 1–8*) The Biblical reference is to John 20: 19. See a letter, JB to his
mother, 'Easter evening' (1971):

> Did you ever notice that Christ was always '*in medio*'—
> central person of Trinity, *among* the doctors in the Temple,
> *among* his followers, etc., and finally 'venit, et stetit in
> medio, et dixit, Pax vobis'—Bishop Andrewes points this
> out in the great 1609 sermon on the Resurrection that I was
> reading at Mass this morning after trying in vain to get
> anything out of the drivel from the goodhearted
> celebrant—anyway it proves that He was *human*—we are
> ever in the *middle* of something or everything. . . . See my
> poem in The New Yorker 'Ecce Homo' this week. (Mrs
> Jill Berryman.)

See also ll. 24–4 of 'The Search', *Love & Fame* (London,
1971), p. 59, and ll. 21–4 of No. 1 of 'Eleven Addresses to the
Lord', *Love & Fame* (London, 1971), p. 83.
Lancelot Andrewes stated that:

> The midst is Christ's place by nature; He is the second
> Person *in Divinis*, and so the middlemost of the other two.
> And on earth, follow Him if you will, you shall not lightly
> find Him out of it; not according to the letter, speaking of
> the material place. . . . a child, *in medio doctorum*, in the
> Temple. . . . His office being to be 'a Mediator,' *Medius*
> 'between God and Man,' where should a Mediator stand
> but *in Medio*? . . . Nor in things natural either combine
> two elements disagreeing in both qualities, without a
> middle symbolizing with both; nor flesh and bone,
> without a cartilage between both. ('A Sermon preached
> before The King's Majesty at Whitehall, on the sixteenth of
> April, A.D. MDCIX, being Easter-Day', *Andrewes' Sermons*
> (1941), vol II, pp. 249–50.)

(*ll. 11–12*)

> When the seventh month came, all the people gathered as
> one man in the square before the Water Gate. They asked
> Ezra the scribe to bring the Book of the Law of Moses

which Yahweh had prescribed for Israel [i.e. The Pentateuch]. . . .

Ezra the scribe stood on a wooden dais erected for the purpose; beside him stood, on his right, Mattithiah, Shema, Anaiah, Uriah, Hilkiah and Maaseiah; on his left, Pedaiah, Mishael, Malchijah, Hashum, Hashbaddanah, Zechariah, and Meshullam [assessors: prominent laymen].' (After Ezra has read the Law, the people begin to weep; but proclamations are issued, and directives readily carried out.) ' . . . the sons of Israel had never done such a thing from the days of Joshua son of Nun till the present. And there was great merrymaking.' (Nehemiah, in *The Jerusalem Bible*, pp. 589– 90.)

p. 67. ' "**How Do You Do, Dr. Berryman, Sir?**" ' (Vermont– New York City– Minneapolis, May 1971)
(*l. 12*) *he can't though*: not in early drafts and T.S.

p. 68. 'The Facts & Issues'
Written in an hour, from 1.15 am. until 2.15 am. in Room 406 of the Shoreham Hotel, Hartford, Connecticut, May 1971. Berryman comments on the manuscript: 'dry as a bone, nearly 4 months'. At the time of writing he was reading Graham Greene's novel, *The Power and the Glory*, and notes that comparable feelings can be found on p. 267 of his edition and 'now at 3.20 a.m. I find *my feeling* on p. 269!!'

p. 70. 'King David Dances' (17 April 1971)
(*l. 4*) 'murder conspiring' (MS.) (the line is a late addition to MS. drafts)
(*l. 6*) 'unutterable dyings bound to bear': 'revolted sons and dead sons bound to bear' (MS.)

Appendix 1: The Chronology of *The Dream Songs*

This appendix is designed to place as many of the Songs as possible in their order of composition. The list is based in large part on Berryman's habit of dating individual manuscript drafts, as well as on information gleaned from letters and from internal evidence. I have tried to avoid speculative dating, which can be seriously misleading, but certain Songs are assigned tentatively to particular years: these are signified by a question-mark prefixed to the month or year in question. After the number of the Song, the first date signifies the first known draft of a Song (or a portion of the Song). Dates in parentheses indicate known revisions or further drafts.

1955
20. 4 December

1956
244. 31 December

1957
12. 16 March (26 March)
23. Autumn (18 November 1958)

1958
5. 29 March (15 May 1964)
54. March (5 April)
1. 8 April
59. 25/26 April (11 June)
30. 17 May
6. 15 June (November–December 1962)
22. 4 July

24.   20 October
73.   1 November
53.   8 November
26.   15 November
31.   18 November
24.   20 November
217. early December
46.   1 December
67.   3 December

1959
103. New Year
74.   15 January
69.   11 February
32.   21 February (?1961; ?1962; ?1963)
48.   22 February
17.   20 April
19.   1 May
10.   revised 23 August (12 June 1962; 16 September 1963)
21.   10 December
71.   20 December

1960
16.   16 January
57.   8 June
221. 18 June
41.   3 September
27.   ?25 November
76.   ?1960

1961
44.   August (2 September 1963)
231. 15 August
250. 20 August
56.   Labour Day
43.   1 November
8.   24 November
34.   ?1961

1962
15.   17 February (12 January 1964)

183. 21/22 March (first two lines)
 49. (23 March)
249. 22 May
210. 11 July
 37, 38, 39. ?Summer
 62. 3 September
107. 7 September (28 August 1966)
  2. 16 September (Thanksgiving)
 61. 12 November
 40. 6 December
 34, 35. ?Christmas
 68. 26 December
 42. 28/29 December
 60. 1962 (27 August 1963)
 45. ?1962
216. ?1962
246. ?1962
 70. ?1962–1963
285. December (1968)

1963
 25. *c.* 19 January
 11. 11 July
115. 13 July
114. mid-July
 66. 19 July
243. 20 July
253. July
228. mid-Summer
225. 10 October
 98. ?Thanksgiving week
 72. 19 December
200. 25 December
246. ?December
254. 1963
219. 1963
113. ?1963

1964
185. 4/5 February
 78. 2 March

80.	2 March
82.	4 March
83.	5 March
84.	6 March
85.	9 March
81.	1/2 April
93.	7 April (22/23 April)
241.	27 April
92.	28 April
128.	Holy Saturday
95.	?30 April (although probably 1967, as No. 97)
270.	16 May
190.	17/18 May
120.	21 May
184.	26 May
122.	29 May
207.	2 June
186.	8 July
195.	7/8 September
212.	25 September
188.	10 October
119.	15 October
140.	16 October
215.	7 November
88.	1964

1965

194.	30 January
209.	14 February
268.	Memorial Day
138.	4 June
195.	5 June
239.	3/4 July
223.	17 July
182.	18 July
211.	25 July
106.	28 July
253.	July
192.	July˙
181.	23 September
180.	?September

191.   17 October
208.   17 October
121.   October, ?1965
134.   (last three lines—'months later, 18 Oct. 65')
104.   25 October
118.   27 October
198.   November
127.   ?Hallowe'en
169.   2 December
166.   14 December
167.   14 December
168.   ?December
163.   ?1965
164.   ?1965
165.   ?1965

1966

Many of the Songs written between July and October 1966 are undated. Some of them were written durng Berryman's residence in Dublin on a Guggenheim Fellowship; others—which Berryman himself designated as 'Gugg'—were written either before his departure from Minneapolis or in transit to Dublin. From September onwards the majority of the Songs were written at 55 Lansdowne Park, Ballsbridge, Dublin: many of those Songs are designated as 'Ballsbridge'. Both 'Gugg' and 'Ballsbridge' groups are frequently numbered in manuscript versions, although Berryman is sometimes only guessing at the order of their composition. For these reasons it is difficult to be precise in dating Songs during 1966, but the following list provides more than an approximate order. It does at least show that Berryman arranged Book VII far more in the order of composition of the Songs than according to the thematic or narrative groupings ventured in earlier Books.

196.   ?May
 89.   June
125.   ?17 June
172.   26 June
278.   30 June / 1 July
160.   3 July
100.   8 July
129.   10 July

130.   10 July
275.   *c.* 11 July
112.   28 July
155.   29 July
175.
265.   2 August
274.
148.
264.
203.
124.
161.
135.
145.
259.
263.
262.
256.
261.
238.
204.
205.
206.
279.
280.
281.   26 August
282.
283.
297.
299.
300.
301.
306.
309.
312.
313.
310.
311.
315.
316.
317.

319.
321.
322.
323. 19 September
294.
287. 20 September
324.
326.
328.
327.
329.
330.
331.
332.
333.
334. 27 September
293.
295.
335.
336.
340. 3 October
337. 5 October
338. 5 October
341. 8 October
342.
343.
344.
290. 12 October
345. *c.* 14 October
346.
347.
349.
350.
352. 15 October
353. 16 October
354. 17 October
325. 22 October
356. 24 October
291. 29 October
314. 2 November
357. 17/18 November

361. 19 November
359. 29 November
360. Hallowe'en
362.
366. December
368. 7 December
369. 7 December
371. 9 December
375. 28 Deceber
374. 28 December
371. 30 December

1967
269. March
381. 29 March
266. 30 March
143. 2 April
303. May
144. 3 May
380. 3 May
142. 1 June
'Note' (p. ix) 30 August

1968
255. 14 February
382. 29 February
193. *c.* 29 February

Appendix 2: Berryman's 'Hunch of Heaven'

Berryman planned that 'Scholars at the Orchid Pavilion',[1] which he began in 1948, should fit into a grand Dantesque design,[2] being the *Paradiso* of a tripartite group in which *Homage to Mistress Bradstreet* would be a type of *Purgatorio*. (*The Black Book*, his ambitious but unfinished sequence of poems on the Nazi persecution of the Jews, would have taken its place as *Inferno*.) In heaven, all should be 'stately', 'vivacious', a domain of 'honour', 'sherry', 'martinis', as well as 'effectless'.[3] Although an early reference to 'Scholars' describes its subject as 'the innocence of age',[4] Berryman settled its eventual theme in another four-word note, 'my hunch of heaven'.[5]

Early drafts of the poem tend to emphasise the exotic, the languorous, and the mandarin:

> The goblets drift our way. I am with you:
> He goes upon too little too far. Watch;
> His beard unmannerly wags from a small chin.
>
> A boat. A lotus. A being unending storm
> We bow before: our thoughts are distinct.

Other fragments similarly show the self-indulgent character of early thoughts in theme, diction, and phrasing, creating an opaque and dreamlike effect:

>   the great sword
> Hangs by the fountain, where a spider gleams
>
> Its essence round the glowing blade
>
> phantasm   dreaming on the minikin

> where the poor winds
> Howl and weep among the highest pines
>
>   of sleep-lorn hours in the thoughtful dark,
> the heartless night
>
>   the sleep lanterns swing. [7]

Like *Homage to Mistress Bradstreet*, the poem started best at second attempt: in this case, in 1960. While Berryman felt that, in the best Chinese tradition, the poem might be meditative, he gave an additional, decisive boost to his sense of purpose for the work in determining that it could also—just like *Homage to Mistress Bradstreet*—present a dialogue. [8] The chief problem for readers of the poem is its allusiveness. For a start, it is peopled with names that ring sonorous and dignified to Western ears, but far from tripping to our tongues. Mo-tzu, for example, is (as Berryman himself once wrote of the Rev. George Gilfillan) 'not a burning name just now', [9] though a mover in his day. On further inspection, beyond the awareness that the poem is dealing with a non-Christian dispensation, the reader has to reckon with a procedure that is anachronistic. All the persons named, that is to say, have an historical reality, but each possibly at a span of hundreds of years from any of the others, and therefore at a distance of social and cultural change. Nor can Berryman rely on an audience that is *doctus utriusque linguae*. Add to these matters the hand and spirit of Berryman himself moving on the material he disposes, and the effect may seem (to borrow a phrase from R. G. Colling-wood) 'not unlike adding a saxophone obligato to an Elizabethan madrigal'. [10] The conduct of the poem is evidently designed to be anti-historical, in a fashion analogous to E. M. Forster's anti-historical examination of the novel—a device that may have us picture Saul Bellow taking tea with Fanny Burney. Furthermore, there is no little difficulty in deciding just what is being done and said. The entire interaction somehow reminds one of Gertrude Stein's last words: 'What is the answer?' followed by 'What then is the question?' [11]

The poem is, strictly speaking, Berryman's fresh look at immortality; he found the question of whether the body and mind survive death a lasting vexation. In a draft fragment for 'Scholars', he asked pertinently:

> We are obliged to consider: does he live?
> or . . . just exist? And if so, does it matter?

From Whitman's 'Song of Myself', Berryman derived a notion of the intimacy and interrelation of mind and body. He understood that the 'I' in 'Song of Myself' often refers only to the body; the soul at once frees and controls the body. In the lecture from which I extract here,[12] Berryman postulates of Whitman the concept 'of a continuous present, which is Eastern', and which the poet 'may have derived from "the ancient Hindoo poems" to which he refers, or he may have invented it'.[13] This concept enabled Whitman to combine past and future in the present moment, so that 'The Kingdom will be here, and now, forever.' It was one solution to the problem of the apparently terrible sundering, the death, of body and soul. Berryman discerned in Whitman areas of assertion and tone which are, like Rilke's view of death, anti-existential and literally true, 'in the following sense: the death a man considers is his own *now*, not his own *then*, when it will actually take place, to himself another man; therefore he can form no just conception of it; and besides . . . always considers it as the ultimate disaster, whereas in practice for a great part of mankind it comes as the final mercy.'[14]

Berryman looked far in search of theories or proofs of the continuity of life and death. From Sir Charles Sherrington,[15] for example, he learned that the perceptible is subject to change from one phase to another, and that accordingly there are no beginnings or endings, because absolute time disappears. In terms of astronomy—always an interest with Berryman—this obviation of starts and finishes also applies. The steady-state theory of the universe[16] supports the idea that clusters of galaxies may change and evolve with time, but that the universe itself does not change. The intrinsic parts of the universe might alter or reconstitute themselves, but the universe in its totality endures without the determination of time. There are no beginnings *de novo*, and no endings.

Regarding the personal life of man, Berryman had to wrestle with a dilemma. On the one hand, he could not conceive of a mind divorced from its body,[17] since he believed that the shock sustained by the mind from the loss of the entire body would be ruinously traumatic. On the other hand, it was, in his own words, 'perfectly amazing to me that such millions calmly believe in reincarnation (= survival)'.[18] What he required for peace of mind now, therefore, was a projection opting for one or the other alternative—complete annihilation or continuance of mind *with* body. Berryman's temperament seemed to preclude a compromise in the matter. Even if, with Julian Huxley,[19] one describes the difference between body and soul as that between an immortal, germinal part and a mortal, somatic part, scruples may occur. There is a continuity from generation to generation, through a substance (known by Weismann's term 'the Germ-plasm') which is able to produce from itself new individualities. The part that dies is known as the soma or body, including in itself a morphe (the individuality of a person). Individuality dies, and substance dies, although substance may continue to function after a fashion, producing new individuals from its undifferentiated state. But one of the difficulties lies in this necessity to distinguish mortal from immortal parts—what may be called, loosely and popularly, mind and body. This distinction, which (as Huxley himself concedes) 'is usual, but not necessary',[20] promotes the very divisiveness that Berryman seeks to avoid. The other feature of this analysis open to scruple is that, while functioning protoplasm—the natural substance—is not necessarily subject to death, in man at least death is most natural. It is, at a point, desired and painless, the natural result of a senescence which seems to be due to internal causes. In sum, Berryman finds himself at odds with any notion which separates out mind and body. Equally, it is hardly reassuring to know that one's germ-plasm—some portion of one's body—may survive, unless it keeps stock of its somatic part—individual character and soul.[21]

On 17 February 1962, Berryman drafted an unpublished Dream Song, 'Henry House',[22] with this final stanza:

> Now for the matter of the other journey.
> If, when I burned to my foundation, flew
> in partial coalesce'
> with a grand swamp-turtle's just dead, also new—
> released, anguisht and muddy, my soul you, turn
> and return to me—yes—

—which alludes to C. D. Broad's[23] notions of the human personality and the possibilities of its survival after death. Like Huxley, Broad hypothesises that an individual is composed of a living body and what he calls a psi-component. It is this psi-component which, to use a phrase of Broad's quite like Huxley's, 'carries traces and dispositions and may persist after the death of the body'.[24] Surmising beyond the simplest, misleading analogies (such as that the dispositional basis of a personality is like the impression a seal makes on a ball of wax), Broad decided that he can 'envisage a number of interesting possibilities of partial coalescence, partial annulment, interference, and so on,

between the psi-components of several deceased individuals'.[25]
Berryman satirically envisages the pairing of his soul, or psi-
component, with the germ-plasm of a turtle. The force of this
bonding derives from the fact that Broad himself recounts the turtle's
limitations of experience:[26] it has no memory or expectation, and
therefore none of its experiences can prompt or modify any other.
Berryman accordingly parodies what is a sad surmise. Like Malvolio,
when asked about the opinion of Pythagoras concerning wild fowl,
he would concur that 'I think nobly of the soul, and no way approve
his opinion.'[27]

But Berryman does not treat Broad as a whole lightly, since the
premise of 'Scholars' is the possibility of survival. Among his notes,
Berryman has occasion to categorise the poem, by reference to
Broad, as 'a testing-out of the idea of Heaven'.[28] Although Broad
seems to traduce the idea that human dispositions could survive
without a body, his summary is concessive: ' . . . the most likely
alternative,' he says, 'seems to be mere dispositional persistence
unassociated with any kind of experience.'[29] It is presupposed that
ante-mortem experience is indissolubly connected with the conscious
body. With the dissolution of the body at death, whatever life
continues—presumably mental or spiritual—must be transacted in a
markedly changed consciousness: so changed as to be radically
different. Broad figures a surviving disposition without any kind of
continuing experience. (Literally, it is to be supposed, a type of
unattached memory endures.)

Naturally enough, the possibilities of a poem charting the existence
of a disembodied psi-component are not compelling. While taking
into account the scientific and philosophical positions, as well as the
dubious status of his premise, Berryman postulates for his poem the
survival of an exclusive, masculine society of painters and philosophers who are dead—as we understand the term—but whose
minds, bodies, and therefore experiences, continue in being. He listed
the effects of this arrangement: 'an assertion', 'a landscape', 'a
scholarly fight', 'a dream', 'a past', 'a present', 'a losing-identity'.[30] It
might allow too for comic results: since experience persists, so might
sexual desire. According to drafts of the poem dating from 1960, the
denizens of 'Scholars' were to wonder if their feelings were pertinent
only to a living body:

> —If it sings, blood. I experiment.
> An ease fulfills my fingers.

Bloodshot, ache not,
hung over Paradise.

Likewise, the pain of the world of men might remain real, even
sadistic or masochistic:

—Howl, said the next, for in the world of man,
whereof we some are veteran, walks pain
measureless, unappeased.
It eats them. I hurt. —You love to hurt,
blurted the next. I love to say the worst,
without reflexion.

Though mortal issues would still be vital, however, they should be
patterned according to different conditions from the waking world.

The most likely pictorial impulse to the poem is a painting known
as 'Scholars of the Northern Ch'i Dynasty collating Classic Texts',[31]
a scroll of ink and slight colour on silk, after Yen Li-Pen (d. A.D. 673).
At the least, Berryman was aware of the picture,[32] and the title
probably cued that of the poem. More prominent in his mind,
however, was the great scroll of 'Nine Dragons'[33] painted by Ch'en
Jung in A.D. 1244. The Dragon, like all other phenomena, was
regarded by the Chinese as an incarnation of the *Tao*. In connexion
with the 'Nine Dragons' scroll, John Lodge wrote: '. . . the *Tao* is the
one ultimate, tireless activity . . . itself unconditioned by time, space,
or matter . . .'[34]

Squarely underpinning this visual stimulus, moreover, was a fair
knowledge of Zen Buddhist philosophy: Berryman read widely in
the appropriate texts.[35] As one result of his research, he decided that
the setting of the poem should be a Sung Landscape. The landscape
painters of Sung Art (A.D. 960– 1279) achieved a consummately fine
expression of atmospheric perspective by means of tone values and
shading.[36] Far from regarding the predominance of haze and mist in
such paintings as an appropriate type of cloud-cuckoo locus for his
unworldly subject, Berryman recognised, on the contrary, that such
properties imaged the concepts of universal impermanence and
insubstantiality proper to both Buddhism and Taoism. They sought
to illuminate the ultimate reality, the ideality, the universal void of
Buddhism (*sunyata*), in which the universe is perceived as the
universal soul. Rene Grousset describes it in these terms: 'The
landscape thus conceived reflected the influence of the mystical

idealism that the Buddhist sect of the Ch'an had propagated since the T'ang.'[37]

The way that Berryman incorporated the spirit of Ch'an Buddhism into the poem must be understood in the context of the first teachings of 'the compassionate Buddha'.[38] Precursory to Buddha, the *Upanishads* taught the concept of Brahman, which is the metaphysical absolute, the transcendent source and embodiment of all reality. The goal of Hinduism was for each individual to discover his changeless *atman*, his true soul or self which is ultimately at one with Brahman. Buddha, as E. A. Burtt tells us, transformed the goal from union with Brahman to entrance into Nirvana. All created things are subject to cycles of birth and decay, and the last body is that in which freedom of mind is attained: 'Some people are born again; evildoers go to hell; righteous people go to heaven; those who are born free from all worldly desires attain Nirvana.'[39]

The Chinese sect known as Ch'an Buddhism developed out of Buddhist teachings, and is in fact more Chinese than Indian. For the Ch'an Buddhist the goal of existence is union with the First Principle, to be attained by an intuitive vision sometimes called 'vision of the *Tao*'. It is this intuition that informs the 'Dragon Scroll' and Sung landscape, as well as Berryman's conceptualisation of 'Scholars'. A growth from within outwards, together with an absence of striving, are fundamental features of the Taoist pursuit—paradoxically, an absence of pursuit.[40] The Tao produces the world, in fact, by 'not-making' (*wu-wei*). The type of 'unconsciousness' involved here is, according to Alan W. Watts, 'what the exponents of Zen later signified by *wu-hsin*, literally 'no-mind', which is to say un-self-consciousness'.[41]

The Buddhist monk reputated to have founded the Ch'an Buddhist sect in China is Bodhidharma, the twenty-eighth Buddhist Patriarch, who taught 'that there is no Buddha save the Buddha that is in one's own nature'.[42] He was officially welcomed to China by Emperor Wu, first ruler of the Liang Dynasty (reigned A.D. 502— 50). Emperor Wu, who 'became an enthusiastic Buddhist and retired to a monastery some years after reaching the Throne, no doubt in the hope of atoning for misdemeanours committed in getting there,'[43] Berryman features in his second stanza:[44]

> Girls came & crouched with tea. Great Wu pinched one,
> forgetting his later nature.

Berryman takes such a licence with Wu because one of the whimsical aspects of the heaven that he postulates is, as I mentioned above, the probability of continuing desire. 'If there are no erections in heaven,'[45] he wrote in a note, and also: 'subject = heaven—desire'. It is clear that Berryman originally aimed to give this aspect of his theme more emphasis than in the published version, as in this fragment dating from 1960:

> My love came awkward in a great red robe,
> for mountain cold, which when we put aside
> her blush like fire, my throat
> stopt did no honour. I think on these things.

Another draft, written at about the same time, Berryman designated as the original first stanza:

> One has an erection. Of her silk-dim tail
> suffering a sudden thought, he lost his theme
> and stammers. Kind, they wait.
> Paths & fountains meanwhile dream, O flat,
> O flashing.[46]

There are notable precedents for Berryman's facetious treatment of 'Great Wu'. During the reign of Emperor Kublai, the Ch'an monk Yen-hui depicted some figures in a vein of 'mystical humour', as well as Buddhist saints. Knowing of his efforts, Berryman included them in this draft stanza:

> We admitted to our company today
> two hermits, one with a cockatoo,
> a very ordinary hermit,
> the other an ecstatic, who in clouds
> saw more than he would say
> Yen-hui put them in ink on silk
> The ghost of Yen-hui coloured them[47]

The paintings to which the stanza alludes are probably those depicting

> '. . . the hermits Te-kuai and Ha-ma in the Chion-in collection,
> Kyoto, the former, in the manner of the Taoist magicians, emitting

a small genie with his breath, the latter sitting in a thicket, holding flowers in one hand, his eyes full of dreaminess and magic power, his toad 'familiar' clinging to his shoulder and lovingly caressing his hair. Also, in the Kawasaki collection, Kobe, the hermits Han Shan and Shih-te laughing, full of monastic malice.[48]

We must try to appreciate just how Berryman makes his own personal rapprochment, as a member of the Western religious communion, with the alien philosophy of Ch'an Buddhism. In a fragment of verse, he asserts:

> intolerable hope the Christians have,
> shameless, unreasoned.[49]

Otherwise, he notes enigmatically:

> our imag[ination] of eternity
>   *only* ours
>   'O, yes; it is the same'

—riddling phrases which surely approach a reconciliation of the First Principles of Ch'an Buddhism and of Christianity, as in another verse-fragment, 'The heart-beat single of the Universe.' Berryman saw no great division between Christianity and Buddhism; the Absolute God of the Western persuasion is not far removed from the vision of the *Tao*. What is at stake is a shift of emphasis away from an Omnipotent Cause, a God who makes (*wei*), to the Taoist intuition of 'not-making' (*wu-wei*). In the Taoist view, God is not The Creator, nor is there *ex officio* sanctity, but all gods are subject (equally with mankind) to the law (Tao), which is a concept rather like the Neoplatonic demiurge. This shift of emphasis is similar in motive to Buddha's own shift of emphasis away from Brahman towards Nirvana. Where Christianity elects a single Absolute God, Buddhism prefers the notion that all participate in the *Tao*.[50] In a sense, Christianity goes one step further than Buddhism; otherwise, it is possible to say, a similar quest for enlightenment informs both faiths. It is this awareness that gives authority for Berryman's gestures towards apparent syncretism, as in the following draft-fragment:

> Soberer, Mot-zu [sic] came on less for less
> which was the stable of our gentleness

in the middle of the wing of the end
'I'll see you later, and I do mean that,
being a Buddhist and Christian

The poem (as Berryman finally chose to publish it) is in four stanzas, but was originally to have been seven stanzas of seven lines each.[51] The first stanza, which Berryman described in the manuscript as 'v. helpful', dates from 1960, the other three stanzas from 1967.[52] Apart from 'Great Wu', whom we have already accounted for, only two other figures are named, the philosopher Mo-tzu and the painter Ch'en Hung-shou. Surviving manuscripts contain references to two other painters, Yen-hui (described above) and T'ang Yin. T'ang Yin,[53] an outstanding landscape artist (A.D. 1470—1523), was to have been included as a type of the gifted man whose life was full of vicissitudes and misfortunes, at least partially self-inflicted. He was not of the scholar-artist class: early in life his degree was withdrawn because of dishonesty in examinations. He spent his career alternating between periods of zeal for and application to his artistic pursuits, dissipation in Su-chou, and seclusion in Buddhist temples. Despite all the misfortunes and vagaries of his life, he left an enduring and sensitive contribution to the world of art. A man with whom Berryman himself might have identified,[54] T'ang Yin is the subject of the following draft-verse:

T'ang Yin next mentioned: 'If the dragon masters
He's knolling us his life, which we all knew.
Nothing is startling: nothing turned out well.
He's here in the midst of us.
The climactic dancers come and they do sing 'All's well.'[55]

Despite the fact that 'Great Wu', the first emperor to adhere to Ch'an Buddhism, is depicted as a grab-ass simpleton, the poem is not trivial, but a subtle and limpid exploration of its central themes. The tone is varied, moving easily from levity to the sublime, from what Berryman himself would have called the 'low-keyed' word 'Sozzled' to the 'high-keyed' 'ensorcelled' (a near-pun). I cannot speak for any technical influence from Chinese sources on the style,[56] but there is, as seen above, considerable substantial influence from Berryman's sources and background material, rather less formal perhaps than Pound's *Cathay*. In its twenty-eight lines, the poem manages the decorous and the argumentative, the patient and the dismissive.

The manner of the poem is defined by a Chinese sense of protocol. Yet the first lines recount an impropriety (I quote from the original draft version):

> Sozzled, Mo tzu, after a silence vouchsafed
> a word alarming:—We must love them all.
> Affronted, our fathers' shades jumped.[57]

In other words, the poem begins with a defiant assertion, but opens out into areas of ideality and reverence within its eschatalogical context. Mo-tzu's outburst conveys a sense of moral violence; though intoxicated and strident, he apostrophises his conviction. His colleagues are discomfited since he has broached a declaration which is inadmissible. According to the unquestioned formality of the proceedings, the session is closed forthwith: 'Whereat upon consent we broke up for the day.'

Mo-tzu, who lived between the death of Confucius in 479 B.C. and the birth of Mencius in 372 B.C., uttered what was tantamount to a heresy—the doctrine of universal love—to which Berryman here refers. It was necessary, he averred, to love other families and states equally with one's own family. His chief antagonist was the philosopher Mencius, who claimed, according to Burton Watson, 'that Mo tzu's doctrine of universal love is equivalent to "being without a father"; that is, it violates the Confucian concept of a graded love that is strongest for one's own relatives and friends and weaker for those less closely related by blood or association.'[58] Mo-tzu's expression of universal love is one that Berryman would share, albeit for more personal reasons. In the following extract (from the manuscript) the word that Berryman eventually published as "fathers" was originally singular, signifying his own father rather than forebears in general:

> —yes, he went madly on, and paused in search
> of his own dreadful subject:—O the father,
> he cried, must not be all.

(The published version also indicates something more of Mo-tzu's exasperation by changing the word 'paused' to 'waved'.)

Among Chinese philosophers and painters down to Mo-tzu, reverence for tradition and the apotheosis of ancestors was absolute in the observance. Ancient values, in art, philosophy and kinship, were a yardstick for all later practices. This theme is the burden of the remainder of Berryman's poem, centring largely on the putative utterances of Ch'en Hung-shou (1598–1652). The facts of the matter are described by Victoria Contag: 'He was primarily a figure painter, but like the six great Ch'ing masters his style, which is peculiar to him, was determined by the masterpieces of earlier ages . . .'[59] His style was shaped on that of Wu Tao-tzu and Li Lung-mien. Berryman thus misrepresents the historical Ch'en Hung-shou for his own purposes: it cannot be that the real Ch'en Hung-shou would have made the following statement:

> The young shoots unaffected by the wind
> mock our love for their elders.

Nor can it be that he would have praised the painting book of 'The Hall of the ten bamboos' (dated 1633, and therefore contemporary with Ch'en Hung-shou's mature work)[60] to the demerit of all bamboo paintings before and after, though Berryman has him declare:

> I cannot find so well
> ensorcelled those of later or former time.
> Let us apply the highest praise, pure wind,
> to those surpassing masters;—
> having done things, a thing, along that line myself.[61]

Berryman takes such valid poetic licence with this figure (a licence similar to that amply justified in *Homage*) because the poem is largely motivated by his wish to contemporise figures from Chinese history and to have them question major aspects of reverence and traditionalism. Originally it was to have included other incidences of what Berryman felt to be a need for the survival of individuality and of personal discrimination: one example survives in this draft fragment:

> Uttered a fourth: 'Wunk.' Oh, we reflected.
> —I fancy, one at last murmured, he means:
> A jungle double afflicts him for it all
> —Hardly. I see desire
> base.—Surely, horror
> is the burden of this withdrawing grunt.

(In other words, as Berryman himself noted, 'they study it'.) The fragment is almost a parody of scholarly debate: interpretation is free for all. Berryman believed that one has the right—living or dead—to think for oneself and to decide one's own standard of values, even though one defies an authority like Goethe's advocacy of ancient truths. The irony inherent here is profound: despite his conviction that a vision of the *Tao* (necessitating, by definition, a denial of ego) was the salient ideal of mortal existence, Berryman could still not resist his equal conviction that personal thought must continue, even to the point of hubris. The following draft-fragment argues for that point of view:

> Austere and grand, among the several ghosts,
> sat thought, and there will come no end to it
> here, in what we have for heaven.[62]

The poem was one that Berryman liked to return to time and time again. Although, like *The Dream Songs*, it did not fulfil his first designs for its structure, the work did provide him with another perspective on themes which he found obsessive. For one matter, its approach to the concept of death and of the possibility of man's survival after death is more droll than in many instances in the Songs. Berryman is hardly systematic, but the breadth of inquiry which lightly informs the work speaks for the fact that he was attempting to balance the grave and the genial. While the poem does not repudiate the anti-Christian, and indeed the general anti-resurrectional bias of *The Dream Songs* (a work with which it roughly coincided in the writing),[63] its tenor is more syncretic. As Berryman originally intended to picture the scene, his heaven was to be a place in which life is apparently perpetuated as on earth—except that the notion of historical discontinuity is collapsed. In consequence of that indiscretion, changing ideas and convictions confront each other in a (presumably ineffectual) disputation. Berryman could not really synthesise the disparities of attitude and conscience which the poem tries to handle, but he could attempt to explode certain historical prejudices and sacred cows—such as undue respect for the dead, for precedence, and for forefathers. The afterlife that he postulates is shorn of its mystique, and of its terror for the living. The conceptual basis of the poem, as I have tried to outline it, is startling, disabusing, and amusing. It deracinates our mythic ideas of death, vents the (often grievous) differences of opinion to which history lends itself, and also relishes the atemporal illogicality of its own hypothesis: that state of life-in-death in which human frailties (including sexual appetite) endure.

Although it is engaging in manner, the fuller implications of the poem are sublimated so well that they may appear to be almost evasive. As Michael Berryhill has observed, [64] the "dreadful subject" (*l. 5*) alludes to the suicide of Berryman's own father, and yet little personal animosity seems to survive in the poem. The most serious aspect of the poem stems assuredly from the rejection of the father, instanced (as I have mentioned above) by the first draft of the sentence, 'O the father / (he cried) must not be all' (ll. 5–6): Berryman disguised the personal animus by changing the noun from the singular to the plural tense. That attitude conditioned the poem's enunciation of disrespect for elders, for kin, and for tradition. In conclusion, I should point out, it was not accidental that in about 1966 Berryman wrote a letter to his own son (from whom he had been separated for some years) in which he copied out his original first stanza—'from a grown-up poem which I was working at in California three years ago (and in Princeton NJ fourteen years ago)'— and then added this significant comment: 'When you come to understand this stanza, and *why I have now quoted it to you*, you will be an educated Poukie or Paul-sensei.'[65]   [my italics]

Notes

I. INTRODUCTION

1. Quoted in Richard Kostelanetz, "Conversation with Berryman", *Massachusetts Review* vol. XI (Spring 1970), p. 345.
2. Robert A. Fothergill, *Private Chronicles, A Study of English Diaries* (Oxford University Press, 1974), p. 154.
3. Roy Pascal, *Design and Truth in Autobiography* (London: Routledge & Kegan Paul, 1960), p. 111. See also: 'One should speak of autobiography in terms of a 'Gestalt' theory. Its truth lies in the building up of personality through the images it makes of itself, that embody its mode of absorbing and reacting to the outer world, and that are profoundly related to one another at each moment and in the succession from past to present.' (Ibid., p. 188.)
4. John Berryman, 'The Poetry of Ezra Pound', *The Freedom of the Poet* (New York: Farrar, Straus & Giroux, 1976), pp. 260, 263; first published in *Partisan Review* vol. XIV (April 1949).
5. *Berryman's Sonnets* (London: Faber & Faber, 1968); *Homage to Mistress Bradstreet* (New York: Farrar, Straus & Cudahy, 1956), most readily available in England in *Homage to Mistress Bradstreet and Other Poems* (London: Faber & Faber, 1959), occasionally cited in notes to other chapters as *Homage AOP; The Dream Songs* (New York; Farrar, Straus & Giroux, 1969), published in England only in the separate volumes, *77 Dream Songs* (London: Faber & Faber, 1964) and *His Toy, His Dream, His Rest* (London: Faber & Faber, 1969); *Love & Fame* (London: Faber & Faber, 1971).
6. *Delusions, Etc.* (London: Faber & Faber, 1972).
7. Berryman, letter to Sarah Appleton, n.d. ('Saturday the 6th—'); in possession of Sarah Appleton.
8. Interview with Kate Berryman, March 1974.
9. Milton Gilman, 'Berryman and the Sonnets', *Chelsea*, vol. XXII/XXIII, (June 1968), pp. 159, 161—2.
10. E.g. John Frederick Nims, 'Homage in Measure to Mr. Berryman', *Prairie Schooner*, vol. 32 (Spring 1958), p. 6: 'Anne Hutchinson her closest friend! This is the kind of impious fraud that drug-store fiction goes in for.'
11. Letter to Henry Allen Moe, Secretary General of the John Simon Guggenheim Memorial Foundation, 17 February 1953. (Carbon copy in John Berryman Papers, Manuscripts Division, University of Minnesota Libraries: hereafter cited as JBP.)
12. Letter to Van Meter Ames, 19 April 1953 (in possession of Van Meter Ames).
13. Interview with Robert Fitzgerald, April 1974.

14. 'Acceptance Speech for National Book Award', New York: The National Book Committee, 1969.
15. Unpub. DS, folder 8 (3 August 1963). (For this method of signification, see preliminary note to footnotes to Chapter 3 below.)

The best critical study to date is Joel Conarroe, *John Berryman, An Introduction to the Poetry*, (New York: Columbia University Press, 1977).

Preliminary studies include Gary Q. Arpin, *The Poetry of John Berryman* (unpub. Ph.D. Dissertation, University of Virginia, 1971) and Patricia A. Brenner, *John Berryman's Dream Songs: Manner and Matter* (unpub. Ph.D. dissertation, Kent State University, 1970). Arpin's chapters on *Homage to Mistress Bradstreet* and *The Dream Songs* are rather weak and cursory; his Dream Song chapter has been ably revised for *Master of the Baffled House: The Dream Songs of John Berryman* (Derry, Pennsylvania: The Rook Society, 1976), where the author is advisedly cautious about making claims for the structural unity of the Songs (see, for example, pp. 42–4). Like Arpin, Brenner did not have the benefit of access to Berryman's manuscripts and working notes, but she was able to interview the poet; although informative, her work is misleadingly schematic, both in her general examination of what she calls (wrongly) 'the three major influences on the songs' ('. . . the ideological components of Whitman's concept of the poetic being and of Hegel's triadic pattern of thesis—antithesis—synthesis as these pertain to Berryman's use of Freudian psychology—and . . . their interrelationship.'), and in charting discretely what she terms the 'three main psychological odysseys (episodes) each of which differs from the others in subject matter in order to show the protagonist's growth and development' (p. vi). Her eagerness to comprehend the Songs in these schemes leads her to such misdirected (in truth, speculative) statements as this:

> The first section of *The Odyssey* is shorter than the other two sections because the content, the background of the Trojan War and Telemachus' search for his father, is not about Odysseus' actual adventures and struggles to return home. Similarly, the first part of Henry's odyssey (*77 Dream Songs*) is shorter than the other two sections because it gives an account of Henry's background and is thus not part of his immediate adventure home. (p. 134, n. 2)

My chapter on *The Dream Songs* shows (mostly, by implication) that I am at odds with such insistent and often fallacious schematism. Susan Thompson's chapter on Berryman (in *Boundaries of the Self: Poetry by Frost, Roethke and Berryman, Considered in the Light of the Language of Schizophrenia* (Unpub. Ph.D. dissertation, University of Texas at Austin, 1974)) is disappointingly un-illuminating, except for occasional insights such as this: 'Berryman is dealing with a fluid boundary, that of the man who flaunts his secretiveness, or privacy, and yet who is paradoxically something of an exhibitionist in doing so' (p. 124).
16. Unpub. DS, folder 2 (26 September 1958).
17. Joseph Haas, 'Who Killed Henry Pussy-cat? I did, says John Berryman, with love, and a poem, and for freedom O', *Chicago Daily News* (Panorama), 6–7 February 1971, p. 5.
18. Jonathan Sisson, 'My Whiskers Fly: An Interview with John Berryman', *Ivory Tower*, 3 October 1966, p. 16.
19. See Appendix 1.

20. Denis Donoghue, 'Berryman's Long Dream', *Art International* vol. XIII, 20 March 1969, pp. 62–3.
21. Letter, JB to William Meredith, 21 September 1966 (William Meredith).
22. Letter, JB to William Meredith, 14 December 1966 (William Meredith).
23. Letter, Kate Berryman to Maris Thomes, 9 March 1967 (Maris Thomes).

2. 'BITTER SISTER, VICTIM!'—*HOMAGE TO MISTRESS BRADSTREET*

All the manuscript drafts of *Homage to Mistress Bradstreet* are in the John Berryman Papers, Manuscripts Division, University of Minnesota Libraries. They consist of several hundred pages, often just scraps of paper, out of any sequence and undated, mostly holograph fragments and notes, as well as early typescript versions with hand-written comments and corrections. It is not possible to identify individual manuscript pages from the collection, which remains unsorted in any close detail. Some of the early typescript drafts are dated, and I have included such information in the text of my discussion. I have worked out Berryman's modes of composition and the development of his themes by a comparison of the various draft fragments, changes in handwriting, types of paper, sometimes by inference, and by retrospective deduction from more finished drafts.

Other documents referred to are also in the John Berryman Papers, including Diaries and Correspondence, except where stated in the notes below. All unascribed manuscript quotations refer to Berryman's own notes and drafts, and cannot be annotated.

1. Most readily available in *Homage to Mistress Bradstreet and Other Poems* (London: Faber & Faber, 1959, 1967; New York: Farrar, Straus & Giroux, 1968), or (without Berryman's notes) in *Selected Poems 1938–1968*, (London: Faber & Faber, 1972). For convenience, I occasionally refer to the poem by a short title, *Homage*; to the volume as *Homage AOP*.
2. Letter to Haffenden, 9 September 1974.
3. Letter to Haffenden, 30 July 1974.
4. See Ralph Wilson Rader, *Tennyson's Maud: The Biographical Genesis* (Berkeley and Los Angeles: University of California Press, 1963).
5. J. M. Linebarger, *John Berryman* (New York: Twayne, 1974), p. 72.
6. Alan Holder, 'Anne Bradstreet Resurrected', *Concerning Poetry* vol. II (Spring 1969), p. 11.
7. Gabriel Pearson, 'John Berryman—Poet as Medium', *The Review* vol. XV (April 1965), p. 10.
8. Holder, p. 17.
9. Linebarger, p. 68.
10. See John Berryman, 'One Answer to a Question: Changes', *The Freedom of the Poet* (New York: Farrar, Straus and Giroux, 1976), pp. 328–9.

11. Gary Q. Arpin, 'Mistress Bradstreet's Discontents', *John Berryman Studies*, vol. I, no. 3 (July 1975), p. 2.

12. From an interview with Berryman: Peter A. Stitt, 'The Art of Poetry XVI', *Paris Review*, no. 53 (Winter 1972), p. 196.

13. Ibid., p. 197.

14. Ibid., p. 198.

15. John Berryman, 'Introduction', in Matthew G. Lewis, *The Monk* (New York: Grove Press, 1952), p. 13.

16. Ibid., p. 14.

17. Ibid., p. 16.

18. Ibid., p. 328.

19. Stitt, p. 196.

20. References to *Homage to Mistress Bradstreet* are given by the inclusion in my text of a parenthetical note of stanza and line no(s).

See Arpin, 'Mistress Bradstreet's Discontents', pp. 3–4, for what seems to me the correct reading of the last three lines of stanza 14. For Berryman's use of the word 'lingeringly', Sergio Perosa identifies the probable source in 'A Commentary on *Homage to Mistress Bradstreet*', *John Berryman Studies* vol. II, no. 1 (Winter 1976), p. 13. (Originally published, with the Italian translation of *Homage*, in *Omaggio a Mistress Bradstreet* (Torino: Giulio Einaudi editore, 1969).) In addition to Berryman's own notes, Professor Perosa provides a number of valuable glosses, some of them based on Berryman's answers in an interview with Mrs Maria Rita Rohr Philmus. Perosa's annotations are best read in the English translation since, curiously, some notes based on Berryman's oral comments were not included in *Omaggio*: notably, those to (28:5) and (49:4).

For another example of Anne Bradstreet's implicit rejection of her husband, the first lines of the whole poem give some evidence:

> The Governor your husband lived so long
> moved you not, restless, waiting for him?   (1:1–2)

Virginia Prescott Clark, in a most useful dissertation, says that 'modern usage would require "didn't you move"' for constructions like 'moved you not' (l. 2). (*The Syntax of John Berryman's Homage to Mistress Bradstreet* (Ph.D. dissertation, University of Connecticut, 1969), p. 48.) I think it likely, however, that the sense of the phrase may be construed to read 'did not move you'. Clark's thesis works convincingly to demonstrate that, despite Berryman's common use of inversions in the poem, the syntactical pattern is far more regular than has been supposed, and that most elaboration occurs after the establishment of a normal subject-verb pattern. Berryman's verbal structures also lack elaboration in terms of mode, phase, aspect, and voice. Another feature to which she usefully points is that Berryman increases the number of primary stresses and clause terminals, which serve more to slow the rhythm of his lines than to thicken their meaning.

21. G. R. Levy, *The Gate of Horn* (London: Faber & Faber, 1948), p. 306. (The

internal quotation is from Empedocles, ap. Ammon, in Arist., *De. Interp.*,
p. 199.)

22. For another view of Berryman's use of the word 'sifting', it is worth considering
what he may have derived from Gerard Manley Hopkins. 'Then the Bradstreet
poem—it is not easy to see the literary ancestry of that poem. Who has been
named? Hopkins. I don't see that. Of course there are certain verbal practices, but
on the whole, not. The stanza has been supposed to be derived from the stanza of
'The Wreck of the Deutschland.' I don't see that. I have never read 'The Wreck
of the Deutschland,' to tell you the truth, except the first stanza. Wonderful first
stanza.' ('The Art of Poetry', *Paris Review* No. 53 (Winter 1972), pp. 184–5.) In
Homage to Mistress Bradstreet, the heroine tends to the view that the fact of her
sinfulness is its own damnation, an attitude of desperate presumption. It is this
philosophy of despair and guilt which seems to speak for the influence of
Hopkins. That in rhythm, metre, and manner, Berryman's poem probably does
owe something to Hopkins has been sufficiently observed by reviewers to need
no further mention here. What strikes me as more important are coincidences of
diction. Hopkins' words 'lull', 'flush', 'flee', and 'sheer', appear in stanzas 30 and
31 of *Homage*, 'sifting' in stanza 38. All these words are shared between the first
two stanzas of 'The Wreck of the Deutschland' (a fact which largely
corroborates Berryman's remark quoted from the interview above) and two
related poems, 'Carrion Comfort' and 'No worst, there is none'.
In stanza 38 of *Homage*, Anne wavers:

> I am *sifting*, nervous, and bold.
> The light is changing.   Surrender this loveliness
> you cannot make me do.   But I will.   Yes.
> What *horror*, down stormy air,
> warps towards me?

(All italics within the quotations cited in this footnote are mine.) She vacillates
between yielding to possession by the devil and vowing herself to Christ. The
echo of Hopkins' feeling of

> The swoon of a heart that the sweep and the hurl of thee trod
>   Hard *down* with a *horror* of height

is, to borrow Berryman's own phrase, ironic and meaningful. The power of God
overwhelms and recovers Hopkins. In contrast, the horror that afflicts Anne
Bradstreet 'warps' towards her. Where Hopkins is 'soft *sift* / in an hourglass', he
has yet the 'vein' of 'Christ's gift' to channel him. Anne is merely 'sifting',
slipping and vacillating, without good guidance. Her self-apprehension inspires
the desperate feeling that she will surely find herself among the chaff that Christ
will burn in perpetual fire (stanza 46:3–4, an allusion to Matthew 3:12, as
Berryman's notes to the poem indicate). In this connection, it seems significant

that in 'Carrion Comfort' Hopkins remits similar feelings of despair, asking Despair why he would

fan,

O in turns of tempest, me heaped there; me frantic to avoid thee and *flee*?
Why? That my chaff might fly; my grain lie *sheer* and clear.
Nay in all that toil, that coil, since (seems) I kissed the *rod*, . . .

A like sense of despair and remorse affects Anne Bradstreet. Hopkins regrets the fact that he wrestled with an angelic incubus or a bestial nightmare—ultimately, of course, with God—in the same manner as Anne fights against her possession by the incubus of sin, as in stanza 28:

Falls on me what I like a witch,
for lawless holds, annihilations of law   (28:4−5)

where the word 'holds', as Berryman told Perosa, signifies 'sexual gropings' (p. 17). In 'No worst, there is none', Hopkins prays to the Virgin Mary for relief from 'Woe, world-sorrow' which would afflict him one moment, 'Then *lull*, then leave off'. He argues that the mind has mountains, 'cliffs of fall, / Frightful, *sheer*, no-man-fathomed', and concludes that the only comfort is that

all

Life death does end and each day dies with sleep.

The sentiment is one that Berryman shared. In respect of Anne Bradstreet, these feelings take the form of a death-wish:

In the article of death I budge.
Eat my sore breath, Black Angel.   Let me die.   (47:4−5)

in case she should plunge into a deeper sinfulness. In stanza 48 she is suffering hallucinations, and in stanza 50 draws towards old age:

I look.   I bear to look.   Strokes once more his *rod*.   (50:8)

In 'Carrion Comfort', Hopkins speaks of the anguish he has endured since he "kissed the rod", that is, submitted himself to the will of Christ. For Anne Bradstreet, Christ's rod is one that he 'Strokes' or fondles, it may be inferred, in pleased anticipation of bringing down in judgement upon her. Holder's observation (p. 16) is also relevant in this context: '. . . we find a woman highly susceptible to what she conceives of as a generalized phallic force. In one of the poem's most memorable moments, she says:

'a male great pestle smashes
small women swarming towards the mortar's rim in vain (37).'

Christ's rod becomes confused in her mind with what the poem seems to insist is the profanity of her sexual rebelliousness.

23. MS. draft. The first two lines quoted were retained in stanza 49 (ll. 1–2), the line 'I do writhe and choke' being replaced by 'Ruined laughter sounds / outside (ll. 3–4). As Berryman told Perosa, the phrase 'ruined laughter' signifies 'the demonic laughter of the dead', and 'outside' marks the transition out of delirium (p. 22).

24. Helen Campbell, *Anne Bradstreet and Her Times* (Boston: D. Lothrop Co., 1891).

25. The use of the work 'stark' in l. 8 (which deliberately includes the connotation of 'stark naked') is true to the psychology of the persona; the 'poet's' chief interest is sexual. He tells Anne Bradstreet that her eyes look 'mild', but he also imputes to her the proposition that her 'eyes look to me' (2:1), i.e. that she herself is already showing an interest in him.

26. See also the phrase 'I lie wrong' (13:6), which, as Berryman told Perosa, 'refers to the hope, again disappointed, of a pregnancy' (p. 12).

27. Although the historical Anne Bradstreet was 'restored' (John Harvard Ellis, *The Works of Anne Bradstreet* (Gloucester, 1962), p. 5) after a bout of smallpox, Berryman distorts the record by insisting that his Anne Bradstreet is scarred by the disease, as Holder points out. I discuss other aspects of Anne's disfigurement below, in connection with stanzas 28 and 29. Here it is important to illuminate the way in which Anne Bradstreet regards her disease as divine retribution for sin in (29:1–4). As Berryman's own notes to the poem explain, these lines contain an allusion to Isaiah (1:5). I have not seen it remarked elsewhere that this biblical quotation concerns God's infliction of sickness—wounds, bruises, open sores— as the wages of betrayal. In a literal sense, the verse speaks of a Judah punished for its sins. Holder, who puts a more secular interpretation on the matter, misapprehends the fundamental importance of Berryman's theological implications: '. . . he might have wanted to brand Anne Bradstreet externally so as to increase our sense of the anguish and displacement that he attributes to her. That is, the smallpox might be intended as emblematic of Anne's alienated condition.' (p. 15)

28. Again, the phrase 'the Atantic wound' (8:1) is a specific reference to Anne's separation from her husband, but is best glossed by comparison with Berryman's short poem 'Canto Amor' (*Homage AOP.*, p. 64) which assimilates sex to death in ll. 19–21. Similarly, in number 77 of *Berryman's Sonnets*, the wedding ring, symbol of wedlock, is viewed with sufficient resentment as to be called 'a wound'. Anne Bradstreet finds her marriage a gall mitigated only later by her children. It is interesting to learn from the typescript of the first ten stanzas sent to Allen Tate on 27 February 1953, that (8:1) originally read: 'That past our Atlantic horror our world is large'. (Allen Tate Papers, Princeton University Library.)

29. Campbell, p. 256. On the question of influence in general, it is clear that Berryman lays himself under a far greater obligation for points of detail (as against texture and style) to Helen Campbell's biography than to anything in

Anne Bradstreet's own work. He stated that 'I was concerned with her though, almost from the beginning, as a woman, not much as a poetess.' ('One Answer to a Question', p. 328.) Later he was even more emphatic: 'The idea was not to take Anne Bradstreet as a poetess—I was not interested in that' (Stitt, p. 195). It is curious and misleading, therefore, that one of Bradstreet's own critics, Elizabeth Wade White, should observe that, 'Although Berryman dismisses Anne's verse as 'bald abstract didactic rime' . . . his own stanzas show that his romantic image of the poet herself grew from a thorough reading of her work,' and that she goes on to note, without reproof: 'The reading of Berryman's poem, as an introduction to the work of Anne Bradstreet herself, is recommended by Hyatt H. Waggoner in his recently published study, *American Poets from the Puritans to the Present*.' (*Anne Bradstreet*, (New York: Oxford University Press, 1971), pp. 378–9.)

30. Cited in Perosa, p. 12.
31. Holder, p. 14.
32. Berryman, 'One Answer to a Question: Changes', p. 329.
33. '(The grammar cannot generate the initial fragmentary part of this sentence; again there is no finite verb.)' Clark, p. 134.
34. Cited in Perosa, p. 10.
35. Berryman's introduction of lines concerning the heresiarch Anne Hutchinson (whose doctrine—really a belief in the 'Inward light'—outraged the Puritan sensibility) serves the same purpose, since he causes Anne Bradstreet to respond intimately: 'Bitter sister, victim! I miss you' (25:2). As Alan Holder has pointed out, Berryman 'is positing a relationship between the two women and a response by the Puritan poet for which there is no evidence . . . in the poet's writings there is no mention at all of that early martyr' (p. 13). Holder proceeds to draw a tentative conclusion—'it is possible to see a connection between Berryman's apparent sympathy for Mrs. Hutchinson, and the description of Dudley's final sickness' (p. 14)—without apparently recognising the personally vitriolic implications of the passage within the larger context of the poem.
36. Letter, Brenda Engel to John Haffenden, n.d. (1973).
37. Carol Johnson, 'John Berryman and Mistress Bradstreet: A Relation of Reason', *Essays in Criticism*, vol. XIV (October 1964), p. 390.
38. Interview with Brenda Engel, May 1975.
39. Perosa, p. 14. The internal quotation refers to John Ciardi's review, "The Researched Mistress", *Saturday Review* vol. XL (23 March 1957), pp. 36–7.
40. Berryman's use of the verb 'greens' in the second line quoted, which survived in the published version (21 : 2), may owe something to Goethe's theory of colours. (Berryman first drew attention to the influence of that theory on Stephen Crane in *Stephen Crane* (New York: Meridian Books, 1962), p. 289 *et passim*, first published in 1950.) According to Goethe, the colour green conveys 'a distinctly grateful impression', one of repose. (See Rupprecht Matthaei, *Goethe's Colour Theory*, trans. Herb Aach, (New York: Van Nostrand Reinhold, 1971)
41. Both Allen Tate letters are in Correspondence, John Berryman Papers.
42. Letter, Berryman to Allen Tate, 6 February 1953 (Allen Tate Papers, Princeton University Library).
43. Berryman, 'One Answer to a Question: Changes', p. 329.
44. Ian Hamilton, 'John Berryman', *London Magazine*, vol. IV n.s. (February 1965), p. 98.

45. Berryman, 'One Answer to a Question: Changes', p. 329.
46. MS. dated 12 February 1953.
47. Cf. 'Thou seest my white hayres are blossomes for the grave', Greene, *Pandosto*, cited in Morris Palmer Tiller, *A Dictionary of the Proverbs in England* (Ann Arbor: University of Michigan Press, 1950), p. 281.
48. Perosa annotates the last line quoted with Berryman's oral statement: 'Invented expression to indicate casually the duration of existence, in contraposition to the religious and providential conception of life held in Bradstreet's time' (p. 24).
49. Richard Kostelanetz, 'Conversation with Berryman', *Massachusetts Review*, vol. XI (Spring 1970), p. 345.

3. 'THE CARE & FEEDING OF LONG POEMS'

The manuscripts of 77 *Dream Songs* and *His Toy, His Dream, His Rest* are in the Manuscripts Division, University of Minnesota Libraries. They run to several hundred pages, including fragments of Songs and note pages as well as more finished versions in holograph and typescript. Since the Manuscripts Division has classified all that material under the head of 'Published Dream Songs', I cannot annotate the notes and quotations which I have extracted from those manuscripts. All manuscript material relating to unpublished Dream Songs, which includes work sheets and notes pertinent to *The Dream Songs*, are contained in separate Hollinger boxes internally divided by numbered folders. In the notes below and elsewhere in the book, I have identified the location of specific sheets with the abbreviation 'Unpub. DS', followed by a folder number. All unascribed quotations refer either to Berryman's miscellaneous notes and drafts of the Dream Songs or to the category of Published Dream Songs.

Additional Berryman material derives from letters or other documents in the possession of other libraries or individuals, which I identify in parentheses.

References to Berryman's work. *The Dream Songs* (published in England only in two volumes as 77 *Dream Songs* and *His Toy, His Dream, His Rest*), are given within the body of the text by a parenthetical note of stanza and/or line numbers.

1. Geoffrey Bullough, *Narrative and Dramatic Sources of Shakespeare* (London: Routledge & Kegan Paul, 1957), vol. I, p. 6. Cited in Unpub. DS., folder 2.
2. Stitt, 'The Art of Poetry XVI', *Paris Review* 53 (Winter 1972), pp. 194–5.
3. Ibid., p. 191.
4. Ibid.
5. Ibid., p. 190.
6. Robert Payne, *The Fathers of the Western Church* (New York: Viking, 1951), p. 137. Cited in Unpub. DS., folder 16.
7. Jack Vincent Barbera, 'Shape and Flow in *The Dream Songs*', *Twentieth Century Literature* vol. 22, no. 2 (May 1976), p. 147.
8. Ibid., p. 148.
9. Ibid., p. 152.
10. Ibid., pp. 150, 154.
11. Adrienne Rich, 'Mr. Bones, He Lives', *Nation* vol. CXCVIII (25 May 1964), p. 538.
12. Ibid., p. 540.

13. Letter, JB to Randall Jarrell, 25 June 1963 (Berg Collection, New York Public Library).

14. Martin Berg, 'A Truly Gentle Man Tightens and Paces: An Interview with John Berryman', *Minnesota Daily*, University of Minnesota (20 January 1960), p. 9.

15. Poetry, vol. LXXV (January 1950), pp. 192—6. See also Berryman's *His Thought Made Pockets & The Plane Buckt* (Pawlet, Vermont: Claude Fredericks, 1958), pp. vi—viii. One section, 'from *The Black Book* (i)', is reprinted in *Selected Poems 1938—1968* (London: Faber & Faber, 1972), p. 32.

16. Jonathan Sisson, 'My Whiskers Fly: An Interview with John Berryman', *Ivory Tower*, vol. XIV (3 October 1966), p. 16.

17. Joseph Haas, 'Who Killed Henry Pussy-cat? I did, says John Berryman with Love and a Poem, and for Freedom O', *Chicago Daily News*, 6 February 1971, p. 5.

18. The only other possibility is that JB intends to refer to the unlikely Emperor Ch'ien-Lung (1736—1796), who was a prodigious but undiscriminating Art collector.

19. Salomon August Andrée (b. 1854); Nils Strindberg (b. 1872); Knut H. F. Fraenkel (b. 1870); their bodies were discovered by a Norwegian expedition. See *The Andrée Diaries*, trans. Edward Adams-Ray (London: John Lane, The Bodley Head, 1931).

20. Barbera, op. cit., p. 150. The internal quotation is from William Meredith, 'In Loving Memory of the Late Author of "The Dream Songs"', Foreword to *John Berryman: A Checklist*, ed. Richard J. Kelly (Metuchen, New Jersey: The Scarecrow Press, 1972), p. xiii.

21. Letter, JB to mother, 25 April 1958 (Mrs Jill Berryman).

22. Letter, JB to Dr A. Boyd Thomes, 14 September 1958 (Dr A. Boyd Thomes).

23. Written *c*. 1945; three of those Songs were originally published in *Partisan Review* vol. XIII (Summer 1946), later collected in *The Dispossessed* (New York: William Sloane, Inc., 1948). Available in *Homage to Mistress Bradstreet and Other Poems* (London: Faber & Faber, 1959), pp. 76—84; two of the Songs are in *Selected Poems*, pp. 20—1.

24. John Berryman, 'Plan for Work', submitted unsuccessfully to the Guggenheim Foundation in 1948 (JBP).

25. Notebook dated 1948, p. 11 (JBP).

26. As note 35.

27. Notebook, 18 October 1948, p. 22.

28. Pub. DS, folder 2.

29. Both works unpublished, in JBP.

30. Unpub. DS, folder 16.

31. Unpub. DS, folder 4.

32. This quotation, and all others in the paragraph, are from Unpub. DS, folder 2.

33. H. T. Wade-Gery, *The Poet of the Iliad* (Cambridge University Press, 1952).

34. Unpub. DS, folder 12.

35. Unpub. DS, folder 2. The substance of this paragraph is drawn from a note dated 5 March 1959.

36. The MS. note reads: 'poss, end of II (an assimilation of "I" and "he" as in I, 1,—v. rare) *or* poss. follow w. "I am, outside" and so end II (Purg.)—*or* even I.'

37. Unpub. DS, folder 2.

38. Ibid.

39. Unpub. DS, folder 2; the schema is dated 26 September 1958. The rest of this paragraph draws on another note in the same folder.
40. Unpub. DS, folder 16.
41. Unpub. DS, folder 1.
42. Unpub. DS, folder 16.
43. The comment derives from Berryman's work 'Self-analysis, Record 2' (unpublished; dated 12 August 1955), p. 107.
44. Paul John Kameen, *John Berryman's Dream Songs: A Critical Introduction* (DA dissertation, State University of New York at Albany, 1976), pp. 43–4.
45. Unpub. DS, folder 2.
46. In connection with the uncollected Song 'The jolly old man', Berryman commented: ' . . . for reasons which I don't remember, I wiped Mabel out and never printed that song. For a long time after that, every now and then Ann would complain that Mabel didn't seem to be taking any part in the poem, but I couldn't find myself able to put her back in the poem, so it has no heroine.' (Stitt, 'The Art of Poetry XVI', p. 194.) Song 30 is called 'Nostalgia, Mabel' in a MS. draft, 17 May 1958.
47. Unpub. DS, folder 16.
48. Unpub. DS, folder 8.
49. Richard Kostelanetz, 'Conversation with Berryman', *Massachusetts Review*, 11 (Spring 1970), p. 341.
50. Ibid., p. 345.
51. 'Auden's Prose', *The New York Review of Books* 1 (29 August 1963), p. 19.
52. W. H. Auden, *The Dyer's Hand* (London; Faber and Faber, 1975), p. 110.
53. See John Haffenden, 'Introduction', *Henry's Fate and Other Poems*, p. xv. Another unfulfilled possibility for which Berryman provided was that Henry's friend should be a type of Proteus (Unpub. DS, folder 16), after the model perhaps of Proteus and Valentine in *Two Gentlemen of Verona*. At least two fragments survive which support the association:

> Proteus and Henry, witty and lovely, doing
> the wings them Proteus and Henry do
> I don't see how they could.
> When the terrible dancers spring to attention, wooing,
> I would not leave them as I must soon screw.
> 'Mercy' said Proteus, 'should—'

and:

> Henry's astonishing friend Proteus
> swarmed to the rescue; else the man was dead.

54. Unpub. DS, folder 2.
55. Unpub. DS, folder 2.
56. Carbon copy in JBP.
57. Letter in possession of Dr A. Boyd Thomes.
58. *The Freedom of the Poet* (New York: Farrar, Straus & Giroux, 1976), p. 330.
59. Ernest C. Stefanik, Jr., 'An Entrance', *John Berryman Studies* vol. 1, no. 4 (Fall 1975), pp. 52–3.

60. In that connection, see a remark in Unpub. DS, folder 11, 'I won't for 5 years publish a book in the U.S.' (21 May 1958).

61. G. R. Levy, *The Gate of Horn* (London: Faber & Faber, 1948), p. 280.

62. Undated letter to A. Alvarez, cited in letter to Haffenden, n.d. (1972).

63. Philip Carrington, *According to Mark* (Cambridge University Press, 1960).

64. William J. Martz, *John Berryman* (University of Minnesota pamphlets on American Writers: University of Minnesota Press, 1969), p. 36.

65. Barbera, p. 157.

66. John Plotz *et al*, 'An Interview with John Berryman', *Harvard Advocate*, vol. CIII no. 1 (Spring 1969), p. 6.

67. Joseph Campbell, *The Hero with a Thousand Faces* (Cleveland and New York: Meridian, 1956).

68. Ibid., p. 69.

69. Unpub. DS, folder 2.

70. Kostelanetz, p. 346.

71. Unpub. DS, folder 2 (MS. dated 2 October 1958).

72. Unpub. DS, folder 8.

73. Unpub. DS, folder 2 (MS. dated 11/12 October 1958).

74. *The World's Great Poets Reading at the Festival of Two Worlds, Spoleto, Italy* (New York: Applause Productions, 1970).

75. Interview with Mrs Jill Berryman, March 1974.

76. Unpub. DS, folder 2 (MS. timed at 5 a.m., 'insomniac in hospital').

77. Unpub. DS, folder 2.

78. Unpub. DS, folder 16.

79. 'One Answer to a Question: Changes', pp. 329–30.

80. Barbera, p. 150.

81. JB, letter to Richard Wilbur, 14 September 1963 (in possession of Richard Wilbur).

82. JB, letter to Allen Tate, n.d. (*c*. April 1963) (Princeton University Library).

83. JB, letter to Allen Tate, 26 June 1963 (Princeton University Library).

84. JB, letter to Valerie Trueblood, 7 July 1966 (in possession of Valerie Trueblood).

85. JB, letter to Ann Berryman, n.d. (*c*. October 1965) (carbon copy in JBP).

86. Barbera, p. 161.

87. Anne B. Warner, 'Berryman's Elegies: One Approach to *The Dream Songs*', *John Berryman Studies* vol. II, no. 3 (Summer 1976), p. 12.

88. See, for example, an anonymous article, 'Pulitzer Prize Once a "Nothing" to Him', *The Minneapolis Star*, Tuesday 4 May 1965; "Showing a visitor a ragged carbon copy of the final song, he said he expects to finish the rest of the poem within a year.'

89. Stitt, 'The Art of Poetry XVI', p. 193.

90. Kostelanetz, p. 341.

91. Ibid., p. 345.

92. "Despondency and Madness: On Lowell's 'Skunk Hour'", *The Freedom of the Poet*, p. 321.

93. William Heyen, "John Berryman: A Memoir and an Interview", *The Ohio Review* vol. XV, no. 00 (Winter 1974), p. 63.

94. Douglas Dunn, 'Gaiety and Lamentation: The Defeat of John Berryman', *Encounter* vol. XLIII (August 1974), p. 73.

95. Jerome J. McGann, *Don Juan in Context* (London: John Murray, 1976), p. 109.

96. Ibid., p. 4.
97. *Henry's Fate & Other Poems* (New York: Farrar, Straus & Giroux, 1977; London: Faber & Faber, 1978), p. 46.

4. *LOVE & FAME* AND BERRYMAN'S LUCK

1. An interview with John Berryman, Peter Stitt, 'The Art of Poetry XVI', *The Paris Review* no. 53 (Winter 1972), p. 200.
2. *Ibid.*, p. 199.
3. *Love & Fame* (London: Faber & Faber, 1971), p. 61.
4. Ibid.
5. J. M. Linebarger, *John Berryman* (New York: Twayne, 1974), p. 129.
6. Ibid.
7. John Bayley, 'John Berryman: A Question of Imperial Sway', in Rober Boyers (ed.), *Contemporary Poetry in America* (New York: Schocken Books, 1974), p. 71.
8. Ibid., p. 69.
9. 'Images of Elspeth', *Love & Fame*, p. 19.
10. J. D. McClatchy, 'John Berryman: The Impediments to Salvation', *Modern Poetry Studies* vol. 6 (Winter 1975), p. 266.
11. Peter Stitt, 'Berryman's Last Poems', *Concerning Poetry* vol. 6 (Spring 1973), p. 9.
12. Ernest C. Stefanik, 'A Cursing Glory: John Berryman's *Love & Fame*', *Renascence* vol. 25, pp. 115–16.
13. Ibid., p. 127.
14. Ibid., p. 121.
15. Ibid., p. 115.
16. Ibid., p. 116.
17. Ibid., p. 121.
18. Ibid., p. 126.
19. Ibid.
20. Jonathan Galassi, 'Sorrows and Passions of His Majesty the Ego', *Poetry Nation* no. 2, pp. 117–120.
21. Ibid., p. 119.
22. Stefanik, p. 115.
23. Final stanza of 'The Home Ballad', *Love & Fame*, p. 80.
24. *Love & Fame*, p. 22.
25. Edward Neill, for example, has called *Love & Fame* a 'morally chaotic work', in which Berryman's 'poetic integrity and authenticity' consists in what Neill has 'tentatively' defined 'as a fidelity to a kind of regressive complacency'. ('Ambivalence of Berryman: an Interim Report', *Critical Quarterly* vol. XVI, (Autumn 1974), pp. 275, 270.) Other notably pejorative notices include those by Robert Phillips, 'John Berryman's Literary Offenses', *The Confessional Poets* (Carbondale and Edwardsville: Southern Illinois University Press, 1973), pp. 92–106, and by Hayden Carruth, 'Love, Art and Money', *Nation*, 2 November 1970, pp. 437–8.
26. *Love & Fame*, pp. 31–33.

27. MSS., and the galley proofs to which I refer next, are located in the John Berryman Papers, Manuscripts Division, University of Minnesota.

28. *Love & Fame*, p. 49.

29. Cf. 'In all the looseness and plainness of *Love & Fame* there is not much successful intensity, but the anecdotes and reminiscences draw you forward at a great clip, keen to see how it all comes out.' (Clive James, 'Two Essays on John Berryman: (2) On *Love & Fame*', *The Metropolitan Critic*, London: Faber, 1974, p. 83.

30. Berryman met Brian Boydell, now Professor of Music at Trinity College, Dublin on 11 February 1937 (JB, letter to his mother, 14 February 1937, JBP). For a time Berryman became closely associated with what Boydell called their 'frightfully aesthetic/intellectual group' (letter Boydell to Haffenden, 13 July 1972), which gathered in his digs on Midsummer Common. On 22 February Boydell first played for Berryman the five records of *The Curlew*, Peter Warlock's melancholy settings for four of Yeats's early poems, 'O curlew, cry no more in the air', 'Pale brows, still hands and dim hair', 'The Withering of the Boughs' and 'I wander by the edge of this desolate lake', Berryman was convinced by the performance that the music needed to be heard in the dark. Peter Warlock was the pseudonym of Philip Heseltine, a mild, conscientious, melancholy man, who, adopting his other name, had assumed a role which was blustering mad, and amorous. As Peter Warlock, he managed difficult, extremely sad music of which *The Curlew* was the consummate type. Norman Stewart, who had been a friend of the composer's, told Berryman on this occasion that he felt Warlock had committed suicide at an early age from the realisation 'that Hazeltine [sic] would return and take possession from time to time throughout his lifetime'. Berryman liked Heseltine's music clearly because of its melancholy aestheticism, and because of what he took to be a bizarre and maudlin pose, a mask. '"The Curlew",' Berryman wrote, 'is beautiful but utterly despairing, the most desolate art I know.' (letter, JB to mother, dated 23 February 1937—actually, a chronicle letter running until 6 March, JBP.)

31. Andrew Chiappe asked Berryman to give the talk on Yeats on 16 January 1937 (letter, JB to mother, 17 January 1937, JBP). The invitations, signed by G. E. Hewan, gave notice that JB would speak on 'W. B. Yates'.

32. *Love & Fame*, pp. 50—1.

33. In view of Berryman's use of the word 'companion', it is interesting to learn from his contemporary account that he was utterly fascinated with the man, whom he first met at the beginning of March 1937:

> . . . 22 but very wise . . . Extraordinary modesty and the most destructive mind I've ever encountered; idea that no one is of the slightest value, but he is worth a little less than anyone else . . . I liked him extremely from the first, but very strange and uncannily silent in company he is. Constant delusions, terror of strangers and people: all, he thinks, believe him mad . . . He will unquestionably be insane in a few months if all continues, but I think it won't . . . Fantastic theories he has and devastating, some of them . . . one day a complete plan for criticism of the novel . . . the next the most profound despair. He was not at the university here but knew Witkenstein [sic], the metaphysician, well, and has been greatly influenced by him. There is a total lack of both conviction and pretension in all that he does. But I am certain that if his balance can be restored in the next year he may do great work. If not, he

will infallibly kill himself. I would do all I can even if we were not, as we already are, *close friends* [my italics]. (Letter, JB to mother, 15 March 1937, JBP.)

Berryman met Dylan Thomas, who figures only in the third line of the same poem ('This guy Dylan Thomas though is hotter than anyone we have in America'), at the same time, but was—then—much less struck by him than by Barton. Thomas was in Cambridge to give a reading at the Nashe Society: disciples gathered about him (as Berryman described to his mother, 'a mad group of people who chanted poetry and drank and argued till all hours' (letter to mother, 6 March 1937, JBP)) and celebrated with a binge that lasted literally for days—from 28 February to 5 March—at Mill Road where, in Katharine Fraser's absence, Thomas was staying. The celebrants included Patrick Barton and Andrews Wanning, who remembers one moment when Berryman, referring to Thomas, told him, 'Hush, the poet's asleep!' (Interview with Andrews Wanning, 11 March 1974.)

34. Linebarger, *John Berryman*, p. 127.
35. 'Images of Elspeth', *Love & Fame*, p. 19.
36. A phrase used by Roy Pascal to characterise St. Augustine's awareness of the problems of remembering (apropos of Book X of *The Confessions*), *Design and Truth in Autobiography* (London: Routledge & Kegan Paul), 1960, p. 69.
37. *Love & Fame*, pp. 23–4.
38. Letter, Dean Herbert E. Hawkes to JB, 2 October 1934. (College Papers, Office of the Registrar, Columbia University, hereafter cited as CP.)
39. Berryman's abridgement of Locke's *Essay Concerning Human Understanding* is 34 pages long ('College Papers', folder 1, JBP). In a published essay, he refers to it as 'a thirty-page digest'. ('Three and a Half Years at Columbia', in Wesley First (ed.), *University on the Heights* (New York: Doubleday and Co., 1969), p. 53.) In the same essay, he states that the notebook in question 'ran to several hundred pages'. Cf. letter. JB to Dean Hawkes, 'a 55,000-word overdue notebook' (16 January 1936, CP).
40. *Love & Fame*, p. 52.
41. Ibid., pp. 19–20.
42. Ibid., p. 43.
43. Ibid., p. 28.
44. Ibid., p. 55.
45. Linebarger, *John Berryman*, p. 132.
46. *Love & Fame*, p. 61. MS. draft in JBP.
47. Ibid., pp. 95–6. This 'Afterword' is substantially the same text as that of 'Scholia to Second Edition' (i.e. of the second American edition, 1972, pp. xiii–xiv), although the 'Scholia' curiously antedates the 'Afterword'.
48. *Love & Fame*, 1st edn. (New York: Farrar, Straus & Giroux, 1970, p. 48 and p. 52 respectively. 'To B— E—' is a poem of twenty lines in five equal stanzas; it is presumably titled on the model of certain of Byron's poems, or of Stephen Dedalus's address 'To E— C—' in Joyce's *A Portrait of the Artist as a Young Man*.
49. Loc. cit.
50. 'The Ironic Title of Berryman's *Love & Fame*', *Notes on Contemporary Literature* vol. 5, no. 4 (n.d.), p. 11. Wilson discusses too the possible sources for the title, whether the last line of Keats's sonnet, 'When I have fears, that I may cease to be',

or l. 40 of Pope's 'Eloisa to Abelard'. Robert Phillips, in *The Confessional Poets* (Carbondale: Southern Illinois University Press, 1973, p. 98) remarks on the Keats possibility; Edward Mendelson ('How to Read Berryman's *Dream Songs*' in Robert B. Shaw (ed.), *American Poetry Since 1960* (Cheadle Hulme, Carcanet Press, 1973, p. 40), on the Pope context. C. D. Corcoran informs me that another possible source is l. 26 of George Herbert's poem 'The Thanksgiving' (see C. A. Patrides (ed.), *The English Poems of George Herbert* (London: Dent, 1974), p. 56), although it seems that none of these 'sources' are of necessary interpretative consequence, since the title is not obviously an allusion.

51. Linebarger, *John Berryman*, p. 132.
52. *Love & Fame*, p. 16.
53. MS. draft in JBP.
54. Interview with Berryman, *The Paris Review*, p. 201.
55. 'After Mr. Bones: John Berryman's Last Poems', *The Hollins Critic* vol. XIII, no. 4 (October 1976), p. 5.
56. Proofs in JBP.
57. *Love & Fame*, p. 95.

APPENDIX 2.   BERRYMAN'S 'HUNCH OF HEAVEN'

All manuscript citations refer to the John Berryman Papers, Manuscripts Division, University of Minnesota Libraries. References are cited simply as MSS. Wherever possible, closer identification includes the date of individual manuscript sheets, and/or their location among the Papers. References to books are to those that John Berryman himself possessed, and that he had in some part read, except where otherwise stated.

1. Published in *Delusions, Etc.* (New York: Farrar, Straus &Giroux; London: Faber & Faber 1972) pp. 34–5; referred to hereafter as 'Scholars'.
2. The parallel with Dante was first sketched by Berryman in manuscript: MSS: (Miscellaneous Poetry, Box 1, folder 3).
3. The terms used in this sentence are Berryman's own, from MSS. cited in note 2 above.
4. The phrase was used by Berryman in an abstract of 'Plans for Work' (?1949), p. 3, submitted to the Guggenheim Foundation in suit of a Fellowship award. Other works mentioned in this schema included 'The Black Book'. A carbon copy of the original submission is in MSS. Correspondence by Subject— 'Guggenheim' folder.
5. MSS. as note 2 above.
6. Misc. Poetry, Box 1, folder 4.
7. MSS. of *Delusions Etc.*
8. MSS: Misc. Poetry (unpublished), folder 28:

Pavilion [sic]
'Scholars at the Orchid ~~Garden~~
Chinese, meditative
a dialogue at last'

(This is an early note, possibly from 1948.)

9. 'T. S. Eliot and France', unpublished article, MSS: Unpublished Prose, n.d.
10. R. G. Collingwood, *The Idea of History* (New York: Galaxy Books, 1956), p. 147.
11. Recorded in *Time*, 16 November, 1959.
12. '"Song of Myself": Intention and Substance', *The Freedom of the Poet* (New York: Farrar, Straus & Giroux, 1976; London: Faber & Faber, 1977), pp. 227–41.
13. Ibid., p. 235.
14. Ibid., p. 237.
15. See Sir Charles Sherrington, *Man on His Nature* (New York: Doubleday, 1953), p. 262; a book cited by Berryman in the reading list for his course. *Humanities 132*—'The Meaning of Life', at the University of Minnesota.
16. Fred Hoyle, *Frontiers of Astronomy* (New York: Mentor, 1957), p. 284. In his own copy of this work, Berryman has marked this page for attention.
17. In a note-page for his course, *Humanities 132*, Berryman wrote: 'But: (me) the *shock* of the loss of the *entire* body, to the mind.'
18. Ibid.
19. Julian Huxley, 'The Meaning of Death', *Essays in Popular Science* (London: Chatto & Windus, 1926), pp. 106–27. This book is also cited in the reading list for Berryman's course *Humanities 132*.
20. Ibid., p. 114.
21. Despite Berryman's disavowal of the notion of re-incarnation, one of his favourite anecdotes (from Hamann by way of Kierkegaard) concerned the return of the dead as posterity. See 'An Interview with John Berryman', *The Harvard Advocate* vol. CIII, no. 1 (Spring 1969), p. 9.
22. MSS, Unpublished Dream Songs. The date of this poem is within a month of some of the draft fragments relating to 'Scholars'. See also another unpublished, uncompleted Song, 'Henry House II', which includes the lines:

you kindly up there, just now, don't forget his soul.
I came on faster, being freely oiled,
at one time.

This poem was written on the back of a reading list for Berryman's course *Humanities 61*, and dates from October 1964.
23. C. D. Broad, *Human Personality and the Possibility of its Survival*, U. of California Press, 1955. (I did not locate Berryman's copy of this work.)
24. Ibid., p. 23.
25. Ibid., p. 24.
26. Ibid., p . 3.
27. Shakespeare, *Twelfth Night* IV. ii. 50–60.
28. MSS. (probably March 1962).
29. Broad, p. 23.
30. As note 28 above.
31. In the Museum of Fine Arts, Boston.
32. In his copy of William Cohn's *Chinese Painting* (London: Phaidon Press, 1948), Berryman marked plates 20–21 which reproduce this painting. He had also

visited the Boston Museum in the early 1940s, when he was teaching at Harvard, and again in 1962–3.

33. Also in the Museum of Fine Arts, Boston. The name 'Chen Lung' in the second line of Dream Song II should read 'Ch'en Jung'.

34. Cited in Laurence Sickman and Alexander Soper, *The Art and Architecture of China* (London: Penguin, 1956), p. 142.

35. He understood, for example, what is known as the *koan* system, the Zen discipline of discovery and awareness. *Koans* are part of the strict physical and moral training of Zen, often by the intuition of answers to problems or precedents. One of Berryman's favourite Zen Stories (acc. to *Recovery*, New York: Farrar, Straus & Giroux, 1973, p. 139) is as follows:

> A Brahmin approaches the Buddha, bearing a gift in each hand. 'Drop it!' commands Siddhartha, and he drops the gift from the right hand. Goes nearer. 'Drop it!' and the left hand gift falls to the ground. Nearer still: 'Drop it!'— and the Brahmin understands.

As a product, like all *koans*, of the Rinzai School of Zen, this anecdote conforms to the practice known as *k'an-hua Zen* (observing the anecdote Zen). In at least one of his classes at the University of Minnesota, Berryman also devised an exercise which would accord with *mo-chao Zen* (silently illuminated Zen): students were told to turn away from the teacher and, in that position, to picture and to think about him without seeing. This is a preliminary *hosshin* type of *koan*, employing a stratagem which conceals the fact that the student is to look inside himself, where the Buddha nature lies.

36. Wang Wei, to whom Berryman had addressed his "Note to Wang Wei" (*Short Poems*, p. 114: written on 22 March 1958), had established the principles of atmospheric perspective.

37. Rene Grousset, *Chinese Art and Culture* (New York: Grove Press, 1961), p. 249.

38. Cf. E. A. Burtt, *The Teachings of the Compassionate Buddha* (New York: Mentor, 1955). I have drawn on this book, which was also included in the reading list for *Humanities 132*, in the discussion that follows.

39. Ibid., p. 59.

40. The Chinese name for this sect is a transcription of the Sanskrit *dhyana*, meaning 'meditation' or 'contemplation'. Dhyana might be attained by motiveless action (wu-wei)—by, for example, 'sitting just to sit'.

41. Alan W. Watts, *The Way of Zen* (New York: Mentor, 1959), p. 35. I am indebted to this work, which was also on the reading list for *Humanities 132*, throughout this paragraph.

42. Sickman and Soper, p. 138. See also the last line of Dream Song 17.

43. William Willetts, *Chinese Art*, (London: Pelican, 1958), p. 309.

44. In the relevant manuscript, which dates from the summer of 1967, Berryman has indicated the source of 'Great Wu' as '309, 178'. Despite the fact that p. 178 of this book describes yet another Emperor Wu (140–85 B.C.), a marginal mark on p. 309 of Berryman's own copy clearly identifies the ruler in question. Michael Berryhill identifies Wu incorrectly as 'Wu Wang, founder of the Chou dynasty'. 'Introduction: The Epistemology of Loss', in Richard J. Kelly, *John Berryman: A Checklist* (Metuchen, N.J.: the Scarecrow Press, 1072), p. xxv.

45. MSS., 1960.

46. The manuscript indicates that the word 'suffering' would not have survived further drafts: perhaps Berryman, on consideration, decided that the emotion was unequal. Another manuscript dating from 13 May 1960 furthers this sensual theme:

    —Their lithest bodies bob in dance . . .
                            raven girls . . .
    across my pleasure; gracing a strange world
    all of elbows and knees

47. MSS., 1960.
48. Grousset, p. 284.
49. MSS., 1960.
50. Cf. 'Konfrontation mit dem Christentum, besonders selner Mystick', in Hugo M. Enomiya, *Zen-Buddhismus*, (Cologne: J. P. Bachem, 1967) (not in Berryman library).
51. The number seven had particular significance for Berryman. We can at best infer the reasons why, but an approach to an answer can be derived from the fact that Berryman himself marked the following quotation (in 1971): 'Throughout the Near East the number seven frequently occurs. This should probably be seen as the sum of three, the divine number, and of four, the number which in the four quarters of the wind comprehended the earth. Seven would then be that which pre-eminently represents the plentitude, perfection, and totality.' (Jan H. Negenman, *New Atlas of the Bible* (London: Collins, 1969), p. 42.) Since Berryman was learned in Biblical studies, we may fairly assume that he had such numerical significances in mind.
52. In view of the fact that Berryman made no significant attempt to work on earlier draft-fragments towards his original seven-stanza conception, we may suppose that his sickness and failing energy in the late 1960s (perhaps even in 1971, when *Delusions Etc.* was being put together) led him to undertake something of a salvage operation. As late as 27 October 1968, Berryman referred to it as a poem 'which I still feel I can do in about fifty lines, but it may work out to be a whole book'. ('An Interview with John Berryman', p. 8.) We may not assume, however, that he was seriously dissatisfied with the finished product, or even considered it a compromise. Declining ambition need not mean decling standards.
53. See Cohn, p. 179.
54. Cf. a draft-fragment (26 March 1962):

    Appointments! Ah: to be passed over. Ah.
    Then the big fame, lasting so little. Ah.
    I wonder at my doings.

55. MSS., 1967.
56. Berryman's only manuscript note on the style of 'Scholars' is as follows: 'one binding (unrhyme) device: a noun in one stanza is a verb later, as 'gorges'—'gorge' (if can keep from mechanical): a principle of activity'.
57. MSS., 1960.
58. Burton Watson, *Basic Writings of Mo Tzu, Hsün Tzu, and Han Fei Tzu*, (New

York and London: Columbia University Press, 1967), p. 10. (Not in Berryman Library.)

59. Victoria Contag, *Chinese Masters of the 17th Century* trans. Michael Bullock (London: Lund Humphries, 1969), p. 43. (Not in Berryman Library.)

60. Cf. Sickman and Soper, p. 164: 'Ch'en Hung-shou made drawings for woodcut illustrations. . . . It was in the late Ming Dynasty, in 1633, that colour printing from wood-blocks reached a peak of perfection in the *Treatise on the Paintings and Writings of the Ten Bamboo Studio*.' Although Ch'en Hung-shou may have contributed woodblock drawings to this work, it cannot be presumed (cf. Berryhill, p. xxv) that he wrote the book.

61. Although Berryman clearly attempted a *leitmotiv* with the use of the wind-image, as: 'a splendid wind', 'the wind howled', 'fearful wind', 'unaffected by the wind', and, in this instance, 'pure wind', I cannot find any strict equivalence or denotation for the symbol. It is possible that Berryman's use of the image was factitious, unsupported by Chinese symbology or tradition, but it does nonetheless suggest the numinous. This possibility is reinforced by the knowledge that the last phrase, 'pure wind', originally read 'at ten', to rhyme simply with 'Ch'en' in the first line of the stanza.

62. MSS., 1967.

63. Ibid. The manuscript notes: 'Athens, evening, *Dream Songs* ended'.

64. Berryhill, p. xxv.

65. Carbon copy in JBP, n.d.

Selected Bibliography

This list does not include all works to which reference is made in the Appendix 2, or other incidental references. For complete lists of works about Berryman, see the invaluable reference works by Arpin and Kelly, as well as the running bibliographies in *John Berryman Studies*.

WORKS BY BERRYMAN

'Acceptance Speech for National Book Award' (New York: The National Book Committee, 1969).
'Auden's Prose', *The New York Review of Books* I (29 August 1963), p. 19.
Berryman's Sonnets (New York: Farrar, Straus & Giroux, 1967; London: Faber & Faber, 1968).
Delusions, Etc. (New York: Farrar, Straus & Giroux, 1972; London: Faber & Faber, 1972).
The Dispossessed (New York: William Sloane, Inc., 1948).
The Freedom of the Poet (New York: Farrar, Straus & Giroux, 1976; London: Faber & Faber, 1977).
Henry's Fate & Other Poems, 1967–1972 (New York: Farrar, Straus & Giroux, 1977; London: Faber & Faber, 1978).
His Thought Made Pockets & The Plane Buckt (Pawlet, Vermont: Claude Fredericks, 1958).
His Toy, His Dream, His Rest (London: Faber & Faber, 1969).
Homage to Mistress Bradstreet and Other Poems (New York: Farrar, Straus & Giroux, 1956; London: Faber & Faber, 1959).
'Introduction', in Matthew G. Lewis, *The Monk* (New York: The Grove Press, 1952).
'Introduction', in Thomas Nashe *The Unfortunate Traveller*, (New York: G. P. Putnam's Sons, 1960).
'The jolly old man is a silly old dumb' (untitled and uncollected Dream Song), *The Noble Savage* I (March 1960), p. 119.
Love & Fame (New York: Farrar, Straus & Giroux, 1970; 2nd edn

revised, 1972; London: Faber & Faber, 1971 (contents as for second American edition)).

Recovery (New York: Farrar, Straus & Giroux, 1973; London: Faber & Faber, 1973).

Selected Poems 1938–1968 (London: Faber & Faber, 1972).

77 Dream Songs (London: Faber & Faber, 1964) (*77 Dream Songs* and *His Toy, His Dream, His Rest* are collected in the single-volume American edition, *The Dream Songs* (New York: Farrar, Straus & Giroux, 1969).)

Short Poems (New York: Farrar, Straus and Giroux, 1967).

Stephen Crane (New York: Meridian Books, 1962).

'Three and a Half Years at Columbia', in Wesley First (ed.), *University on the Heights* (New York: Doubleday and Co., 1969), pp. 51–60.

'Thursday Out', *The Noble Savage*, no. 3, May 1961, pp. 186–194.

WORKS OF REFERENCE

Arpin, Gary Q., *John Berryman: A Reference Guide* (Boston, Mass: G. K. Hall, 1976).

Kelly, Richard J., *John Berryman: A Checklist* (Metuchen, New Jersey: The Scarecrow Press, 1972).

Stefanik, Jr., Ernest C., *John Berryman: A Descriptive Bibliography* (University of Pittsburgh Press, 1974).

MONOGRAPHS AND LONGER STUDIES

Arpin, Gary Q., *Master of the Baffled House: The Dream Songs of John Berryman* (Derry, Pennsylvania: The Rook Society, 1976).

Arpin, Gary Q., *The Poetry of John Berryman* (unpub. Ph.D. dissertation, University of Virginia, 1971).

Arpin, Gary Q., *The Poetry of John Berryman* (Port Washington, New York: Kennikat Press, 1978).

Berndt, Susan G., *Berryman's Baedeker; The Epigraphs to The Dream Songs*, (Derry, Pennsylvania: The Rook Society, 1976).

Brenner, Patricia A., *John Berryman's Dream Songs: Manner and Matter* (unpub. Ph.D. dissertation, Kent State University, 1970).

Clark, Virginia Prescott, *The Syntax of John Berryman's Homage to*

Mistress Bradstreet (Ph.D. dissertation, University of Connecticut, 1969).

Conarroe, Joel, *John Berryman, An Introduction to the Poetry* (New York: Columbia University Press, 1977).

Kameen, Paul John, *John Berryman's Dream Songs: A Critical Introduction* (D.A. Dissertation, State University of N.Y. at Albany, 1976).

Linebarger, J. M., *John Berryman* (New York: Twayne, 1974).

Martz, William J., *John Berryman*, University of Minnesota Pamphlets on American Writers (University of Minnesota Press, 1969).

Thompson, Susan, *Boundaries of the Self: Poetry by Frost, Roethke and Berryman, Considered in the light of the Language of Schizophrenia* (unpub. Ph.D. dissertation, University of Texas at Austin, 1974).

OTHER WORKS CONSULTED: BOOKS AND ARTICLES

Alsop, Joseph and Stewart, *We Accuse: The Story of the Miscarriage of American Justice in the Case of J. Robert Oppenheimer* (New York: Simon and Schuster, 1954).

The Andrée Diaries, trans. Edward Adams-Ray (London: John Lane, The Bodley Head, 1931).

Anon., 'The Madman in the Tower', *Time*, 12 August 1966, pp. 20–5.

Anon., 'Trial of a Young Poet', *Encounter* vol. 23, no. 3 (1964), pp. 84–91.

Arpin, Gary Q., ' "I Am Their Musick": Lamentations and *The Dream Songs*', *John Berryman Studies* vol. I, no. I (January 1975), pp. 2–6.

Arpin, Gary Q., 'Mistress Bradstreet's Discontents', *John Berryman Studies* vol. I, no. 3 (July 1975).

Auden, W. H., *The Dyer's Hand* (London: Faber and Faber, 1975).

Barbera, Jack Vincent, 'Shape and Flow in *The Dream Songs*', *Twentieth Century Literature* vol. XXII, no. 2 (May 1976), pp. 146–62.

Barbera, Jack Vincent, 'Under the Influence', *John Berryman Studies* vol. II, no. 2 (Spring 1976), pp. 56–65.

Bayley, John, 'John Berryman: A Question of Imperial Sway', in Robert Boyers (ed.), *Contemporary Poetry in America* (New York: Schocken Books, 1974), pp. 59–77.

Beethoven, Impressions by his Contemporaries, ed. O. J. Sonneck (New York: Dover Publications, 1967).

Berg, Martin, 'A Truly Gentle Man Tightens and Paces: An Interview with John Berryman,' *Minnesota Daily* (University of Minnesota), 20 January 1970, pp. 9, 10, 14, 15, 17.

Berryhill, Michael, 'Introduction: The Epistemology of Loss', in Richard J. Kelly (ed.), *John Berryman: A Checklist* (Metuchen, New Jersey: The Scarecrow Press, 1972), pp. xxi–xxxi.

The Book of Psalms from the version of Miles Coverdale as published in the 'Great Bible' of 1539 (London: The Haymarket Press, 1930).

Broad, C. D., *Human Personality and the Possibility of its Survival* (Berkeley & Los Angeles: University of California Press, 1955).

Burtt, E. A., *The Teachings of the Compassionate Buddha* (New York: Mentor, 1955).

Campbell, Helen, *Anne Bradstreet and Her Times* (Boston: D. Lothrop Co., 1891).

Campbell, Joseph, *The Hero with a Thousand Faces* (Cleveland and New York: Meridian, 1956).

Carrington, Philip, *According to Mark* (Cambridge University Press, 1960).

Carruth, Hayden, 'Love, Art and Money', *Nation*, 2 November 1970, pp. 437–8.

Casey, T. J., *Manshape that Shone, An Interpretation of Trakl* (Oxford: Basil Blackwell, 1964).

Cervantes, Miguel de, *Three Exemplary Novels*, trans. Samuel Putnam (London: Cassell, 1952).

Ciardi, John, 'The Researched Mistress', *Saturday Review*, vol. XL, 23 March 1957, pp. 36–7.

Cohn, William, *Chinese Painting* (London: Phaidon Press, 1948).

Conarroe, Joel, 'After Mr. Bones: John Berryman's Last Poems', *The Hollins Critic* vol. XIII, no. 4 (October 1976), pp. 1–12.

Contag, Victoria, *Chinese Masters of the 17th Century* (London, 1969).

Daniélou, Jean, *Origen*, trans. Walter Mitchell (London, 1955).

Dodsworth, Martin, 'John Berryman: An Introduction', in *The Survival of Poetry* (London: Faber & Faber, 1970), pp. 100–32.

Donoghue, Denis, 'Berryman's Long Dream', *Art International*, vol. XIII (20 March 1969), pp. 61–4.

Dunn, Douglas, 'Gaiety and Lamentation: The Defeat of John Berryman', *Encounter* vol. XLIII (August 1974), pp. 72–77.

Ellis, John Harvard, *The Works of Anne Bradstreet* (Gloucester, 1962).

Ferrari, Enrique L., *Goya: Complete Etchings, Aquatints, and Lithographs* (London, 1961).

Fitzgerald, Robert, *Homer: The Iliad* (New York: Doubleday-Anchor, 1974).

Fothergill, Robert A., *Private Chronicles, A Study of Diaries* (Oxford: University Press, 1974).

Freud, Sigmund, *The Ego and the Id* (London: Hogarth Press, 1972).

Galassi, Jonathan, 'Sorrows and Passions of His Majesty the Ego', *Poetry Nation* no. 2 (1974), pp. 117−24.

Gilman, Milton, 'Berryman and the Sonnets', *Chelsea* vol. XXII/XXIII (June 1968), pp. 158−69.

Goguel, M., *The Life of Jesus* (London, 1933).

Grousset, Rene, *Chinese Art and Culture* (New York: Grove Press, 1961).

Guignebert, Charles, *Jesus*, trans. S. H. Hooke (London: Kegan Paul and Co., 1935).

Haas, Joseph, 'Who Killed Henry Pussy-cat? I did, says John Berryman, with love and a poem, and for freedom O', *Chicago Daily News*, 6 February 1971, pp. 4−5.

Haffenden, John, 'Berryman's "Certainty Before Lunch"', *John Berryman Studies* vol. I, no. 3 (July 1975).

Haffenden, John, 'A Year on the East Coast: John Berryman 1962−63', *Twentieth Century Literature* vol. XXII, no. 2 (May 1976), pp. 129−45.

Hamilton, Ian, 'John Berryman', *London Magazine* vol. IV n.s. (February 1965), pp. 93−100.

Heim, Karl, *The Transformation of the Scientific World View* (London: SCM Press, 1953).

Heyen, William, 'John Berryman: A Memoir and an Interview', *The Ohio Review* vol. XV, no. 2 (Winter 1974), pp. 46−65.

Hobson, Wilder, *American Jazz Music* (London: J. M. Dent & Son, 1941).

Holbrook, Stewart H., *Ethan Allen* (New York: Macmillan, 1940).

Holder, Alan, 'Anne Bradstreet Resurrected', *Concerning Poetry*, no. 2 (Spring 1969), pp. 11−18.

Homer, *The Odyssey*, trans. Robert Fitzgerald (New York: Heinemann, 1961).

Howard, Jane, 'Whiskey and Ink, Whiskey and Ink', *Life* vol. LXIII (21 July 1967), pp. 66−76.

Hoyle, Fred, *Frontiers of Astronomy* (New York: Mentor, 1957).

Huxley, Julian, *Essays in Popular Science* (London, 1926).

James, Clive, *The Metropolitan Critic* (London: Faber & Faber, 1974).

Janouch, Gustav, *Conversations with Kafka* (New York: Frederick A. Praeger, 1953).

Johnson, Carol, 'John Berryman and Mistress Bradstreet; A Relation of Reason', *Essays in Criticism* vol. XIV (October 1964), pp. 388–396.

Kierkegaard, Soren, *The Last Years: Journals 1853–1855*, ed. and trans. Ronald Gregor Smith (London: Fontana, 1968).

Kostelanetz, Richard, 'Conversation with Berryman', *Massachusetts Review*, II (Spring, 1970), pp. 340–47.

Levy, G. R., *The Gate of Horn* (London: Faber and Faber, 1948).

Linebarger, J. M., 'Dream Song 6: "A Capital at Wells"', *John Berryman Studies* vol. II, no. 1 (Winter 1976), pp. 36–7.

Lowell, Robert, 'The Poetry of John Berryman', *New York Review of Books* II (28 May 1964), pp. 2–3.

Lundegaard, Bob, 'Draft-Raid Defendants Convicted', *The Minneapolis Tribune*, 19 January 1971.

McClatchy, J. D., 'John Berryman: The Impediments to Salvation', *Modern Poetry Studies* vol. VI (Winter 1975), pp. 246–77.

McGann, Jeromy J., *Don Juan in Context* (London: John Murray, 1976).

Mackenzie, Lewis, *The Autumn Wind*, selection from the poems of Issa (London: John Murray, 1957).

Matthaei, Rupprecht, *Goethe's Colour Theory* (New York: Van Nostrand Reinhold, 1971).

Mendelson, Edward, 'How to Read Berryman's *Dream Songs*', in Robert B. Shaw (ed.), *American Poetry since 1960* (Cheadle Hulme: Carcanet Press, 1973), pp. 29–43.

Meredith, William, 'In Loving Memory of the Late Author of "The Dream Songs"', Foreword to Richard J. Kelly ed., *John Berryman: A Checklist* (Metuchen, New Jersey: The Scarecrow Press, 1972), pp. xi–xx.

Negenman, Jan H., *New Atlas of the Bible*, ed. Harold H. Rowley (London: Collins, 1969).

Neill, Edward, 'Ambivalence of Berryman: an Interim Report', *Critical Quarterly* vol. XV (Autumn 1974), pp. 267–76.

Nemerov, Howard, *Journal of the Fictive Life* (New Brunswick: Rutgers University Press, 1965).

Nims, John Frederick, 'Homage in Measure to Mr. Berryman', *Prairie Schooner*, no. 32 (Spring 1958), pp. 1–7.

O'Connor, William Van, *Obsessive Images* (Minneapolis: University of Minnesota Press, 1960).

Oesterley, W. O. E., and H. Theodore Robinson, *An Introduction to the Books of the Testament* (London: SPCK, 1949).

Origen on First Principles, trans. G. W. Butterworth (London: SPCK, 1936).

The Oxford Annotated Bible with the Apocrypha (New York: Oxford University Press, 1965).

Panofsky, Erwin, *Tomb Sculpture* (New York: H. N. Abrams London: Thames & Hudson, 1964).

Parkman, Francis, *The Jesuits in North America in the Seventeenth Century* (Boston: Little & Co., 1880; London: Macmillan & Co., 1885).

Pascal, Roy, *Design and Truth in Autobiography* (London: Routledge and Kegan Paul, 1960).

Payne, Robert, *The Fathers of the Western Church* (New York: Viking, 1951).

Payne-Gaposchkin, Cecilia, *Stars in the Making* (New York, 1959; rpt: Cambridge, Mass.: Harvard University Press, 1961).

Pearson, Gabriel, 'John Berryman—Poet as Medium', *The Review* vol. xv (April 1965), pp. 3—17.

Perosa, Sergio, 'A Commentary on *Homage to Mistress Bradstreet*', *John Berryman Studies* vol. ii, no. 1 (Winter 1976), pp. 4—25.

Perosa, Sergio, *Canti onirici e altre poesie* (Torino: Einaudi, 1978).

Perosa, Sergio, *Omaggio a Mistress Bradstreet* (Torino: Giulio Einaudi editore, 1969).

Phillips, Robert, *The Confessional Poets* (Carbondale and Edwardsville: Southern Illinois University Press, 1973).

Plotz, John *et al.*, 'An Interview with John Berryman', *Harvard Advocate* vol. ciii, no. 1 (Spring 1969), pp. 4—9.

Pope-Hennessy, John, *The Complete Works of Paolo Uccello* (London: Phaidon Press, 1950).

Porterfield, Jo., 'Berryman's "A Strut for Roethke"', *The Explicator* vol. xxxii (December 1973), item 25.

Rader, Ralph Wilson, *Tennyson's Maud: The Biographical Genesis* (Berkeley and Los Angeles: University of California Press, 1963).

Ramsey, Jr., Frederic, and Charles Edward Smith, *Jazzmen* (London: Sidgwick & Jackson, 1957).

Rich, Adrienne, 'Mr. Bones, He Lives', *Nation* vol. cxcviii (25 May 1964), pp. 538, 540.

Ricks, Christopher, 'Recent American Poetry', *Massachusetts Review* vol. XI (Spring 1970), pp. 313–38 (esp. 313–15, 333–8).

Sanctis, Sante de, *Religious Conversion: a Bio-Psychological Study*, trans. Helen Augur (London: Kegan & Paul, 1927).

Schindler, Anton Felix, *Beethoven as I knew him*, ed. Donald W. MacArdle, trans. Constance S. Jolly (London, 1966).

Sherrington, Charles, *Man on His Nature* (New York: Doubleday and Co., 1953).

Sickman, Laurence, and Alexander Soper, *The Art and Architecture of China* (London: Penguin, 1956).

Silz, Walter, *Heinrich von Kleist: Studies in his Works and Literary Characters* (Philadelphia: University of Pennsylvania Press, 1961).

Sisson, Jonathan, 'My Whiskers Fly: An Interview with John Berryman', *Ivory Tower* vol. XIV (3 October 1966), pp. 14–18, 34–35.

Stahl, E. L., *Heinrich von Kleist's Dramas* (Oxford: Basil Blackwell, 1948).

Stefanik, Ernest C., 'A Cursing Glory: John Berryman's *Love & Fame*', *Renascence* vol. XXV (Summer 1973), pp. 115–27.

Stefanik, Ernest C., 'An Entrance', *John Berryman Studies* vol. I, no. 4 (Fall 1975), pp. 52–3.

Stekel, Wilhelm, *Sadism and Masochism*, English version by Louise Brink, (London: The Bodley Head, 1953), vol. I.

Stitt, Peter, 'Berryman's Last Poems', *Concerning Poetry* vol. VI (Spring 1973), pp. 5–12.

Stitt, Peter A., 'The Art of Poetry XVI', *Paris Review*, no. 53 (Winter 1972), pp. 177–207.

Wade-Gery, H. T., *The Poet of the Iliad* (Cambridge University Press, 1952).

Waggoner, Hyatt H., *American Poets from the Puritans to the Present*, (New York: Oxford University Press, 1971).

Warner, Anne B., 'Berryman's Elegies: One Approach to *The Dream Songs*', *John Berryman Studies* vol. II, no. 3 (Summer 1976), pp. 5–22.

Wasserstrom, William, 'Cagey John: Berryman as Medicine Man', *Centennial Review* vol. XII (Summer 1968), pp. 334–54.

Watson, Burton, *Basic Writings of Mo tzu, Hsun Tzu, and Han Fei Tzu*, (New York and London: Columbia University Press, 1967).

Watts, Alan W., *The Way of Zen* (New York: Mentor, 1959).

White, Elizabeth Wade, *Anne Bradstreet* (New York: Oxford University Press, 1971).

Willetts, William, *Chinese Art*, 2 vols (London: Pelican, 1958).

Wilson, Patrick, 'The Ironic Title of Berryman's *Love & Fame*', *Notes on Contemporary Literature* vol. v, no. 4, pp. 10–12.

Wittke, Carl, *Tambo and Bones* (Durham, N. Carolina: Duke University Press, 1930).

The World's Great Poets Reading at the Festival of Two Worlds, Spoleto, Italy (New York: Applause Productions, 1970).

Zervos, Christian (comp.), *Catalan Art from the Ninth to the Fifteenth Centuries* (London and Toronto: William Heinemann, 1937).

Index

Berryman's works are listed by volume in alphabetical order under his name in the index, which does not include reference to the chronology of Appendix 1.